*A Wonderment
of Mountains*

John —
Hope you enjoy these
mountain travels with
Carson as your guide —

Sam Venable
10/7/13

A Wonderment of Mountains

THE GREAT SMOKIES

CARSON BREWER

With a New Foreword by

Sam Venable

The University of Tennessee Press / Knoxville

Stories copyright © 2004 by Alberta Brewer.
Foreword copyright © 2004 by The University of Tennessee Press.
All Rights Reserved. Manufactured in the United States of America.
First Edition.

These stories originally appeared as columns in the *Knoxville News
Sentinel* on the dates accompanying each story. Columns are slightly
edited and thus differ slightly from their original form. Reprinted by
permission of the *Knoxville News Sentinel.*

This book is printed on acid-free paper.

Library of Congress Cataloging-in-Publication Data

Brewer, Carson.
A wonderment of mountains, the Great Smokies/Carson Brewer;
with a new foreword by Sam Venable.— 1st ed.
    p. cm.
Collection of columns written for the Knoxville News Sentinel.
Originally published: Knoxville: Tenpenny Pub., c1981.
ISBN 1-57233-240-9 (pbk.: alk. paper)
1. Great Smoky Mountains (N.C. and Tenn.)—
    Description and travel—Anecdotes.
2. Great Smoky Mountains (N.C. and Tenn.)—
    Social life and customs—Anecdotes.
3. Mountain life—Great Smoky Mountains (N.C. and Tenn.)—
    Anecdotes.
4. Natural history—Great Smoky Mountains (N.C. and Tenn.)—
    Anecdotes. 5. Brewer, Carson—Anecdotes.
6. Great Smoky Mountains (N.C. and Tenn.)—
    Biography—Anecdotes.
I. Title.

F443.G7 B74 2003
976.8'89—dc21   2003011955

To Alberta,
companion on
mountain highs

CARSON BREWER has been a reporter
and columnist of *The Knoxville News-Sentinel*
for thirty-five years. In recent years
his columns on conservation issues and
on the Great Smoky Mountains have won
widespread recognition:

● E.J. Meeman Conservation Awards
(twice) from the Scripps-Howard Foundation

● Golden Press Card Award from Sigma
Delta Chi professional journalism fraternity

● Journalism Award of the Tennessee Society
of Professional Engineers

● Forestry Recognition Award, Kentucky-
Tennessee Section of the Society of American
Foresters

● Special Citation of Maryville College
Alumni

● Public Service to Conservation Award
of the Tennessee Association of Conservation Districts

● First Place for Best Local Columns, in
the United Press International Tennessee
Association of Newspapers (UPITAN)
competition, twice—1979 and 1980

● In 1980, Brewer was appointed by Gov.
Lamar Alexander to a five-year term on the
Great Smoky Mountains National Park Commission.
The five-member commission represents
Tennessee in meetings with the National
Park Service, and furnishes information
to Congress about park needs.

Contents

Contents

Foreword to the Paperback Edition

For more than two hundred years, and for a wide variety of reasons, writers have been drawn to the Great Smoky Mountains of Tennessee and North Carolina. No matter their specific discipline—biology, geography, crafts, folklore, fishing, nutrition, history, government, politics, economics, and dozens more—authors never fail to find rich sources of material in these misty ridges and fertile valleys.

For pioneer naturalist William Bartram of Pennsylvania, the highlands—as well as the low country of South Carolina, Georgia, Alabama, and Florida—proved to be a vast, uncharted territory, bristling with previously unknown species of trees and shrubs. Here, Bartram traveled freely among tribes of native people who befriended the gentle Quaker. His four-year journey in the 1770s culminated in a work now known as *The Travels of William Bartram*.

More than one century later, a wanderer with a different agenda discovered the Smokies. Horace Kephart was running away from alcoholism and his stifling life as a librarian in St. Louis. He searched for the most distant outpost in the East and in 1904 arrived by train in the tiny hamlet of Bushnell, North Carolina, now covered by Fontana Lake. Virtually at death's door, Kephart was nursed back to health by mountain man Granville Calhoun. For the next three decades, Kephart documented this wild land and its rugged people through magazine stories and two classic books, *Camping and Woodcraft* and *Our Southern Highlanders*.

Not long after Kephart's death in 1931, a California linguist named Joseph S. Hall ventured into the Smokies, burdened with primitive recording devices. Over portions of the next twenty years, Hall lived and worked alongside the locals, capturing their speech patterns, customs, and mannerisms. This effort culminated in the publication of *Smoky Mountain Folks and Their Lore,* in which Hall simply but eloquently "let the mountain people tell their own stories."

In the more modern era, these mountains have summoned writers like Carlos Campbell, Michael Frome, Margaret Lynn Brown, and Daniel Pierce to chronicle the long, arduous struggles, cultural and political, that culminated on June 15, 1934, when Congress authorized establishment of the Great Smoky Mountains National Park.

Campbell sold insurance to feed his family, but the mountains were his life's passion. He hiked more than four thousand miles of trails and worked tirelessly in the park campaign. These experiences led to his well-received *Birth of a National Park* plus co-authorship of *Great Smoky Mountains Wildflowers.* After his death in 1978, a collection of Campbell's previously unpublished stories was released as *Memories of Old Smoky.*

Frome, a writer, author, college professor, lecturer, and longtime proponent of wilderness legislation, penned the definitive *Strangers in High Places,* which has been in continuous print since 1966. In 2000, Brown, also a college professor and author, added her own thorough history of the "re-created" Smokies, *The Wild East.* This was the same year that Pierce, yet another professor and author, weighed in with *The Great Smokies,* drawn from the unique perspective of previously unexplored archives.

These are but a few of the more than two thousand books that have been written about the Great Smokies. In 1981, Tenpenny Publishing added to this impressive list with a collection of essays by *Knoxville News Sentinel* columnist Carson Brewer. Its title, *A Wonderment of Mountains,* spoke volumes about Brewer's regard for the area.

Brewer's name was no stranger to Southern Appalachian readers, especially those with an interest in the national park. His byline had appeared over thousands of Smoky Mountain newspaper articles, and his *Hiking in the Great Smokies,* a trail guide that debuted in 1962, long was considered the standard by which others were judged. But in *A Wonderment of Mountains,* this fascination soared to new heights.

Born February 2, 1920, in the Hancock County, Tennessee, community of Luther, Brewer came to the *News Sentinel* in 1945, shortly after discharge from the United States Army. He had shown a penchant for newspapering in high school and concentrated on English and social studies at Maryville College and the University of Tennessee. In a *News Sentinel* career that spanned more than half a century, he covered every news beat at one time or other—courts, police, politics, education, features, obituaries, weather. But the assignment that would eventually make Brewer's name a southeastern legend came in the late 1950s, when city editor Joe Levitt suggested he visit the relatively new national park, maybe take a few hikes, poke around with the locals, then write a column or two.

It was love at first sight.

Brewer threw his physical energies into hiking Smoky Mountain trails, fishing Smoky Mountain streams, and talking to Smoky Mountain people. Then he used his writing talents to reduce these experiences to paper. The formula continued year after year, column after column, book after book. Although he retired from the daily newspaper grind in 1985, Brewer continued to write a regular *News Sentinel* column—often dealing with mountain topics—until shortly before his death on January 15, 2003.

These efforts resulted in a number of professional honors, many of them for environmental writing. In 1972, Brewer won the Edward J. Meeman Conservation Award from the Scripps Howard Foundation. (Fittingly, Meeman had served as *News Sentinel* editor in the 1920s and was a staunch supporter of the national park's creation.) In 1974, he earned the Forestry Recognition Award from the Kentucky-Tennessee section of the Society of American Foresters. That same year, the Tennessee Society of Professional Engineers bestowed its journalism award on him. Maryville College alumni added a special citation in 1976. The UPI-Tennessee Association of Newspapers awarded Brewer first place in the "local columns" division in 1979 and 1980. The Tennessee Association of Conservation Districts gave Brewer its 1980 public service award for columns he wrote about the loss of farmland. Another newspaper series, this time about the Tennessee Valley Authority, garnered Brewer the 1982 Golden Press Card award from the Society of Professional Journalists. The society also named a scholarship in Brewer's honor in 1984. The Knoxville Writers Guild presented its inaugural Lifetime Achievement Award to Brewer in 2002.

Other honors did not involve plaques and formal dinners. In 1980, Tennessee Governor Lamar Alexander, a fan of Brewer's writing since his own boyhood hiking days, appointed the columnist to a five-year term on the Great Smoky Mountains National Park Commission, an advisory group to the National Park Service. Shortly before Brewer retired from active newspaper work, the park service named a black bear cub in his honor. And in 2001, the Norris Watershed Board unveiled the Carson Brewer Hiking Trail.

In addition to *Wonderment* and his trail guide (incorporated into *Day Hikes in the Smokies* by the Great Smoky Mountains Natural History Association in 2002), Brewer was the guiding force behind four other books about the mountains. In 1975, he and his journalist wife, Alberta Trulock Brewer, wrote *Valley So Wild: A Folk History*, which is still available from the East Tennessee Historical Society. His tour guide of Southern Appalachia, *Just Over the Next Ridge,* was published by the *News Sentinel* in 1987 and eventually expanded into three editions. Brewer's text for *Great Smoky Mountains National Park* (1993, Graphic Arts Center Publishing Company) accompanied the artwork of acclaimed Gatlinburg photographer Ken Jenkins. And in 1999, he wrote *A Tour Guide to Cades Cove* for the natural history association. His only non-mountain book was *The Heartbeat of a City,* a history written in 1989 under contract for the Knoxville Utilities Board.

Yet of all these volumes, *A Wonderment of Mountains* stands out in my mind as Carson Brewer at his absolute best. I enjoyed the book when it appeared in 1981, just as I did earlier this year when I blew the dust off my dog-eared copy and began compiling excerpts for an article in the wake of his death.

This was an easy, yet frustrating, exercise. Easy because I could literally close my eyes, point a finger at virtually any page, and find a perfect quote. Frustrating because I soon realized there was no way to funnel two hundred pages of book text into a twenty-inch newspaper column.

Within days, there was a groundswell of response from readers. "Where can I buy a copy of that book?" they wanted to know.

Nowhere, unfortunately. *Wonderment* was out of print by the early 1990s, and Tenpenny Publishing had gone out of business. Except for library editions and the rare copy that might show up at a garage sale or second-hand bookstore, it was not to be found. But through an agreement between the University of Tennessee Press and Carolyn Nichols, founder of Tenpenny Publishing, this Southern Appalachian classic has now returned to the marketplace.

As you will see in the pages that follow, Brewer's presentation of people, places, and events in the Great Smoky Mountains ranged from whimsy to pathos, historical to contemporary. He was at the same time a casual observer and an active participant.

He had a naturalist's eye for detail and a poet's gift for description. On a February hike to Rainbow Falls, Brewer noticed the reflection of sunlight on snow and remarked that the entire landscape was "littered with diamonds." One October, while relaying word about the change in foliage, he began, "Autumn in the Great Smokies is a mad artist in a crazy hurry to splash on all his paint before he runs out of time and tree leaves." And then there was this encounter with a common mountain songbird: "A winter wren is a little brown bird that looks like somebody ran out of material before he finished it. But when it tilts back on a fir branch and sends its song rippling out into the cool dampness of the highlands, there is nothing unfinished about it. It's the best. And this morning, when the sun sent shafts of light down through the mists and the mountains looked all clean and wet and new as if the Maker had just finished making them, winter wrens seemed to be having a convention. I listened to their songs for maybe thirty minutes, till I walked down below their summer altitude range."

Clearly, Brewer believed in foot power. "Walk," he preached in a special *News Sentinel* outdoor section in 1979. "It's good for you. Burns up calories, defogs the brain, makes the blood flow faster, lifts the spirit."

Over the years he hiked every trail in the park, often leading organized nature tours. Legions of other readers traversed the Smoky Mountains vicariously after Brewer had pounded the ground with his boots and returned to the office, notes in hand. He tempted them with early-morning journeys on late-autumn paths freshly carpeted with leaves. This was the best time to hit the trail, he reckoned, "before somebody else wore all the new off of it."

Yet he was just as quick to point out the downside of human activity in the delicate highland environs. He particularly abhorred hard-soled boots with knobby treads. "The worst thing about them is that they cut up trails," he once groused. "Only thing worse for a trail is horseshoes."

Thus, as enthusiastically as he encouraged readers to participate, Brewer sometimes bluntly advised them to stay away. "I'm not trying to lure anybody into Whiteoak Sink," he columnized in 1977. "For it's a place that can be quickly ruined by too many hogs [wild boar] or too many people. And I suspect unpleasant things could happen to one there. I'd guess at least a thousand copperheads live in those old stone fences and walls and half that many rattlers in Blowhole Cliff. With no markers to guide you and no maintained trails, you could get lost. And if you should venture into one of those caves, you might get lost for a long time. If I were you, I wouldn't go near the place."

Most of the time, however, his resounding message was a hearty "Come on along and see this gorgeous country!"

Brewer could stand atop a mountain crest and revel in the grandeur below him, such as this 1971 account of sunset from Cliff Top, near the summit of Mount LeConte: "Below the bright sky, the scene darkens by degrees, mountain by mountain. The main range of the Smokies is darker than the sky; Sugarland Mountain is darker than the main range. The hues shade down through blue-gray, blue-purple to blue-black. Then dramatic change. Rising out of the narrow upper valley of Little Pigeon River's West Prong is fog nearly as white as snow. It mushrooms up in humps and peaks like sheeted goblins. While the rest of the scene is as still as a painting on a wall, the fog moves, mostly upward but sometimes horizontally, in ghostly ballet against the dark bulk of the mountains."

Just as easily, he could change gears and inspect his surroundings, one micron at a time, from twelve inches away. On a May hike in 1974, Brewer made a casual stop at trailside and took a few minutes to study an ancient, rotting hemlock log, covered in spring wildflowers. The paragraphs that subsequently flowed from his typewriter could find a home in any classroom discussion of theology, botany, art, literature, or entomology. "You can bury your nose deep in the cool violet bed and smell the mix of life and death while pondering the unceasing cycle of each into the other," he concluded. "A nearby creek keeps singing over the old gray stones in its bed. A breeze tickles the little rabbit ears of the violet blooms. And it is time to walk some more."

Brewer was a stream fisherman. No boats and motors for him, thank you. Commenting in 1985 about his upcoming retirement, he reasoned that spring was the best time to cut loose from the shackles of the workplace: "The waters of all the creeks and rivers start warming in April, and the trout and smallmouth and redeyes need my attention. It's good for fish to have some foolish fisherman to laugh at."

Yet he ladled quite a bit of laughter upon himself. Although he was an accomplished fly fisherman, Brewer loved to poke fun at his sporting foibles. Such as this memory from 1978: "There I was, in the middle of the Raven Fork of the Oconaluftee River, trying to stay upright as I crossed. Then this trout had to go and complicate things." He shared every angler's frustration about bum luck: "I sometimes think I always get to the right creek at the wrong time." And surely any fisherman who ever suffered through one of "those days" can empathize when Brewer wrote, "I began mouthing cuss words stronger than I had tasted in years. The rocks that weren't slippery were unstable. Step on them and they immediately tilted in the wrong direction. I fell, going down with all the grace of an elderly horse. I was lucky. No broken back. Only a stove-up left little finger resulted from the fall. After that, I snagged a hook in the finger next to it. When I wasn't falling I was stumbling, making too much commotion in the water. That's not the way to catch trout. Little fish start racing around like junior-grade Paul Reveres, telling everybody with fins that a catastrophe is coming up the creek."

No mention of Brewer's abundant lifestyle would be complete without the inclusion of food. Especially breakfast. He stayed trim throughout adulthood, owning in no small part to his steady regimen of walking, but the man had a voracious appetite and believed in taking on copious amounts of morning fuel. On more than one occasion, he regaled readers about gorging on "a breakfast of sausage, eggs, pancakes, honey and syrup." Not just any kind of honey, either. Brewer was addicted to sourwood, straight from mountain apiaries, and he critiqued each year's production like a wine connoisseur grading vintage.

Personality profiles were another of Brewer's strong suits. Raised on a mountain farm, he was accustomed to, and felt comfortable around, rural folk. He spoke their language. He knew their ways. Historian John Rice Irwin, founder of the Museum of Appalachia in Norris, knew Brewer for most of his life. Upon the writer's death, Irwin remarked,

"Nobody else will come along that will know all about the early rural and mountain life like he did. He not only knew the area and the region and the background of the people, but he also had an abiding interest in it."

This relationship gave Brewer tremendous latitude. He could scold or praise in his column, and his lessons were invariably on target. He could get away with good-natured ribbing, too, such as his 1975 retrospective cataloging of the Whaley families in Greenbrier Cove. This took a bit of organizing, Brewer pointed out, because it might be "Speckle Bill Whaley, Vander Bill Whaley, or White Head Bill Whaley. When somebody told Mrs. Leander Whaley that Leander said he wouldn't be home from the bear hunt till after dark, she might have to ask which Leander—husband Leander, father Leander, or brother Leander."

He also wrote tenderly of these national treasures as, one by one, they began to slip away. When 103-year-old Granville Calhoun—yes, the same Granville Calhoun who nursed Horace Kephart back to health—died in 1978, Brewer realized the mountain man "was more than half as old as the nation. He was one of the few who lived throughout both the country's centennial celebration and its bicentennial."

Of Lem Ownby, last of the old-time permanent residents inside the park, Brewer crafted these words: "He has plowed oxen, mules, and horses on the forty-four-acre farm on Jakes Creek. But he has never owned or driven an automobile. He worked for Little River Lumber Company when it was harvesting the big trees of the virgin forest of the mountains around him. But he has never held a job outside the Great Smokies. Lem has crossed only one state line, the one at the top of the mountain dividing Tennessee from North Carolina, going as far as Tow String Creek, still in the Great Smokies, 'to buy a dog from a feller.'"

Brewer closed the story quietly, reverently, yet with a gentle nod to the old ways: "With the pride of mountain men of an earlier era, Lem says he's never been on relief. He said he's eligible for food stamps, and some have tried to persuade him to use them. He has refused. Will he live to be one hundred? He doubts it. He doesn't seem much concerned about when he departs. He says he's 'got the rocks bought' for his grave. He's going to 'a better place.' But don't bet that he'll like the water when he gets there."

These and all the other delightful entries in *A Wonderment of Mountains* are timeless. They are both a link to the past and a gateway to the future. I'm confident this book will still be an excellent resource fifty years down the road. It came from the heart of an authentic friend of the mountains and resonates just as clearly today as it did more than two decades ago.

Carson Brewer may not have realized it when he penned these words in 1975, but he summed the situation perfectly: "Most history books are written about great men and great events. But we learn little of the common sweat-and-dirt things that made up day-to-day living."

In this one, we surely—and thankfully—do.

Sam Venable, Columnist
Knoxville News Sentinel

A WONDERMENT OF MOUNTAINS: THE GREAT SMOKIES

TENPENNY PUBLISHING, Knoxville, Tennessee

1

At Home in the Great Smokies

The first time Lucinda Oakley saw her future husband, Earnest Ogle, was when he came to the Oakley home in the Great Smoky Mountains to hunt a bear.

Earnest didn't find the bear. But a small joke that has lasted more than a half-century is that Earnest "came looking for a bear and found a dear."

She was fifteen; he was eighteen. She was the eldest of twelve children born to Wiley Oakley and Rebecca Ogle Oakley. The Oakleys lived in a six-room house that sat at about the point where now begins the Bullhead Trail to Mt. Le Conte.

Lucinda was the first to see the bear that Earnest never found. She was sitting atop the drawbars of the fence, watching her father do the evening milking. Glancing toward the barn, she saw a black animal, and said to Wiley, "Dad, I didn't know we had a black calf."

"We don't," he said. Then he looked and saw that the "calf" was a bear. It escaped, up toward the Bullhead, before Wiley could do anything about it.

Word of the bear spread. And after a few days, Earnest Ogle and some other boys, with guns and dogs, stopped at the Oakley home. It was a Friday, and Lucinda had just come home from the Pi Beta Phi School. She saw the strange boys and walked on into the house.

Earnest came to the door and asked about the bear. Lucinda told him where they'd seen it, which way it went. Earnest and his fellow hunters went in search of it.

A few days later, Earnest asked Crockett Maples, the Gatlinburg mailman, the name of that "oldest girl of Wiley Oakley." Crockett told him. And pretty soon, Crockett carried a letter from Earnest to Lucinda.

Several days passed and Lucinda had written no answering letter. Crockett finally said to Lucinda, "That boy's pinin' his life away for you. Why don't you answer him?"

Lucinda told him she didn't have the money to buy a stamp.

"You don't need a stamp," he told her. "I won't take the letter to the post office; I'll just put it in his box."

So Crockett Maples carried the love letters between Lucinda and Earnest, his letters stamped, hers unstamped.

Earnest began coming to see Lucinda. The Oakleys liked him. He and Lucinda went places in his second-hand T-Model Ford.

In 1926, the whole flock of Oakley children had measles. Wiley Oakley didn't have the money to pay a doctor to treat them. Lucinda was very sick.

"I wouldn't break out. I was out of my head and running a high temperature," she said.

Earnest came to see her, found her delirious. A younger sister was giggling at Lucinda's incoherent talk. Mrs. Oakley told the little one it wasn't funny, that Lucinda might die.

Earnest asked about a doctor. Mrs. Oakley said they couldn't afford one. Earnest left and came back with Dr. John Ogle. He stayed with Lucinda until her fever broke. Earnest paid him.

This Wiley Oakley who was so poor in 1926 that he could not afford a doctor for his seriously ill eldest child, later was to become more prosperous as the "Roamin' Man of the Mountains," the colorful Great Smokies guide and storyteller. When Gatlinburg was getting its tourist industry started, Wiley Oakley was its biggest human attraction. Gatlinburg sent him to the big cities of the nation, to tell his stories and lure visitors to the little town at the foot of Mt. Le Conte.

I phoned Lucinda several weeks ago, when I was writing about oldtime mountain weddings. I thought she and Earnest might have had one of those colorful mountain weddings.

But they didn't. In fact, it was almost the wedding that wasn't.

In the fall of 1926, after Lucinda had nearly died in the spring, she and Earnest did some serious talking. She'd finished at the Pi Beta Phi school. Her teachers thought she should go on to college. But there was no money for college.

She and Earnest decided to get married. And on a cold Nov. 17, they got into his T-Model and drove to the courthouse in Sevierville to get the license. She was seventeen and he was twenty. Their families knew what they were doing. They approved.

Perhaps only half jokingly, Lucinda said her parents "thought I was going to be an old maid," and they wanted one fewer mouth to feed.

The parents left the wedding entirely to Lucinda and Earnest. It would be very simple.

At the courthouse, a little justice of the peace named Trotter (Lucinda doesn't remember his first name) wanted to marry them. He told them it was starting to snow and they might not be able to find a preacher.

Declining the offer, Lucinda said maybe they could find a preacher.

They got back into the T-Model and started back up the road. Lucinda was quieter. She was having second thoughts, doubts, fears.

She was thinking of her mother, putting herself in her mother's place years later. Thinking of all those babies and no money for a doctor. All that child-bearing had been hard on her mother (but not fatal, for she's still living at ninety). It had been hard on Lucinda, too. She had to help rear all those younger brothers and sisters. "They took me out of school every time she (her mother) had a baby."

As the T-Model rattled up the bouncy road, Lucinda looked at Earnest and told him she didn't want to get married and have a dozen babies.

He pulled the T-Model off the road and stopped. He said the boys back home would laugh at him if he came home unmarried. He said he guessed he'd "just keep goin' as far as the road's trimmed out."

She looked at Earnest and knew she loved him very much. There'd been no doubt of that—almost from the time he came looking for the bear. She began changing her mind again.

"After all, you did save my life, when I had the measles," she said.

And he said they didn't have to have a dozen children. "But we do want one or two, don't we?" (They had three.)

He turned the T-Model around and started back to the courthouse. Snow was falling thickly by now.

They found Trotter again. He took them into a room with a big open fire for the brief ceremony.

They didn't go back to Gatlinburg. Earnest's maternal grandpa,

John Ramsey, lived in Pigeon Forge. Earnest had arranged for them to stay there for a time. John Ramsey had just killed hogs. There was fresh pork tenderloin for the wedding supper.

A foot of snow lay in Pigeon Forge the next morning, but it "didn't make a bit of difference" to Lucinda and Earnest.

Before Earnest died Oct. 17, 1979, they'd been married fifty-three years and eleven months, "with never a regret."   —6/8/80

0000

This Halloween is a good time to tell the story of the ghost that came out of the loft. It's a true story, and because it is, the names of those involved will have to be changed.

About seventy-five years ago, or so, two young mountain men of Lower Le Conte Creek, in Gatlinburg, heard about two "right purty" girls in the family of Ol' Man Higgins, who lived way over the ridge on the head of Baskins Creek, now in Great Smoky Mountains National Park. And they decided they would go and "spark" these girls.

Let's call the young men Joe and Henry and the girls Sarah and Nancy. Incidentally, Henry is still living at the age of ninety-six.

One cold winter day, Joe and Henry lit out over the mountains. It was late when they reached the clearing where the Higgins family lived in a little log cabin. Blue smoke curled from the chimney, and the old man was out chopping wood to make more smoke.

"Howdy," Henry and Joe said, a little nervously.

"Howdy," the old man returned. "What you boys doin' so fur from home?"

Joe stammered and stuttered and turned red in the face and finally said, "If you don't care, we thought we would come sparkin' with your daughters."

"I don't know as how I would care," the old man said. "Jist pick up a load of wood and we'll go in."

The girls were pretty, all right, but awfully bashful.

The old man piled wood on the fire, and everybody sat watching the sparks go up the chimney. The old man and his wife asked lots of questions and the boys answered. The girls giggled.

Before long, the old man and woman went back to a corner of the one-room cabin and went to bed. Henry and Joe and Sarah and Nancy were left by the fire. The boys whispered to the girls and the girls mostly giggled back. Once in a while, one of the boys would punch the fire and they would watch the sparks fly.

The boys finally rose and said they had to start back home.

The old man raised up and said, "Nope. You will stay the night with us. You might get lost and freeze to death out there on a dark night like this."

He told one of the girls to take the lantern and show the boys the way outside to the ladder that led up to the loft. That's where the boys were to sleep, just above the girls and their parents.

They got up into the loft and moved close to the warm chimney before stripping down to their long-handled underwear and crawling into bed.

After their eyes became accustomed to the darkness, the boys noticed big cracks in the loft floor over toward the middle. The light from the fireplace was shining through them.

The boys decided they'd crawl slowly and silently over to one of those wide cracks and watch the girls get ready for bed. After all, if a girl got careless in those petticoats as she stuck her feet toward the fire for a last warming, a fellow might see her leg half way to the knee.

Joe crawled ahead of Henry. Suddenly, his weight was off center on a broad loose plank. Down they went, Joe and the plank, into the middle of the cabin floor. What a racket!

The girls screamed and jumped into bed and covered their heads, shutting out the sight of that frightened ghost in long-handles.

The old man raised up and asked, "You hurt, son?"

"Nope." Joe said. He jumped up and ran out the door and back up the ladder as fast as he could go.

Down the ladder Joe and Henry went at first light the next morning. Without eating breakfast, or saying "good-morning," they lit out over the mountain as fast as they could run.

And they never again went sparkin' on Baskins Creek.

—10/31/76

Shivaree!

If you've taken part in a shivaree and played post office and spin-the-bottle, chances are you've been around a half-century or more.

In fact, you've been around so long the anthropologists may come looking for you to get information about those fine old East Tennessee customs of courtship and marriage.

Dr. Charles H. Faulkner, a UT anthropology professor, sent me a copy of a book called *Glimpses of Southern Appalachian Folk Culture*. It is a memorial collection of term papers by students of the late Dr. Norbert Riedl. Before Bert Riedl died of a heart attack, he and his students were studying folk culture in the Southern mountains.

It has chapters on several subjects, but the one that got my attention first was Philip Conn's piece on "Traditional Courtship and Marriage Customs in the Appalachian South."

Philip talked with his elders in Hardin Valley, Shady Valley, Ocoee, Birchwood, Tellico Plains, Tennessee, and Damascus, Virginia. He came up with lots of courtin' and marriage customs before most people here had "dates" and went on honeymoons after the wedding. They walked home from church together, sat up together with dead neighbors. They met at candy-pullings and corn-huskings.

After all the candy was pulled or the corn shucked, the young folks played post office. (Girl in separate room would call a boy and say he had a letter. He'd go and kiss her.) Or they'd play spin-the-bottle. (Boy spins bottle and kisses girl to whom it points when it comes to rest.)

When a couple married, they didn't go on a honeymoon. Most went to live temporarily with the groom's parents, or, less frequently, with the bride's parents.

The young folks in the neighborhood gave them a shivaree, called a "serenade" in some communities. Nearly always, the groom was given a rough ride on a fence rail, and the bride was carried around in a big zinc wash tub.

All this was good-natured fun. But, according to the findings of Philip Conn, people in some communities went farther. They would abduct the bride or groom or both and keep them awake and apart "until both became thoroughly disgusted with the institution of marriage . . . The common denominator of shivarees was a ransom given either in the form of money, food, or wine to buy peace and privacy."

A girl usually married a boy of her own community. Young men of some communities helped enforce this custom by hiding in ambush and throwing rocks at any outsider who called on a neighborhood girl.

One of the superstitions concerning weddings was that a bride should not bathe on her wedding day, because if she gets her belly wet, her husband will be a drunkard. Another was that if the bride's father tapped her lightly on the left cheek with an old shoe, it would bring good fortune to the marriage. The bride's mama sometimes gave her a poke of wheat to make certain mama would have many grandchildren.

Church weddings were rare back then. Lots of weddings were at the bride's home, often outside in the yard if it were a spring wedding. Engagements were brief and sometimes not at all. When a boy and girl decided to get married, they wasted no time doing it. Without telling anybody, they sometimes went to a preacher or justice of the peace and got married.

But marrying at home was better. For it was considered good luck in some communities if the family cat was at the wedding.

Then there was the elopement, in which the boy ran off with the girl, usually against the wishes of her parents. "In cases of elopement, the ceremony was very simple, with the couple usually getting married in their everyday clothes," Mr. Conn wrote.

I can verify that. For I once drove the get-away car for an eloping couple. I think it must have been in the late 1930s that this young fellow came to my uncle's general store in Mooresburg. I'd never seen him before. He wanted to borrow a car and a driver. My older cousin Bill was tending store and couldn't go. So I took the fellow in Bill's car.

He wore an old black hat, overalls, and a beard that must have escaped the razor for at least a week. I have seen people nearly as clean come off a day's work with a threshing machine.

I drove him to within about 100 yards of his intended's home. He got out of the car and headed toward the house. He was bent over, hurrying, trying to make no noise. He looked like a fellow hurrying to get a shot at a deer about to move out of range.

Pretty soon, he came back with her. Both were hot, sweaty, excited. I took them to the nearest justice of the peace. The ceremony was very brief. And the groom never took off his hat.   —*11/26/78*

Foretelling Death

This next story is also from Gatlinburg, from Lucinda Ogle. Jane Whiting, a retired Wisconsin teacher, came to live in the Gatlinburg area several years ago. She was a friendly, likeable person who made lots of friends. One of her close friends was Lucinda.

Jane once did some work for the National Park Service. It involved research into the old sayings and superstitions of oldtimers of the Great Smokies. And one superstition several of these oldtimers told her was this:

"If a bird flies through your house, one of your close friends or a member of your family will die."

Later, Jane drove into the Ogle yard one day and chatted a few minutes with Lucinda. She said she'd just bought a bag of cement and she was going home to mend a culvert below her house. This was on a Thursday.

That same afternoon, there was a hard storm. Lucinda rushed to close the windows in two Ogle cabins.

Lucinda hurried on to close the bedroom windows. Then back she went to the living room. And there, flying around in fright and confusion was a little wren. She "shooed" it into the kitchen and it flew out the temporarily unscreened window, which apparently was where it had entered.

Minutes later, Lucinda said, she remembered something Jane Whiting had said after listening to the oldtimers' superstition about a bird in the house. Jane had said she'd like to "come back as a happy little wren."

The following Sunday, Lucinda missed Jane at the meeting of the Smoky Mountain Historical Society. "I asked Bob Kennedy if he would drive by and see about her," Lucinda said.

"He found her lying against the bank, with her trowel in hand and cement in a little red wagon close by," Lucinda said. "The police and officials said she had gone instantly. I was glad of that part, since it was three days afterwards.

"Now," Lucinda continued, "I wonder about the old sayings ... I don't want any more birds in my house. It would worry me and give me the creeps, almost like a ghost."

That's all the spooky stuff for today. But Lucinda has another subject that's seasonally timely, if you've just taken down the firescreen:

When Lucinda was a little girl, she would go with her mother to visit various relatives. And in some of their homes, the "old black fireplace would be covered with a white cloth." And on this cloth would be "different designs, according to the ideas and tastes of the woman of the house, whether it was a humble log cabin or a more modern weather-boarded house."

Lucinda thinks the screen served two purposes: It kept the wind from blowing soot out into the room, and it was something pretty to look at.

"The one Great Aunt Lindy Ogle had in front of her fireplace is the one that stands out in my memory to this day, some sixty years later," Lucinda said. It had a graceful design of fern fronds, in a "dark and light smoke color."

Lucinda remembers being told it was made with buttermilk and soot from the fireplace. This mixture was placed over real ferns brought in from the woods.

"This must have been the first of what's called screen printing," Lucinda said. She wants to know whether anyone living now remembers exactly how it was done.

This discussion of soot and buttermilk started Lucinda and me into other uses of soot. Both of us remembered that some people once used soot for treatment of wounds. And Lucinda remembered that mountain people used to use it for heartburn or "soured stomach"— indigestion.

They ate it, Lucinda said. She said she'd eaten soot for indigestion and "it works."

She told of a little mountain boy who'd heard his mother talk of taking soot for "soured stomach." But he got his words mixed up. His mother saw him in the fireplace, his face black, and asked what he was doing. "I'm getting me some soot because my stomach's moldy," he said.   —*10/31/76*

Claude Hyde Day

We may as well call this Claude Hyde Day, for you won't find much in this piece not connected, one way or another, with him. We're interested in many of the same subjects. He began one of his letters like this: "It seems that every time I read your articles, you speak of something I am familiar with."

And his last letter starts, "The last few lines in your article reminded me of what happened to the first purebred Angus cow my father ever owned."

This was a reference to a mention of those old stories about cows falling out of the field on some of the steep hillsides of East Tennessee, Southeast Kentucky, Southwest Virginia and Western North Carolina.

Mr. Hyde went on to say that the cow's name was Madge and that his father had bought her from Sim Hooper, who owned the first Angus herd in the South.

"My father sent me to the pasture to hunt this cow," Mr. Hyde continued. "She had not showed up for her feed at the barn with the rest of the cattle. I could not find her. She had a bell on (but I) could not hear it. Father went to hunt her. There was a branch between the pasture and cornfield. We had built what was called a pole and rider fence up the branch—rolled logs in, drove stakes across the logs, and put poles between the stakes.

"This cow was heavy with calf. There was a steep bank in the pasture. She had started down this bank, started sliding and went over the fence into the cornfield. She rammed her head between two chestnut logs . . . about two feet apart in the cornfield, turned a flip-flop and broke her neck."

In another recent letter, Mr. Hyde said, "I thought I'd write you about something you may have never heard of. This is the disease called milk sickness in humans and trembles in livestock.

"Lots of the early settlers here in the mountains died from this disease. Lots of them didn't know what caused it. My ancestors, the Hoopers, learned about it just after they settled here and became good at detecting it . . .

"This disease is caused by a plant that grows on the north side of these mountains in shaded areas. It will not grow where the sun hits the ground. It is called white snake root. It has a fuzz underneath the leaves, like beard."

Mr. Hyde points out that the poison in the plant will kill a dry cow but not one giving milk. But any human or animal drinking the milk may die or become very sick.

"The Hoopers learned years ago that you could kill the poison with castor oil, raw eggs and Epsom salts by drenching humans with this mixture. But you can hardly ever cure an animal if they get down past walking," Mr. Hyde said.

"Sim Hooper discovered this plant by cutting cattle stomachs open that had died with the trembles. The drug paralyzed the nerves in the stomach.

"Sim Hooper gathered several bundles of white snake root on Santeetlah Creek, just across the creek from the old Stewart log cabin, and sent the plants to North Carolina State College, where they discovered the drug."

Yes, Mr. Hyde, I had heard of milk sickness. I think I read of it first in John Preston Arthur's *Western North Carolina*. One of many stories Mr. Arthur tells is about the death from milk sickness of a man named W. W. Rhinehart. Mr. Rhinehart became sick atop the Great Smokies. His companions carried him down Bradley Fork, and he died at the base of a big poplar tree on Oconaluftee River.

But the man who told me most about milk sickness was an old fellow named Ralph Hunter, another Western North Carolinian. I saw him about three years ago at his farm home on Caney Fork of the Tuckasegee River, in Jackson County.

He attended North Carolina State from 1905 to 1909. He said one of the professors once asked members of the class whether they had any peculiar problems back home. Mr. Hunter said he told the professor about milk sickness and the trembles.

After class, Mr. Hunter said, one of his classmates came to him and said that milk sickness was a problem where he lived, too.

The young man said his father believed he knew the plant which cattle ate that caused the disease. Mr. Hunter and the other student then went to the professor, who arranged to have some of the plants sent to him. And, with those plants, they ran down the poison which caused the disease.

Mr. Hunter could not remember the name of the other student, but he said he was from Graham County. I'll bet his name was Hooper.

Incidentally, Mr. Hunter had a different home remedy for treating humans with milk sickness—baking powder. He told of saving a woman's life with it.

I think we don't hear about milk sickness much any more because few cattle graze in the woods as they did years ago.

You know where I last saw cattle grazing in the woods? Just down the slopes from Hooper Bald, which got its name from Sim Hooper's father or grandfather. This was three or four summers ago. The area is part of Nantahala National Forest, and the U.S. Forest Service has since banned grazing there.

Hooper was the last big grassy bald in this region on which livestock grazed. Consequently, it is much better preserved than the balds of the Great Smokies—Gregory Bald, Spence Field, Andrews Bald, Russell Field, and Parsons Bald—where grazing ceased in the 1930's.

—11/4/73

Sam Ownby Memoirs

Sometime before the Civil War, Jake Evans and his son-in-law James Ownby sold their property in the Glades, in Sevier County, and moved to the Ducktown area on the Tennessee-Georgia line.

"They bought a farm there and were doing quite well," Sam Ownby, son of James, said later. "But Grandmother Evans . . . was so dissatisfied that she started walking back to Tennessee. Dad and Grandfather Evans got on their horses and overtook her. They told her if she would go back home and stay until they harvested their crops, they would sell out and go back to Tennessee. So they sold their land that fall and moved back to the Glades . . . They sold down there for $400. In less than a year the same property sold for $10,000. Ducktown Copper Mining Co. bought it. It is now called Copper Hill."

This is one of the stories Sam Ownby dictated to his daughter, Mrs. Reaford (Velma) Lamons, Sevierville, before he died ten years ago at the age of ninety-three.

Carlos Campbell, long interested in the Great Smoky Mountains area and its people, learned of these dictated memoirs of Mr. Ownby, obtained a copy and passed it along to me. Sam Ownby was one of a dwindling number of oldtimers whose memory went back to a way of life that differs greatly from the one now. As the nation's 200th birthday celebration approaches, Carlos thinks it is particularly appropriate that people of today know more about that road our parents and grandparents and great-grandparents traveled to get us where we are. Most history books are written about great men and great events. But we learn little of the common sweat-and-dirt things that made up day-to-day living.

Sometimes I think the picture that has come down of the mountain woman has been a little out of focus. Because she bore several children, worked in the house, barn and field, often died young, the feeling has crept in that her husband did not hold her in high esteem and perhaps felt little tenderness toward her. Otherwise, the reasoning seems to go, how could he subject her to such a life?

Sam Ownby's wife, the former Sarah Whaley, died before Sam dictated these memories to their daughter. Let's look at some of the things he said about her:

"Your mama got sick that fall after we moved down here and never was able to do much more work. The year(s) of 1950-1951 she layed in bed a year. Then in the fall of '51 Dr. Yarberry came to see her and she slowly started getting better. In the spring of 1952 she got up again and we celebrated our sixtieth wedding anniversary in March . . .

"Toward the last of June, Sarah and me went to town one afternoon with Marion in his truck. He took us to Walter's and Lillie's where we spent a night or two. This was the first and only time your mama went anywhere, and we came back home and Sarah got sick about the first week of July and died 23 of July . . .

"I still miss your mama, so bad sometimes I just can't stand it . . . always when I was sick or worrying about something she could always cheer me up . . . Lots of nights yet, when I start to turn over in bed I'll think just a second, 'I must not pull the covers off of Sarah.'"

Let's look at some more topics covered by Sam Ownby. Here are some hunting stories:

"One winter while Dad lived in the Glades, on Dudley Creek, he hunted a lot with Uncle Aaron Whaley. He was Dad's brother-in-law

(Aaron married Sally Ownby, a sister of Dad's). That winter Dad killed fifteen deer.

"Dad and brother John went deer hunting another time. They lost the deer the dogs were after and returned home. They were telling Mother about the chase. She laughed and said she got their deer. That she was outside doing the family washing when the deer came, so fast it got caught with its head fastened in the fence. She ran and killed it with her battling stick.

"Another time Dad and Aaron Whaley were deer hunting, on Round Top Mountain. They killed three deer. Aaron carried the two smaller deer and Dad carried the larger one and their two guns. This meant plenty of meat for a long time.

"On this same mountain—Round Top Mountain—John (Black-smith) Whaley and Chris Parton were deer hunting, and John got bitten by a rattlesnake. Chris carried him home on a stick litter, and he got well. He drank a gallon of moonshine in the meantime and before being bitten."

On the Civil War:

"When the Civil War started . . . Dad was too old to have to go. But my brother John was drafted. So Dad went along with him. When Dad and John got a six-day furlough they came home. There was just one way to cross the river at Knoxville and that was on a ferry boat. When Dad and John got back to the ferry boat after their six days leave, the Rebels had it under control. So Dad and John couldn't get across to go back to their company. So they just came back home and it was a month or longer before they got back to their company, and their captain had them marked up as deserters. They asked the captain to reinstate them. He kept saying he would . . . but he never did. So finally they were ordered to go to Red Clay, Georgia, into battle, still marked up as deserters, and then they did desert . . .

"Not long before peace was signed, the Rebels brought a cannon up to Gatlinburg where a bunch of them were staying. They were almost starving. One man said they were cooking red clover and eating it. So they started making raids on most every house around Gatlinburg and through the Glades . . .

"One day a gang of Rebels was coming, and Mother gave what money she had to my sister Patty and told her to go throw it in the brier patch. Another time they came and Mother had wove sister Patty a dress. One of the Rebels stretched the cloth up and remarked, ' This would make me a damn pretty shirt.' Patty held onto one end of the cloth till the man turned it loose, then she ran and hid it. They took Mother's feather beds out on the ridge, ripped them open and let the wind blow the feathers away. Dad owned a pretty young mare. The Rebels took her and left a scrawny old pony. Dad named her 'Reb.' One day I was riding her from the field to the house for dinner and I fell off her. Dad finally swapped her for a yoke of steers.''

On the problems of buying a new home and moving:

"We lived on the Cowflat (Branch) two summers, and I swapped places with Jim and Caldonia Whaley and moved to the right-hand fork of the river in the fall of 1912. We also swapped all our household furnishings that we could because we had no way to move them, only by sled, off the Cowflat Branch. When I moved there, this house had only one big room and a lean-to kitchen. I tore this kitchen down and built more rooms to the house, with porches practically all around it. In this land swap with Jim I got lumber to build my house and barn.''

On the death of a child:

"The next fall, Rosalia was born, but she only lived two days. I was building on the barn when Sarah sent Evalena . . . to tell me the baby was dying. We buried her in the Ownby Cemetery, straight across the river from our house. We just carried her in the casket across the river. Mark carried Evalena and Walter carried Estel. Uncle Bradford Whaley (a Primitive Baptist preacher) held the graveside service.''

On hard times:

"One time during Grover Cleveland's presidency, I had to sell a yearling for two dollars to get money to pay my land taxes. The man to whom I sold it kept it for a few months and sold it for $2.25 . . . Times were hard, and sometimes it looked like there was no way I could get enough money to buy shoes for you children to wear to school in the winter time. We depended mostly on getting you shoes and clothing with money we got from our dried beans and chestnuts we sold to stores to be sent by wagon to market in the city.

"But none of you ever had to go barefooted (in winter). Your mama kept reminding me that we had never had to beg or go hungry.''

—11/16/75

The Whaleys of Greenbrier

When a stranger in Greenbrier Cove sixty-five years ago asked where did Bill Whaley live, he had to specify which Bill Whaley—Speckle Bill Whaley, Vander Bill Whaley, or White Head Bill Whaley.

When somebody told Mrs. Leander Whaley that Leander said he wouldn't be home from the bear hunt till after dark, she might have to ask her which Leander—husband Leander, her father Leander or her brother Leander.

Of course, some families besides Whaleys lived in Greenbrier Cove. Most of the other were Ownbys, but there was one Ogle family, plus Cantrells, Proffitts and Mayeses. And, according to one account, there was a family named Guess.

A peddler came to the Guess home late one afternoon, after he had visited most of the other homes in the community. He called at the Guess gate and Mr. Guess came to the door.

"And what is your name, sir?" the peddler asked.

"Guess," Mr. Guess replied.

Without hesitation, the peddler said, "I'd guess Whaley."

According to one authority, seventy per cent of the children in the Greenbrier School were Whaleys, and most of the others had Whaley mothers.

This piece on the Whaleys of Sevier County—and, especially, of Greenbrier Cove—is not the result of any research of mine. It is the work of Carlos C. Campbell. Carlos, you know, is an authority on the history of Great Smoky Mountains National Park and on the wild-flowers of the park. And now he apparently is becoming an authority on the Whaleys of the Great Smokies.

With the help of Mrs. Glenn (Joyce) Whaley, whose husband descended from the Greenbrier Whaleys, and Glenn Cardwell, a knowledgeable Sevier Countian and able technician of the Great Smoky Mountains National Park, Carlos has assembled lots of Whaley facts and maybe even a little Whaley fiction.

The Whaleys came to this country from England in the 1700s. By the early 1800s they were getting in each other's way in North Carolina. So two brothers, William and Middleton Whaley, set out for Sevier County, Tennessee.

The Whaleys probably settled where they did as a result of the route they chose for crossing the mountain. According to one source, they crossed at what's now called Dry Sluice Gap. This would have brought them down into Tennessee by way of Porters Creek and right into Greenbrier Cove.

William stopped and built a house in the Cove and Middleton went on down a bit farther and selected a spot in the Glades.

An odd thing about Dry Sluice Gap is that it was known once, apparently not long after the pioneer Whaleys crossed it, as Indian Gap. Of course, the present gap by that name is the first one west of Newfound Gap.

Maybe Dry Sluice Gap once was known as Indian Gap because some Indians crossed it from North Carolina into Tennessee and took that same Porters Creek route down into the Cove that the brothers Whaley took. For high up in the Cove, on the west side of Porters Creek, was an area called the Indian Nation community. The story handed down verbally through generations of Whaleys is that some Cherokees lived there for a time. They may have come over the mountain to hide there at the time of the Indian Removal in 1838.

The Indian Nation community was in the neighborhood of the Fitified Spring, earlier called the Spasmodic Spring. Both names come from the irregular off-and-on flow of the spring. It was said to be having fits or spasms.

The Whaleys and the Ownbys who soon followed probably were typical of the best of the pioneer life we think of when we consider the Bicentennial celebration. They cut trees, built log homes, grew corn in the bottoms, hunted deer and bear. They built churches and attended them, built schools and filled them.

They weren't overly burdened with money in the early days, for there wasn't much a mountaineer could do to make money. But Greenbrier Cove residents could sell logs. Some of the basswood, poplar and oaks were hauled by wagon over the rough, rutted roads to Sevierville.

Carlos gave me a map of the Cove, showing the site of every house and who lived in each in the 1904-1922 period. It also shows the four grist mills, three cemeteries, two churches, two stores, two blacksmith shops, and one school.

I like some of the notes keyed to the map. For instance: "Joel Ownby gave this place to his son Walter Ownby. He sold it to Vander

Bill and Sallie Whaley for a pair of mules, wagon and $300."

In the houses lived eleven Whaley families, ten Ownbys and five others. That's twenty-six families. These twenty-six apparently produced a remarkable number of children. For Glenn Cardwell learned from a former teacher in the Cove that there were 225 pupils in the school. That's more than eight school-aged children per family. It's quite a crop of children, especially when you stop to consider that many of these families probably had other children too young for school, a few of the families probably were newly married, and others were too old to have children.

Elijah Whaley, son of William, donated land for the first school and church, time uncertain.

The second school, built in 1880, had two rooms. So did the third, built in 1908, but the rooms were bigger.

After the third was built, young Haynes Whaley bought the second and tore it down and used the material to build a house for himself and his bride. But before he tore it down, he used it briefly as a skating rink. He had bought a pair of roller skates in Knoxville. These were the only skates in Greenbrier and probably the only ones in all the Great Smoky Mountains. Some people still remember the fun it was to be held in the arms of Haynes Whaley as he zoomed around the room on his roller skates.

By about 1915-1919, the two big rooms in the new school weren't big enough. Pupils overflowed into both churches and into what was called "Granny's College." This was a one-room building formerly occupied by Kathern Brown (Granny) Whaley. It was the Cove's post-graduate school—for eighth graders.

A big four-room school was built, but it burned in 1926. The students went back to the churches. They could not go back to the old two-room school because Kimsey Whaley had bought it and converted it into Greenbrier's only hotel, the Le Conte.   *—9/28/75*

Mash Better than Grass

Here's a story about a steer that apparently thought mash was better than grass, corn, or just about anything else. This story about the mash-gulping steer is in a history report on Great Smokies balds. Mary Lindsay wrote it. Dr. Susan Bratton helped her gather the information in interviews with Great Smokies oldtimers. Both Susan and Mary are with the Uplands Research Laboratory.

It was Roy Myers, who has lived all his eighty-six years in Tuckaleechee Cove, who told them about the mash-slurping steer. It was a white steer owned by Mr. Myers' father. The Myers family grazed their cattle on Defeat Ridge in summer. And there was a moonshiner who had a still somewhere up the valley of the Middle Prong of Little River. The steer found it and evidently liked what he'd found. It is not recorded whether his fondness for mash was from the very first taste or whether it was an acquired taste, such as some have for Scotch whisky, olives, and women with green eye makeup.

"He'd drink . . . fifty gallons of mash every night," Mr. Myers told his interviewer. "Drive him two miles from one holler to another, but he'd come back that night . . . That liquor or mash made him fat."

Though I'm not positive, I don't think Mr. Myers meant that fifty-gallon consumption per night to be taken literally. I'd guess it was his way of emphasizing that this steer put away a lot of mash.

Mr. Myers said Tom Sparks, who was the herder for many years at Spence Field, "grew the biggest cabbage heads that I've ever seen" in a cleared patch in the woods near the bald.

"I can remember I come out of North Carolina one time and met him comin' round from Bone Valley towards Thunderhead . . . He made cornbread and put it in the oven and went out there and got a cabbage head and drenched it and just quartered it and put it in a big iron kettle and got about two pounds of butter and put on it. I thought it was the best meal I ever eat, that cornbread and . . . cabbage."

Various oldtimers told the girls that cattle were taken up in the mountains to graze when the lambs tongue was up and ready to eat. But the girls didn't find out what lambs tongue is until one of them interviewed Dr. Randolph Shields, chairman of the Biology Department at Maryville College. Randy Shields is not as old an oldtimer of the mountains as some of the others. But he did herd cattle up there.

In fact, I think I recall his telling me that he and Kermit Caughron were the last herders up there.

And lamb's tongue, Randy said, is trout lily. Or dogtooth violet, or adder's tongue, or fawn lily. Cattle liked it and it was the first thing available in the mountains for them in spring.

What we call various plants depends somewhat on the point of view of those doing the calling. For instance, there's Dutchman's-breeches. At least, that's the name most wildflower fans use for the beautiful little plant whose blooms look remotely like a pair of britches. But a farmer or cattleman may call it stagger weed. For when a cow eats heartily of it, she gets sick and staggers. And a couple of botanists talking to each other, such as Susan and Randy, call it by its botanical name, *Dicentra cucullari.*

Here's Randy telling about the summer of 1934, when he and Kermit herded: "I graduated from college about the last week in May, and I just put a pack of grits on my back and set out—I lived in Walland at the time—and walked through the mountains and on up to there and stayed up there pretty much all summer. I still had folks living in Cades Cove; my grandmother and aunt were there and I'd go off to the Cove and get food from time to time. At least, my share of the food, and Kermit would go off and bring up food, too. But we killed (game). We never went out in the day without taking a rifle with us, and any game we saw was fair game. Turkeys. By the middle of July, the turkeys were good eating size and they'd come out on the bald late in the evening to chase grasshoppers and various insects that lived in the grass . . .

"I don't think Kermit or I . . . will ever forget the time we went off down Twenty-Mile (Creek) looking for some cattle that strayed off, and we were coming back up what's now called Long Hungry Ridge . . . used to be a nice trail up there, pretty steep. And we met a big gobbler coming down the trail. Turkeys are sort of like DC3's or something. They've got to have a pretty long runway before they can take off. Well, we surprised him . . . He was coming down, coming around a bend in the trail, and we just met. Well, it was a little brushy along the side of the trail, so he didn't attempt to take off. He just decided he had to turn around and head back up the trail, you see, to get up enough speed so he could take off. And we almost caught that old gobbler, until he hit a cleared space along the side of the trail where he took off to the side. We chased him, I guess, for 100 yards up that trail trying to catch him.

"But we did get young turkeys. We'd have to slip out, of course, around the edge of the bald and come right up from the cabin late in the evening and get ourselves a young turkey for supper."

People who grazed cattle, sheep, hogs and horses in the mountains had to worry about quite a few hazards.

Late spring snowstorms and weather froze lots of cattle to death a time or two. Bone Valley Creek, tributary to Hazel Creek, on the North Carolina side, gets its names from all the cattle bones left there after such a late storm.

People now trying to fix the dates of some of those things that happened so long ago have problems. Mary Lindsay, in a conversation with Arthur Stupka, said Jim Shelton of Maryville remembered that one such bad storm started on the evening of May 19 and continued the next day. But he couldn't remember what year. I'd bet a nickel or two on 1894 being the year.

The record low temperature here for May 20 was a 34 in 1894. And until we logged a 38 the past May 19, the record was 39 for that date and it also was in 1894. Only a little snow was recorded in Knoxville then, but much more could have fallen in the mountains. And in my "weather" file, I find some scribbled notes I probably made from a phone conversation several years ago. Somebody reading the records of Heritage United Methodist Church, in Blount County, said the Sunday School class did not meet on May 20, 1894, because of snow.

Several people told Mary and Susan about lightning killing stock. Randy Shields said that lightning sometimes killed whole herds of sheep. He recalled that his family used to take their sheep up Eka-neetlee Creek all the way to the mountaincrest at Ekaneetlee Gap. Lightning killed most of them one year.

"So my grandmother took all of us kids and my aunt and started early one morning and we went up to Ekaneetlee Gap and pulled the wool off all those dead sheep," Randy said. "They'd been dead long enough until the hair had loosened up very well. Of course, they didn't smell very well, either, but she salvaged the wool from the sheep."

So sometime when you're fussing about some messy job, remember the Shields children pulling that wool off all those overripe sheep.

—*6/13/76*

Smokies Maple Sugar

Ask for information from people who read this column and you'll get it. Maybe more than you asked.

For instance, I asked about a month ago when and why East Tennesseans stopped tapping sugar maples to make syrup and sugar. I got the answers, plus a claim for who invented lollipops, or suckers.

Lucinda Ogle, Gatlinburg, claims her maternal grandpa, Henry Oakley, invented suckers.

Grandpa Oakley would have his grandchildren gather some birch twigs and pans of snow when he was making maple syrup on cold early March days.

Then he would boil the maple sap a little longer than if he were making syrup to pour on pancakes. This would be thicker syrup. He would pour it in thin strips across those pans of snow.

And as the snow chilled it, the Oakley grandchildren each would stick one end of a birch twig under one end of one of those strips of cooling syrup and start rolling it.

The result was a little ball of very thick maple syrup of a taffy-like consistency on the end of a twig. A lollipop. Or, a "sucker," as the Oakley grandchildren called them.

Lucinda thinks that was about sixty-five years ago, when she was a child of about four. Later, when she was fifteen, which would have been in about 1924, she thinks the practice of making maple syrup and sugar had about died out in the Gatlinburg area. How does she fix the time?

It was the year before she and Earnest started courtin' and she was attending the Pi Beta Phi School. One of the teachers, Marian Folsom, from Vermont, had several youngsters helping her make orange marmalade one night.

"She put sugar in," Lucinda said. "Then she decided she hadn't put in enough. She went out in the dark and got another little bag and put it in. But when we tasted it, it was salt."

To make up for that disaster, Marian Folsom brought maple syrup all the way from Vermont to make maple syrup lollipops the way Lucinda remembered them. She had to bring it from Vermont because maple syrup wasn't available any longer from local trees, Lucinda said.

And the reason it wasn't available, according to Earnest Ogle, is that the timber industry had cut most of the big sugar maples by that time. Sugar maple lumber was in great demand for flooring.

Somebody else who remembers tapping sugar trees and making syrup is Woodrow Kirk, Route 1, Lenoir City. His wife Ruth wrote me about it. He told more over the phone.

When he was eight or nine years old, living near New Zion Church, in what is now Oak Ridge, he helped his father, Walker Joseph Kirk, make syrup. Three big sugar maples stood up a hollow on the Kirk farm. This was in the early 1920s.

When the sap started rising, Walter Kirk would bore holes in the trunks of those maples. Then he'd stick elderberry stems in the holes. Elderberries have pithy centers. He would punch out the pith with a wire, leaving the stem hollow. Then he'd place buckets under the stems. (Mrs. Walter S. (Lola) Thompson earlier told me that the hollow piece through which the sap drains is called a "spile.")

Mr. Kirk said it took about twenty-four hours for a gallon bucket to fill. They poured the sap into an iron kettle and boiled it into syrup.

He put wooden plugs in the holes in the trees to stop the flow of sap. After about three weeks, he could remove the plugs and get about as much sap as he got the first time.   —12/18/78

CCCCC

Jim Bohanan, an oldtime Gatlinburger, lost his life carrying maple sugar to the market in Knoxville.

Back in the nineteenth century, according to Lucinda Ogle, Jim Bohanan had "gathered up everybody's sugar" and was carrying it in a flour sack. These were molds of brown maple sugar, very sweet and flavorsome.

Jim Bohanan was carrying the results of lots of work and time. About forty gallons of maple sap are required to make a gallon of syrup. I don't know how much sap it took to make that sack of sugar Jim was carrying, but it probably was more than forty gallons.

Besides his own sugar, he probably was carrying some Ogle sugar. For he was married to Easter Ogle, daughter of Thomas Ogle, one of the five Ogle brothers who settled in Gatlinburg. (She was given that name for being born on Easter.)

As he walked down West Prong of the Little Pigeon toward Pigeon Forge, he came to a ford where he had to cross the river. It probably was in March, which generally has lots of rain. Anyway, the river was up and Jim had trouble picking his way across on stepping stones. He apparently slipped and fell. He drowned. When they found his body, the sack was wrapped around his neck. And the river had melted all the sugar.

They buried him where Polly Bergen's store stands today, Lucinda said. And Easter later married William Trentham.

I don't know how widespread was the practice of making maple syrup and sugar in East Tennessee. But it must have been pretty common in the Great Smokies. I've always heard that's how Sugarland Mountain got its name. That's the long, high ridge that runs southward from Fighting Creek to the top of the Great Smokies at Mt. Collins.

I looked at the Cades Cove quad map, trying to find Becky's Sugar Cove. For I have a notion somebody once told me there is a cove by that name and it was named for Becky Cable. Anyway, I didn't find it. But I did find Tiptons Sugar Cove, Tiptons Sugar Cove Branch (which runs into Forge Creek), Sugar Cove Ridge, and Sugar Cove Branch (which runs into Mill Creek). So I'd guess that lots of sugar used to be made near Cades Cove. But no more.

According to the 1968 edition of Encyclopedia Britannica, West Virginia is the closest state to East Tennessee that still produces maple syrup in commercial quantities.

Britannica also says maple syrup is "one of the few crops produced solely in North America and is one of the oldest, having been produced by Indians of the Great Lakes and St. Lawrence River regions prior to the arrival of white settlers."   —*12/21/78*

Old Time Beliefs

In this modern world nobody believes in much of anything any more. Not even superstitions. But somebody will become a believer sometime when he opens an umbrella in the house and the roof falls in on him.

That's one of the superstitions Carlos C. Campbell, insurance executive, Great Smoky Mountains enthusiast, author and goodness knows what else, got up recently for David Hamilton. David, a fourth grader at Bearden Elementary School, studied superstitions in connection with the school's Creative Learning in a Unique Environment (CLUE) program. That shows how much times have changed. A few generations back people didn't study superstitions. They lived by them.

Not only is it bad luck to open an umbrella in the house, according to Carlos, but it's also bad luck to twirl one. I never knew that second one before, and I suppose that's why I never amounted to anything. For I've been known to twirl an umbrella.

It's also bad luck to carry an axe into the house, Carlos and I agree. Even so, Carlos says, some people believe that an axe or a butcher knife placed under the bed of a pregnant woman will prevent, or reduce, pains of childbirth.

Did you know it's bad luck to leave a house by any door other than the one through which you entered?

Back when I used to smoke cigarets, I knew—but did not always observe—the belief that it was bad for three persons to light cigarets on one match.

Nearly everybody used to know it was bad luck to give a pocket knife (or any other sharp instrument) to a sweetheart or close friend. It would "cut the friendship."

If you take the ashes from the fireplace on Friday, someone will steal something from your house before the next Friday.

If you gather eggs after sundown, the hen will stop laying.

And don't burn eggshells. That also will make the hens stop laying.

If you worry about Friday the thirteenth being unlucky, carry a pinch of salt in your left hip pocket. That'll make it lucky, or at least not unlucky.

If you want your dog to be a good watch dog, cut some hairs from the end of his tail and bury them under the front door steps.

A flint rock kept warm in the fireplace will prevent hawks from carrying off small chickens.

To remove a wart, rub a dishrag over it and bury the dishrag. When the dishrag rots, the wart will be gone. (I've heard of a quicker way, which we'll discuss some day.)

Don't thank anyone who gives you a plant or cutting. To do so will make the plant die.

A jaybird (blue jay) is unlucky. A long time ago he sold himself to the devil for a grain of corn, and he's been in trouble ever since.

If a baby sees itself in a mirror before it is six months old, it'll die during the next six months.

Fish won't bite while the cows are lying down in the pasture. (I think some people still believe this and perhaps offer some semi-scientific argument about it.)

The first woodtick that fastens itself to the body of a baby must be killed with an axe or other tool if the parents want the baby to grow into a clever workman. If it is killed on a bell or banjo, or on some clear-ringing object, the child will develop a good singing voice. If the tick is killed on a book, the baby will grow up to "speak all kinds of proper words."   *—4/12/76*

QQQQ

Doug Myers, who works in The News-Sentinel Mail Room, came by my desk one morning several months ago and asked whether I'd ever heard that a man born after the death of his father had psychic powers.

Doug said his wife Wanda's great-grandfather, David Shackleford, is reported to have been such a person. He was born in Harlan County, Kentucky, after robbers killed his father.

One of the powers David Shackleford is said to have had was to cure thrush by blowing into a baby's mouth. He also sometimes could foretell the future.

I told Doug I'd never heard of such a thing. For that matter, I don't think I'd ever heard of "thrush," except as a bird. But I have since been educated.

It was only a few weeks after Doug mentioned the subject that I came across the same thing again. Mrs. A.D. (Edith Holt) Sams, of Knoxville and formerly of Clinton, died. I was looking through her News-Sentinel library file, preparing to write a story about her death. In the file was a story Betsy Morris, Living Today editor, had written about Mrs. Sams years earlier. In her younger days Mrs. Sams had been a social worker in rural Kentucky. One day she had met a woman who had taken her baby far up the branch to have a man blow in its mouth to cure the "thrash." This fellow was one of those born after his father's death.

And now, I'm looking through *Glimpses of Southern Appalachian Folk Culture*, from which came the piece on courtship and marriage customs of East Tennessee. And I find several versions of this belief in a paper on "Superstitions and Beliefs Concerning Babies in Southern Appalachia," by Joan Morton. (Joan, like the authors of other papers in this book, was an anthropology student of the late UT professor, Dr. Norbert F. Riedl.)

Some samples:

"If a baby has hives have someone whose father died before he was born to breathe into the baby's mouth."

"To cure thrash, take the child to someone who has never seen its father and have that person blow in the child's mouth."

Here are some a little different:

"If a baby has the thrash, have a man who has never seen his father—an illegitimate child—blow his breath in the mouth."

"The seventh child in a family can cure the thrash by blowing in the baby's mouth."

Some other baby cures:

"To stop a baby's slobbering, go to the brook and get a minnow and let the baby suck the minnow's tail."

"To cure a very young baby of croup, tie a black silk cord around its neck."

Some people in Loudon County used to believe that a pregnant woman who drinks lots of grape juice will bear a dark-skinned baby. But if she eats lots of fish, the baby will be blonde and blue-eyed.

Before moving on to something else in the book, I'd better report that I looked up "thrash" in the dictionary and could not find it as any kind of ailment, but "thrush" is listed as a mouth ailment of infants. It's caused by a fungus.

Let's look a bit at the paper on "The Care of the East Tennessee Dead," by Myra Bettis, Michael Blackwell, Robert Hoffman, Patty Sonka and Loretta Swingle.

Before embalming and professional undertakers became common here earlier in this century, friends and neighbors generally prepared the body and dug the grave when a person died. But in some communities, the first thing to do after a death was to stop the family clock, "because if the clock stopped by itself while a corpse was in the house, a member of the family would die within the year . . . Another reason for stopping the clock was to limit the power of death by stopping the cycle and introducing a new period of time."

In Morgan and Scott Counties, the body of a dead person was laid out on what was called a "cooling board." Many families had their own cooling boards. These were passed down through the family and used by several generations.

The board was about the size of a twin bed. It often was made of some hard wood like oak. It sometimes was placed on saw horses and used as a table at church picnics or barn raisings. Some families also used it as an ironing board.

It was common for a dead person's personal effects such as wallets and combs to be buried with him. It was less common if a fellow's favorite shotgun or chewing tobacco went with him to the great beyond, but they sometimes did. And a Chattanooga man told the students of a fellow who died at nearly the same time his dog died. So the dog was buried at his feet.   —*12/3/78*

2

Mountain Christmases Remembered

It is a cold, dark night. No moon, but a billion stars. A freezing crust is already forming on the rutted road along which a half-dozen young people walk.

Except for whispers and half-muffled laughter, they are silent. Lamplight glows yellowish from the window of a house ahead. As they reach the house, the young night-walkers veer off the road and start circling the house.

Suddenly, no more silence. There is bedlam: Rifle shots, firecrackers, cow bells ringing, yelling.

The front door is opened, and a grinning head of the house passes out an apple and a few chestnuts to his noisy guests.

Although this may sound like a combination of the Fourth of July and Halloween, it was the night before Christmas in Cades Cove fifty years ago.

At least, that's the way Kara Gregory remembers one of the Christmas customs of the Cove. Kara, now of near Maryville, is a native of the Cove. His early-settler ancestors left the family name on Gregory Bald and Gregory Ridge, high above the Cove.

If someone inside the house had spotted the "serenaders" and rushed outside and fired a gun into the air first, he would not have been obligated to treat the visitors. But they'd have circled the house and rung their bells and shot their guns and firecrackers, anyway.

There was more emphasis then than now on Christmas fireworks. Charlie Myers, a Cove native whose memory goes back to about 1900, says young men sometimes got hold of dynamite and set off rumbling blasts.

Of course, Christmas wasn't the only thing different fifty to seventy-five years ago. The same landscape that now sparkles at night with electric lights then was largely dark, broken only by bobbling lanterns of late travelers or coon and possum hunters, as well as by the lamplight glow in windows.

Generally, people worked longer and harder for less. Christmas had to be different. As a rule, grownups did not exchange presents. Presents were for young children who hung their stockings from the fireboard on Christmas Eve.

Next morning, while a crackling fire was just beginning to take the chill off the front room, they'd find their stockings lumpy with oranges, sometimes a rare banana. A doll for girls, a Barlow knife or a few marbles for a boy.

A father's entire Christmas spending might amount to no more than three or four dollars.

Children then didn't get long Christmas vacations. If Christmas fell on Thursday, they'd go to school on Wednesday, have some sort of Christmas program and then be out of school only until the following Monday.

Different families followed different customs about working on Christmas Day. Charlie Myers said people in his family normally did not work on Christmas. But Kara Gregory said that if the weather was good and the ground dry, his father might plow for a half-day.

Men and boys often went hunting Christmas morning. The squirrels, rabbits or quail they brought home became Christmas supper. Or if they returned early enough before the mid-day meal, their game became an "extra" for Christmas dinner.

Someone driving the loop around the Cove now and seeing all the deer might wonder why the hunters back then hunted only small game.

But no deer were in the Cove then. The number left in the mountains above the Cove were so few and a hunter's chances of getting one were so slim that few residents bothered to hunt. However, it was from this remnant herd that today's much larger herd developed.

But quail were plentiful. Charlie Myers remembered killing eighteen quail one day, and he recalled killing eight with one shot on another occasion.

Farm folk back then weren't quite so wedded to turkey as the major

Christmas dinner dish. They had a choice of several domestic fowl which roamed about the farm. My mother, who spent her girlhood on a farm on Yellow Branch, not far from where that little stream runs into Clinch River, remembers eating chicken, turkey, duck, and guinea fowl on various Christmases. Her favorite, though, was pork tenderloin. However, it was unusual on Christmas Day, for hogs usually were butchered in November and the tenderloin would be gone by Christmas.

Both Mama and Kara Gregory mentioned American chestnuts as an ingredient nearly always in the dressing for chicken or turkey. Kara said his family usually ground the chestnuts in a sausage mill. Mama remembers using them boiled but whole.

Sweet American chestnuts were a prodigious blessing to the people of the Southern Appalachians. Millions of bushels fell to the forest floor and were free for the gathering. Kara Gregory remembers his father sometimes gathered a wagonload of chestnuts and took them to Maryville to sell. Of course, the family kept a good supply for home consumption. Hogs ran wild and thrived on chestnuts. Turkeys ate them. Bears and squirrels fattened on them.

One thing on nearly every Christmas dining table was a stack cake, with apple sauce or cooked dried apples or dried peaches between the layers.

Farm families dried lots of apples and sometimes peaches in summer. From my childhood, I remember seeing apple slices drying in racks placed on the roof of some farm building.

Mama said her father, my Grandpa Jake Winkler, built a drying house. In it was a small stove, so drying could continue even in rainy weather. It must have been gone before I came along, for I don't remember it.

You may remember the subject of sulfured apples came up here a year or so ago. I've forgotten the details, but this was a method of drying apples by which the whiteness is retained. Ordinary dried apples are sort of brownish red. But good, especially when cooked and used in Christmas stack cakes.

Christmas trees then were rare in East Tennessee mountain homes. This may have been a hold-over from the early years of the nation when the Puritans believed the Christmas tree was a pagan symbol.

"Most of the mountain folks said it was 'Tom Foolery'—wasting your time," says Mrs. Earnest Ogle of Gatlinburg.

She was one of the fortunate children. Her father was the legendary Wiley Oakley, the Roamin' Man of the Mountains. Wiley believed in Christmas trees.

"When we had our log cabin decorated with a tree and holly on the fireboard, a homemade cornstalk manger scene placed under the tree, and a little bunch of mistletoe hung over the door (children would kiss each other), our many cousins and neighbors' children would come to see our tree and to hear Wiley's tales," Mrs. Ogle remembers.

"For Dad could keep us hypnotized with all sorts of stories about the outdoors. There were fairies, dwarfs, angels, and Santas, and all sorts of things happening in the deep, dark woods.

"Some of the cousins would use the excuse they were going possum hunting and came by our house to see the tree and play games around the big fireplace . . .

Some games I remember were fox and geese, played with corn geese and the fox a black button. He could move anywhere. We also played checkers. We made our own boards and used two colors of buttons. Also guessing games—pass the thimble and Jack in the bush. (Hold chestnuts in your hand and say a little rhyme.)

"We popped corn, made molasses candy and pulled it, roasted chestnuts, and parched corn if the popcorn was all used up. Sometime later, there was peppermint and horehound stick candy for us all. We always had gingerbread and always had plenty of apples in the cellar."

Another Christmas custom Mrs. Ogle remembers is "Christmas gift." If you said, "Christmas gift" to somebody on Christmas morning before they said it to you, they had to give you a present before the end of the day.

"We dozen Oakley children would get out of bed at the crack of day and run half a mile down the road to get 'Christmas gift' on our Great Aunt Lindy (Ogle) because she made the 'bestest' sweetbread. She later told me she would hear us coming but didn't let on, for she loved to see our happy faces when we thought we had tricked her."

Then there was Old Christmas, Jan. 6. Twelfthnight, the eve of Epiphany. According to an old belief in East Tennessee and probably many other places, the animals—cows, horses, sheep, pigs—all knelt and prayed on Old Christmas.   *—12/23/73*

Santa Visits the Sugarlands

Santa Claus didn't always get to every house on this map (page 37) fifty years ago. It wasn't the easiest place in the world for him to reach. Sometimes he busted a sleigh runner on rocks in the road along West Prong of the Little Pigeon. Dave Newman's bear dogs once took out after Santa's reindeer and chased them all the way to Elkmont.

And there was just no way Santa could slither down the stovepipe at the Fred Newman home and store beside the river.

Alie Newman Maples lived there. She made the map and sent it to me. She's Fred Newman's daughter. She is married to Millard Bruce Maples, a son of Crockett Maples. Crockett Maples was the carrier who brought the U.S. mail to the people on this map more than five decades ago. Crockett didn't travel in a fancy sled such as used by Santa Claus, so he was able to deliver the mail without great hardship.

Sometimes Crockett brought a letter to Alie from her mother, who had split up with her father.

Her father didn't remarry for a year or two. And it was because of this that Alie and her brother, Ray, spent a lot of time at the nearby home of their grandparents, Dave Newman and Nancy Ogle Newman.

And Newman grandchildren who spent much time at the grandparents' home didn't miss Santa Claus much. For Dave Newman was a bear hunter, full of tales of bear hunts. He was about as good as Santa. He was nearly bald, and he sometimes had a mustache and sometimes not. There was a great black bearskin rug in front of the fireplace. And every Newman grandchild put in lots of time on that rug. Especially Alie and Ray. For all of Dave's and Nancy's children were grown and gone. So they were glad to have Alie and Ray walk down the lane and spend time with them.

You wouldn't recognize the features of this map if you looked at the place today. For it's up in Great Smoky Mountains National Park, above what is now Park Headquarters and east of what is now U.S. Highway 441. (The highway and park headquarters weren't built at this time, but they're shown on the map, at upper right, to help you.)

Alie says the road down along the river was new then. Lots of people were talking about the park that was sure to come. And people must have thought they'd get lots of business if they built stores along this new road.

"My dad, in good hopes for better days, built a little store beside the new road," Alie said. "About 200 yards above us, Uncle Will Newman built a store. About a quarter of a mile up the road, Earnest and Lucinda Ogle built a store. About a quarter of a mile down the road, Uncle Sam Huskey and Aunt Alice built yet another store and a rooming house, called Skyuka." (Skyuka was an early tourist establishment in the area.)

Alie sometimes thinks of what might have been. "If we still owned all this land, we would have what Gatlinburg has today. Only in a nicer and cooler place," she said.

But that was not to be. This area, called the Sugarlands, was bought for the park. Trees have been growing nearly fifty years in what are shown here as Dave Newman's fields.

He owned more than 100 acres of land. It stretched up the river to a point opposite the present trailhead for the Huskey Gap Trail. Though his acres were rocky, the soil was good and reasonably level down there along the river.

The Newmans grew corn on that land. Their cows and mules grazed there.

They carried some of the corn up to Uncle Burt Ogle's grist mill, powered by Little Pigeon water.

You won't find much of all this now if you walk from U.S. 441 down toward the river.

Alie said she went to the old spring recently. She found it covered "and nearly choked to death" with the leaves of many seasons. But she remembers when the water welled up a foot deep in the spring. And the Will Newmans, Fred Newmans, Dave Newmans and Alex Coles all carried drinking water from it.

She said her father, who now lives in Jefferson County, sometimes talks about the good water from the spring. He says a rabbit or a squirrel cooked without that mountain water just doesn't taste quite right.

Part of the stone fence still stands. Alie says that when spring comes, "you can still find Easter flowers around my grandmother's old home place. You still find . . . old wagon skeins from the little blacksmith shop my grandfather used to own."

Alie thinks people from outside Sevier County who drove along that road were "sorry for the bare-footed kids playing along the roadsides.

But we were the happiest kids in the world. We would climb our grapevine mountains, make Indian hats out of the mountain laurel now called rhododendron, which back then I had never heard this name. Gosh, what a word, anyway! Mountain people like mountain laurel. That's good enough for me. Mom agrees with me yet about laurel and ivy."

(People back then also used "ivy" for what we now call "laurel.")

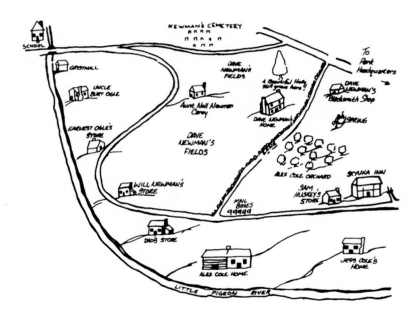

The Newmans kept milk in crocks set in deep places of a small stream. Ramps stored in the same cold water stayed fresh for weeks.

Fred Newman built his little store and then added a one-room lean-to, in which the family lived. It contained two beds, the kitchen stove, tables—nearly everything they owned. It was covered with tarpaper.

Someone wrote—and Alie read it in later years—that tarpaper shacks were springing up along the road and would soon ruin the mountains. "But as Aunt Debby Newman would say, 'If we could have built a mansion, we wouldn't have needed the shacks.' "

Grandpa and Grandma Newman had a better house: Three downstairs rooms and a big upstairs, plus two porches. And it had that big fireplace.

It was at this big house that the Newman clan gathered on Christmas Day. They would kill the biggest rooster in the yard and have chicken and dumplin's. And for dessert they would have stack cake, usually made with molasses instead of sugar.

Alie remembers the first orange she ever tasted. She received it near Christmas at the Pi Beta Phi School. "It was the best smellin' thing I ever smelled."

She remembers decorating a Christmas tree with strings of popcorn and with sycamore balls wrapped in foil. The foil was saved over the year from sticks of chewing gum.

Santa missed a lot by not getting to the Sugarlands more often.

—12/16/79

A Doll Big as a Baby

The first Christmas present James Willis Tucker can remember buying was a doll. He was twenty-six years old. His wife, Louise, was eighteen. They'd been married two years and had no children. The doll was for Louise.

It was a big doll, big as a baby. He was in Tellico Plains and happened to see it in a store. So he bought it, for two or three dollars. "It was sort of a joke," he said.

He's eighty-seven years old now and she's seventy-nine. They live in South Clinton, but they grew up in the Rafter community of Monroe County. He is a sturdy, square-shouldered man, not very tall.

On Thanksgiving Day I wrote about Mrs. Tucker's memories as a logging camp cook in the Tellico River region. Nothing special about it. Thanksgiving was just another work day for the loggers.

Now, Mr. Tucker, born in 1890, puts his memory to work on what Christmas was like when he was a youngster in the foothills of the Unicoi Mountains.

It was a little like Christmas now. But only a little. Christmas carols in church on the Sunday nearest Christmas. And Santa Claus. But the Santa who worked the Rafter territory was not overburdened.

Nevertheless, the stockings were hung on each side of the fireplace. Four pairs of them, for four Tucker brothers. Mr. Tucker, then called "Tuck," was the oldest. These were long stockings their mother had knitted, and they usually were the color of natural wool.

The family all slept in one room of the log house—parents in one bed, Tuck and a brother in another, and the two younger brothers in a third bed. The fire burned low by the time everybody was in bed. And by early the next morning, the big room was cold.

Tuck and the brother who slept with him usually were the first to wake up. Always before dawn. Out of bed they hopped. They'd light one of the coal oil lamps and head for the stockings beside the chimney.

Their usual find was an apple or two, some stick candy, and an orange. Oranges were special. The stores in Rafter and Tellico Plains stocked them only at Christmas. The apples came from the family orchard. Some escaped being sliced and dried, or made into apple butter, and were hoarded till Christmas.

Only after they'd explored their stockings did the boys get the fire going. Of course, everybody in the room was awake soon after the first two boys got up.

There were no toys in the socks. (None under the tree, either. In fact, there was no tree.) Mr. Tucker became acquainted with store-bought toys only after he and Mrs. Tucker had children of their own. What toys he had as a youngster were those he made. He remembers making a sled. It was a toy sometimes and sometimes not. It was a toy when he slid down hill on it in snow. But it was something else when he hauled wood on it.

He remembers getting no clothes at Christmas, and the reason probably was that new clothes had to be made or bought a little earlier, at the beginning of cold weather. He went barefooted until frost, but shoes were necessary before Christmas to prevent frostbite. Even so, his toes were frostbitten one cold winter when he was going to school early enough to build the fire in the school stove.

But all this doesn't mean that Christmas was not a special day. It was very special. It was a day relatives got to see each other. It was the day the children made those oranges and apples and candy last as long as possible. It was the day somebody killed a chicken. Sometimes it was fried, sometimes stewed and served with dumplings at mid-day.

One reason Santa traveled light in the Rafter region was that most people there didn't make much money. Mr. Tucker remembers when his father made as little as $8 a month.

But conditions improved a bit by the time Tuck was eighteen. He was working then, had a three-day-week job carrying the mail from the post office at Tellico Plains to the one at Rafter. The pay was $13 a month.   *—12/25/77*

3

Getting There on Foot

[Advice to persons preparing advertisements for the lodging and tourist businesses:]

Why not color shots of azaleas on Gregory? Deer and wild turkey in Cades Cove? Rhododendron on Thunderhead? Abrams Falls? Ramsey Cascades? And boast of the fact that you must walk to see most of these. And boast that people can walk seventy miles in the Great Smokies and cross only one public road.

People will come, and they'll walk.   *—6/20/71*

00000

Walk. It's good for you. Burns up calories, defogs the brain, makes the blood flow faster, lifts the spirit.

Call it hiking if you'd rather. Most people do if the trip is more than a mile or two, if it's on a foot trail and if you wear a small pack containing a snack and rain gear.

If you are a beginning hiker, don't overdo it. Don't walk till your muscles ache or until you're exhausted. But walk at a good clip till you're breathing deeply. Head up, shoulders back, arms swinging, long steps.

Walk at least twice a week for twenty to thirty minutes. Four or five times a week is better. After a couple of weeks, find time to walk two hours once a week. After a month or six weeks, extend it to four or five hours. By the end of summer, you'll have no trouble with a fifteen-mile hike.

If you are reasonably healthy, you should have no trouble. But if you've got a health problem—particularly one involving the heart—check with your doctor before you start hiking. This doesn't mean heart patients should not walk; it just means a doctor should advise them.

Walk in comfortable clothes. Comfortable shoes and socks are most important. Wear heavy socks that absorb moisture and cushion your feet. Hiking boots are not a must for short walks around home. But you need them for hikes in the mountains. Get boots about ten inches high for ankle support and with thick soles to protect your feet.

You need treaded soles. But you do not need those rock-hard soles that became popular a few years ago. They're fine for bare-rock hiking in New England and the Rockies, but they are not necessary for hiking in this region. The worst thing about them is that they cut up trails. Only thing worse for a trail is horse shoes.

For cold-weather hiking, wear three or four thicknesses of shirts, sweaters and jackets. When you get hot, you can take off a layer and stash it in your pack. Summer hikers need only comfortable trousers and shirts, enough to resist snags. Be sure your hiking clothes fit. You don't want tight clothing that restricts your movements or chafes you. You need rain gear, and most hikers prefer ponchos.

Get a day pack for carrying your lunch and poncho, plus a few safety items: a compass, though you probably won't use it once a year; flashlight; matches in a moisture-proof container; some small bandages for blisters; a strong, sharp knife; and quadrangle maps.

The maps help keep you from getting lost. They also add much to your enjoyment. From them, you learn the name of the ridge or valley where you walk, its elevation, its relationship with adjoining places. You can buy the maps at the TVA map office on the first floor of the West Tower.

You also may want to buy hiking books that describe some of the trails. These are available at visitor centers in the Great Smokies and at most local book stores.

For safety, you should not hike alone. A companion can make a lot of difference if you fall and break a bone or become ill.

Nevertheless, some like to hike alone and accept the risk. A silent hiker walking alone is likely to see more bobcats, foxes, bears and birds than several gabby hikers. But the least a lone hiker can do is leave word with a family member or friend where he is going to hike, where he'll leave his car and when he expects to return.

If you like companionship on the trail and want to learn from veteran mountain roamers, consider joining Smoky Mountains Hiking Club. It's more than just an association of hikers. Established in 1924, it has a long record of effectively championing outdoor causes.

The club usually hikes about twice a month, sometimes on Saturday, sometimes Sunday, and sometimes overnighters involving both days.

Spring probably is the best time to start hiking, though fall is a close second. It's wildflower time, time for lots of birds to be busy in field and forest.

Get out there and try it.   —*4/1/79*

Champion, Veteran Hikers

I get tired just thinking of Margaret Stevenson and Dr. Elgin P. Kintner. My knees ache. My feet blister. And I break out in a bad case of admiration for these two long-walking Maryvillians.

There are nations in Europe and possibly in other parts of the world that these two could walk across in a day without shedding much sweat. But they do most of their walking in the Great Smokies and other East Tennessee mountains.

In a letter a while back, Dr. Kintner said he and Margaret would like to know how many people have hiked all the maintained trails in the park. "This fall we completed such a goal and have enjoyed doing it," he said.

"It all started several years ago when Leslie Webb, librarian at the TVA (now retired), and several others of us wanted to see if we could hike from Newfound Gap to Davenport Gap in one day," he said. "We did. And after a few weeks to get over the painful memories of the hike, the pleasant memories became a challenge for other long hikes. We hiked the trip out to High Rocks from Clingmans Dome and back. With the help of my wife in driving cars, I hiked from Newfound Gap to Maddron Bald and out to Tennessee 73."

Dr. Kintner, I have no idea how many have hiked all the maintained trails in the park. I know I have not. My guess is that you and Mrs. Stevenson are members of a pretty small group.

And I'm sure that few hike as far as you do in a day. Some of the through hikers on the Appalachian Trail (AT) put in up to thirty miles a day. I recall that Branley Owen did as many as forty miles a day when he broke the AT record. But Branley is a good deal younger than you and Margaret.

My own longest hike in the Smokies was from Newfound Gap to Cosby Campground, by way of the AT and the Low Gap Trail. Including a side trip to Mt. Guyot's summit, the total was about twenty-seven miles.

Margaret is the wife of Rev. William R. Stevenson, a retired minister. They moved to Maryville from Tryon, N. C., about three and a half years ago. Since coming to Maryville, Margaret has hiked more than 6000 miles.

But, you say, that can't be. That's nearly five miles per day, seven days a week, fifty-two weeks per year.

It can be. Margaret is the walkingest woman you're likely to meet on a trail around here. She hikes nearly every day. She hikes some with Dr. Kintner, and she has other regular hiking companions for different days of the week. Her husband, like Dr. Kintner's wife, hikes occasionally, but he's not as enthusiastic about it as Margaret.

Dr. Kintner says they made fifteen hikes twenty to twenty-four miles long, thirteen from twenty-five to twenty-nine miles and twelve from thirty to thirty-five miles. "The advantage in long hikes is that you can leave your car at one point, hike down, around, up, over, and back, all on different trails—and without the help of another car or person to pick you up or leave you off."

I would mention another advantage: Putting in that many miles in a day often rules out the necessity of carrying a heavy pack and spending the night at one of those little bare-earth primitive campsites where you wear a little more skin off the mountain.

Dr. Kintner, who is fifty-nine years old, says he started hiking twenty-five years ago, and then he started "serious hiking" five to seven years ago. Once your body is conditioned to these long walks, you don't suffer much, he says.

Mrs. Stevenson started hiking regularly in 1958. Not the long hikes then, but about eight miles a day, nearly every day.

Since moving to Maryville, she's got into long hiking.

She's sixty-four years old, a tall, tough, good-looking gray-haired woman. She carries about one hundred forty pounds, spread fairly thinly over five feet, nine inches.

Margaret described two or three of the routes of their long hikes. This will be more meaningful to people familiar with the Great Smokies. But maybe we can get the general idea across to others.

Nearly everyone knows where Clingmans Dome is. OK. Margaret and the doctor started from the parking lot there, went for a short distance on the Andrews Bald Trail, and then down the Forney Creek Trail—all the way to Fontana Lake. That's quite a hike, nearly anyone will agree. But that's not all. They had to come back.

On the return, they switched westward from the Forney Creek Trail to the Jumpup Ridge Trail, following it to Welch Ridge. They took a side trip off the Welch Ridge Trail to High Rocks. Then back to Welch Ridge Trail and on up the mountain to Silers Bald, then back eastward on the AT to the car in the parking lot. They had hiked about thirty-three miles and they got back to the car fourteen hours after they left it.

Or how about this for one day's walking: Out of Smokemont Campground and up the Hughes Ridge Trail, down across Raven Fork and up Hyatt Ridge to the Balsam Mountain Trail, then to Tri-Corner Knob and the AT, west on the AT to Pecks Corner, then down Hughes Ridge to Bradley Fork and back to the car?

Margaret says it's thirty-five miles. How far is thirty-five miles?

Well, for example, it's approximately the distance from Knoxville to Pigeon Forge.

It's exactly the same as the east-west distances across Luxembourg at the widest point.

And if there is a good trail around the borders of sixty-one-square-mile Liechtenstein, Margaret Stevenson and the doctor could walk completely around that principality in a day and have time left for a short hike.

Sometime this year, after I work myself into better shape, I may go hiking with those two. *—3/13/71*

Properly tuned, maintained and fueled, the human body is a marvelous machine. A trio of Maryville residents who had done all the right things demonstrated the results to me, who had not.

I mean they walked me into the dirt up in the Great Smokies last Monday, ground me down to a nubbin. And those who did it were older than I, up to ten years older than I.

They were Margaret Stevenson, sixty-five, who can keep right on walking into tomorrow and never lose her cheerful charm; Dr. Elgin P. Kintner, sixty, who wants to do all seventy miles of the Appalachian Trail inside the park in two days; and Ralph Collins, sixty-seven, who only started serious hiking since he retired a year or two ago.

I wrote about the long hikes of Margaret and Elgin back in March. I wound up that piece by saying, "Sometime this year, after I work myself into better shape, I may go hiking with those two."

I didn't get myself into better shape. I just went, anyway. When they introduced me to Ralph, there was something vaguely familiar about his smile and the line of his nose. Some conversation confirmed he was the fellow who tried to teach me German at Maryville College more than three decades ago. It wasn't Ralph's fault that the effort wasn't more successful.

We were hiking to High Rocks, a stoney wart high on Welch Ridge, about seven miles south of Silers Bald. We started from Clingmans Dome. Ralph and Elgin changed shoes at the car. Since Margaret and I were already in our hiking boots, we headed on toward the tower.

Margaret immediately established superiority. We started at a fast pace, both walking and talking. Pretty soon I knew I'd have to stop one or the other. I didn't have enough breath for both. I stopped talking.

We got atop the tower for half the sunrise. The red disc was exactly half above the horizon. I'm sure Margaret would have seen it all if she hadn't slowed for me. Elgin and Ralph arrived.

A wind took Elgin's hat and a plastic bag belonging to Margaret and hurled them into fir trees. We recovered the hat.

We hit a good pace from Clingmans to Silers. We didn't have to climb Silers, for the Welch Ridge Trail branches off the Appalachian Trail just east of Silers. But we climbed Silers, anyway, for these Maryville folks do things thoroughly.

Welch Ridge has some of the finest oaks in the Great Smokies. But there was little fall color up there. Many of the oak leaves were still green, but they had a weathered, bedraggled look left from a freeze. Colors of beech and birch leaves were dulled. But we saw patches of color far down in the valleys.

Not much wildlife was out in the wind. We saw occasional juncos, several ravens, one kinglet (I don't know whether golden-crowned or ruby-crowned), a few boomers. Heard red-breasted nuthatches. Saw a monarch butterfly who'll never make it to Mexico or wherever he was going. He was grounded with a torn right wing.

We ate lunch at High Rocks, sitting on the porch of the fire lookout's cabin. While there I borrowed tape from Elgin to put on my left big toe where a slight tenderness was developing. Elgin tapes part of the bottoms of his feet to ward off blisters.

This is one of several things Elgin does to make possible long hikes in relative comfort. He'd already given me a sample of a spread of honey, peanut butter and dry milk. It tastes pretty good and supplies quick energy. Later in the afternoon, he broke out a quart of Gatorade and divided it among us. He studies the various physiological effects of food, liquid, heat and the like on long-distance hikers.

Elgin and some friends have hiked the eastern end of the AT in the park—Newfound Gap to Davenport Gap—in a day. But he has tried twice and failed both times to hike the western end—Newfound Gap to Fontana Dam—in a day. He gave up once because he found he was going to arrive at Fontana far behind schedule. The other time he was affected by hot sunshine. Later, with four other Maryville residents, he hiked the thirty-two miles from Clingmans to Fontana. That time he used an umbrella to shelter himself from the sun.

He's now considering using Mt. Collins as the starting point for both the east-end and west-end hikes, since it's nearer the middle of the AT in the park. And he'll use the umbrella if he has to. It doesn't bother Elgin that somebody might think it a bit odd for a fellow to be rolling along the AT under an umbrella.

Elgin walks some nearly every day. But since he still works for a living, he can schedule the long hikes only every couple of weeks. On the other hand, Margaret and Ralph can hike nearly every day. Margaret does hike about every day except Sunday, when she teaches Sunday school. Those two roll on endlessly, effortlessly.

Margaret and Ralph wore pedometers. When we got back to the car, Ralph's said we'd walked a little more than twenty-three miles.

Margaret's said we'd walked twenty-four miles. I'm sure hers was right. We'd been on the trail about ten hours. The worst mile of the twenty-four was the twenty-third, up steep Mt. Buckley. We were widely separated. I was behind. Margaret was next, holding back to baby me along. Then Elgin. And one hundred yards up ahead in the lead was Ralph, moving steadily, never faltering.

If Buckley had been fifty feet higher, they'd have had to carry me. Oh well, I'll work myself into shape before the next one. —*10/30/77*

Transmountain Hike

The balls of my feet are still a trifle tender, one or two muscles remain a bit sore, but I've got some good memories that will outlast the aches. The aches and memories are from walking across the Great Smoky Mountains Sunday and Monday—from Park Headquarters near Gatlinburg to and through Deep Creek Campground and southward almost to Bryson City.

The distance is about thirty-six miles, as best I can figure it. Hiking time: fourteen hours and thirty-seven minutes—eight hours for the first sixteen mostly uphill miles and six hours and thirty-seven minutes for the next twenty mostly downhill miles.

Besides not having seen parts of it before, I had a couple of other reasons for taking this transmountain walk:

1. Much of the Appalachian Trail along the crest of the Great Smokies is becoming a ditch worn into the earth by too many hikers. I wanted to suggest a good alternative for those who want a hard hike.

2. I'm weary of listening to able-bodied humans complain that they have no way of seeing the beauties of the Great Smokies unless somebody builds more highways into it. I'm fifty-three years old, slightly flat-footed, and I spend most of my time in bed or playing a typewriter. If I can walk across Ol' Smoky, nearly anyone with reasonably good health and the desire to do so can walk the five to fifteen miles necessary to see a great deal of this national park. No more blacktopping is needed.

Because State Highway 73 is closed to cars westward from the intersection with U.S. 441 at Park Headquarters, I walked from the intersection along the road to Fighting Creek Gap. From there, I took the Sugarland Mountain Trail up to its intersection with the Appalachian Trail (AT) on top of Mt. Collins. Then to Clingmans Dome, by way of the short Spruce-Fir nature trail.

I saw only one person on the Sugarland Trail until I reached the spring near the AT shelter on Mt. Collins. This one fellow was still snoozing inside an orange tent at 11 a.m.

Unlike the AT, worn down to hard-packed earth and bare rock, most of this trail is easy on the feet and eyes. It is paved variously with pine needles, hemlock needles, and leaves of many kinds. Sometimes it's only a path a few inches wide winding through tall grass that often doesn't dry from one dew or one shower to the next.

The trail is in rather bad condition only at the two ends—near Fighting Creek Gap and near the AT. The latter section is badly eroded because of the AT traffic down to the shelter and the spring.

The best display of laurel bloom I've seen in years ranged from post-maturity at low altitudes to bud stage in the high country. Scattered flame azalea and a few rose-purple rhododendron blooms were open. Patches of bluets and foam flower were showing off up in the high country, and a few witch hobble blooms were open high on Mt. Collins.

I saw no bears or other large animals. However, wild hogs have rooted up moist sections of the trail and made them pretty messy in a few places. A ruffled grouse exploded into flight less than five yards from me. Squads of snails in lovely tan-brown shells all seemed to be traveling toward Clingmans Dome.

This trail sticks pretty close to the crest of Sugarland Mountain, that lofty divide separating the valleys of Little River and West Fork of the Little Pigeon. One walks part of the time along the narrow crest, listening to the music of both streams thousands of feet below.

I gave up heavy backpacking after back surgery a few years ago, and I carried only a lunch, binoculars, camera, extra socks and a few emergency articles in a daypack. I've also just about given up camping in the mountains. Camping areas that are much used are the most unattractive spots in the park—worn bare of vegetation, often muddy, sometimes littered.

When I reached the Clingmans Dome Road, Alberta met me and we drove back to Gatlinburg to spend the night.   *—6/14/73*

Next morning, after I filled up on a breakfast of sausage, eggs, pancakes, honey and syrup, Alberta drove me back to the top of the mountain and I started down the North Carolina side on the Fork Ridge Trail.

Before I'd taken two steps down the trail, I heard a winter wren singing. A winter wren is a little brown bird that looks like somebody ran out of material before he finished it. But when it tilts back on a fir branch and sends its song rippling out into the cool dampness of the highlands, there is nothing unfinished about it. It's the best.

And this morning, as the sun sent shafts of light down through the mists and the mountain looked all clean and wet and new as if the Maker had just finished making it, winter wrens seemed to be having a convention. I listened to their songs for maybe thirty minutes, till I walked down below their summer altitude range.

The first six and a half miles of this hike were fast and easy, except for a great deal of blowdown the trail maintenance crews hadn't got around to clearing.

Long stretches of the narrow path are so cushiony soft you're tempted to run barefooted.

This part ends abruptly when the trail plunges off the ridge and into Deep Creek. It's one of the major large creeks that glides and jumps over its rocky bottom, draining this highland wilderness garden. I crossed it on the trunk of a fallen tree.

A few yards beyond the crossing, the Fork Ridge Trail intersects the Deep Creek Trail, which swings northeastwardly along the creek up toward a connection with U.S. 441 on Thomas Ridge. In the other direction, the Deep Creek Trail stays fairly close to the east side of the creek for the next 10.5 miles downstream.

The Poke Patch Campsite, the first of four or five primitive campsites strung out along the creek, is just beyond the creek crossing.

Laurel bushes—some as large as average sized dogwoods—were shedding showers of bloom into the creek.

The trail along the creek is wider, wetter, and of gentler grade. It is so wet in places that it's soupy. In other places, it is washed out, the result of the rampaging creek during the March and May floods.

About seventeen miles from the Dome Road, the trail connects with a motor road that leads down through Deep Creek Campground. I walked about three miles on down through the campground and beyond before Alberta, hauling a load of fried chicken, picked me up.

For anyone wanting a long hike in the Great Smokies, I suggest this transmountain trek. It has the variety that comes with an elevation range of about 4500 feet. It has far less traffic than the worn and widely known Appalachian Trail section through the park. —*6/18/73*

An Old Indian Trail

Monday was the right day to head up Ekaneetlee Branch on one of the last scraps of trail still distinguishable of the great Cherokee Indian trails system of two hundred years ago.

Long before dawn, I picked up fellow Norrisonian Bill Allen, possessor of a brand new law degree, and we drove to Maryville and picked up John Stiles, who informed us the weatherman was advertising an eighty percent chance of rain for the day.

By the time we'd taken on a good load of breakfast at Sambo's Restaurant, dawn was near enough for us to see lots of black clouds. They were still up there when we reached Cades Cove. But things were beginning to break right for us.

For instance a park employee unlocked the gate to the loop road the minute we arrived. You can't beat that for timing.

Deer were grazing all over the Cove. We estimated we saw seventy-five.

We once watched a dozen scampering deer and probably thirty wild turkeys at the same time. The turkeys were closely bunched, and they flew when we were within twenty-five to fifty yards of them. Counting as fast as I could, I got up to twenty-five before they were out of sight.

The next day, Ranger Kent Higgins said the Cove now has three turkey flocks—one of forty-one, one of thirty and the other with fewer members. Kent hasn't been able to get an exact count on the smallest.

He estimated one hundred fifty to two hundred deer live in the Cove and the wooded hills immediately surrounding it.

But there is one fewer now than before last Sunday. Kent said somebody shot and killed a deer and left it lying where it fell about 11 a.m. Sunday. The killer was riding in a car.

With the rain threat in mind, we hurried up the Gregory Ridge

Trail—the part along Forge Creek—till we reached the stump of the so-called Giant Poplar.

Ekaneetlee Branch enters Forge Creek a few yards from where that big poplar stood. And I wonder how many Cherokees stopped for a minute to rest against that old tree before heading up the branch toward Ekaneetlee Gap. At 3842 feet above sea level, this gap is one of the lowest spots along the crest of the Great Smokies. Those Cherokees knew how to pick the best spot to cross a mountain. The Indian trail then continued southeasterly down the Carolina side of the mountain. Most of the way it followed another stream, Ekaneetlee Creek, to where it enters Eagle Creek. Then it went down Eagle to where it flows into the Little Tennessee River, not far upstream from the present Fontana Dam.

But lumbering in pre-park days wiped out most of the old trail on the Carolina side.

However, the valley of Ekaneetlee Branch, on the Tennessee side, was never logged. But the good Lord himself came close to clear-cutting a great swath of it in April 1974. A fierce windstorm—perhaps a tornado—ripped into the virgin forest, breaking off and uprooting poplar and hemlock giants nearly as large as the big fellow down on Forge Creek. Fortunately, the storm didn't get all the big trees. Some magnificent ones remain.

I think, maybe, we shouldn't fuss about such storms. Over the long, long period, they may wear white hats. I suspect they're part of the answer to an argument advanced by some opponents of wilderness. They say that the big poplars eventually will die and not be replaced in a forest unlogged or unburned. The reasons given, if I remember correctly, are that poplar seeds need bare earth to germinate. And the seedlings must have sunlight to live.

Well, after a storm like this one, there is bare earth where the old trees were uprooted. And when a storm knocks down so many trees, it leaves unshaded places for young poplars to grow.

The trail was easier than we'd expected. One reason was that a man with a chain saw had sawed a path through the downed trees across the trail. My gratitude for what he'd done kept clashing with my resentment at his bringing the saw into Ekaneetlee Valley. One thing is certain: It would have taken us lots longer to reach the gap if that fellow hadn't used the saw.

It was still so early when we reached the top that we decided not to go back the same way. Instead, we followed the Appalachian Trail westward to where it leaves the crest at Doe Knob. We stayed on the crest, following the old AT route of about thirty years ago, to Gregory Bald.

The clouds were still up there. A south wind was whistling out of North Carolina, always tugging at the treetops. Rain drops spattered us lightly several times. Always bothered by the rain threat, we kept a pretty good pace most of the time.

A deer bounded down into Tennessee as we neared Gregory.

What was he doing up there, where he had nothing much to eat but acorns, when he could have been down in the Cove, grazing like a steer? Maybe he was a radical. Or a hiker.

Bill and John said they'd never failed to see deer on Gregory Bald. I said I'd never seen one there. When we left the bald this time, it was my record that remained intact.

Maybe the deer didn't like the Gregory weather. It was the only cold place we found. The wind blew hard, hurling ragged blankets of fog across the bald at ground level. We dug sweaters and heavy shirts out of our packs before we finished lunch.

We saw lots of bronzed galax on dry ridges. Flame azaleas carried lots of buds for next spring's bloom.

The last leg of the hike was the six downhill miles along Gregory Ridge and Forge Creek. My toes started hurting. They still hurt. We stopped once and stretched out in luxury on dry oak leaves in a galax patch.

It was somewhere on Gregory Ridge that the last drop of rain hit us. But we never got damp enough to iron all day. Nor was the day too hot or too cold. It was nearly perfect.

We got back to Forge Creek and filled up on sweet, cold water. Then back to the stump of the big poplar, where we'd left this trail in the morning.

On down to the parking area, we were still on the old Indian trail. For the Indians continued down Forge Creek and across the Cove and on to the vicinity of the present Maryville, according to park researchers.

With plow and fire and bulldozer and blacktop, white people over the past 200-plus years have obliterated nearly everything that was

Indian east of the Mississippi. So it is good to find a scrap of Cherokee footpath in the forest and walk on it and wonder how many seasons past it was that the first human walked that same route.

It probably isn't exactly the same route. I suspect the man with the chain saw may have rerouted the path in a place or two to suit his convenience. And, 600 or 700 years ago, the Indians may have changed it a bit here and there to go around giant poplars cast down by a similar storm. But it is nearly the same, as much the same as anything can stay in a time span stretched over centuries.

There are two other scraps of old Cherokee trails in or near the park. One is at the eastern park boundary. What's left of it now goes by the name of Asbury Trail, for that outstanding early Methodist bishop who used the same route the Cherokees used. The other is the old Indian road, down the north side of the mountain from Indian Gap 2.5 miles to a junction with the Chimney Tops Trail.

Of course, woods bison and smaller animals probably walked those routes before the Indians. And bear and deer and an occasional white traveler have kept the Ekaneetlee path from fading into the forest over the past two hundred years.

The odds are great against such a narrow, fragile path lasting so long. I-40 probably will not last a third of that time.   *—12/21/75*

Winter Woods

John Stiles and I went walking in the winter woods Monday. Up, up, up from the Big Creek Ranger Station, at the eastern end of the Great Smokies. Up to Walnut Bottom. Then up the Gunter Fork Trail to the crest of Balsam Mountain.

It was a round-trip of just under twenty-two miles. Pretty good mountain walking for two News-Sentinel typewriter operators. We'd been trying for a month to make this hike. But things kept getting in the way of it. And a good thing this turned out to be. For if we'd had the weather experts working on it six months, they couldn't have come up with a better day for our purposes than the one we finally got. Generally, this is the best season for local walkers to walk in the Great Smokies. Most of the horde of summer hikers have gone wherever summer hikers go. You can walk now without sweating gallons.

Also, there's a new leaf carpet on the trails, cushioning the rocks, hiding the erosion. And John and I wanted to get on it before somebody else wore all the new off it.

Some may question the term "winter woods." True, the calendar says this is still autumn. But the ice up there in the mountains and the bare tree branches say it's winter.

So does the thermometer. So will your next heating bills. Use of TVA power hit a peak of 17,356,000 kilowatts Oct. 28. It was Nov. 30 last year before it topped 17 million kw. The national Weather Service station here logged 320 heating degree days in October, compared with only 172 the previous October. This past October was the coldest one since 1917. Temperatures averaged 6.4 degrees below normal. The early days of November were even colder—averaging about eight degrees below normal the first twelve days.

And this day we walked in the woods was the coldest up to that time. The low at McGhee Tyson Airport was twenty-five. It was eight at Newfound Gap and zero at Mt. LeConte. I don't know what it was along Big Creek and Gunter Fork, but it was well below freezing, for the creeks were fringed with ice. Icicles a foot long were suspended from overhung banks. The wind blew all day. And on top of Balsam Mountain, it screamed and moaned like the devil's choir and must have sent the chill factor far below zero.

We started walking from the ranger station at about 7 a.m. We hurried to keep half-way warm. It would be an hour before we saw the sun warming some of the peaks above us and nearly two hours before we'd walk in sunshine.

We walked an easy grade, used years earlier by logging trains of the old Crestmont Lumber Co. To our left, Mouse Creek tumbled down from Mt. Sterling over Mouse Creek Falls. On our right was a great clutter of house-sized gray boulders which must have tumbled down from the south side of the main ridge of the Great Smokies a few millennia ago. Some of the boulders are in Big Creek. The water swirls around the big ones and goes jump-jumping over the smaller.

We stopped and drank from a small stream that comes bubbling and sliding down a deep rock wrinkle. A marker there says it is Brakeshoe Spring. Did some railroader cool a hot brakeshoe with some of that water? Or did a brakeshoe have to be replaced there?

We hadn't intended to go all the way to the mountaintop. We planned to go up Gunter Fork to a waterfall that John Smartt had mentioned to Carlos Campbell and which Carlos mentioned to me. But at Walnut Bottom we came to a marker which said it was only 4.5 miles to the top. It also said we'd already walked 6.5 miles. We looked at our watches. It wasn't yet 9. It'd be a shame not to go on to the top, we agreed. Should be no problem in getting there by about 11.

Well, that wasn't to be. We'd been misled by the easy grade along Big Creek. I don't mean the grade up Gunter Fork is any backbreaker, but it's a lot steeper than the one along Big Creek.

Nobody provided bridges across Gunter Fork, as they had on Big Creek. The boulders were icy at our first Gunter Fork crossing, and we each slipped and wet a boot.

The higher we hiked the colder it got. We could tell, not so much from the way we felt, but from the way the rhododendron leaves looked. Up here they were curled tight like little green cigars.

Nearly all the deciduous leaves were down up here and the wind was putting the hook to the few that remained. It's a young forest, grown up since Crestmont logged it forty or fifty years ago. Lots of poplar and birch whose straight, light-colored trunks were beautiful in bright sunshine.

We reached that waterfall, a mile and a half or two above Walnut Bottom. And I think we could have camped up there six months without finding a more appropriate moment to look at it.

This is sort of a combination waterfall-waterslide. I wouldn't fuss with anybody who wants to call it a cascade. It starts maybe seventy-five yards up the mountain as a waterfall. Then it slides several yards and then hits a steeper section from which it both falls and slides into a catch basin beside the trail. The rock underlying this falling, sliding water is yellow-brown.

The Great Smokies have lots of pretty falling-water scenes. Abrams Falls is outstanding, more for the pool below than for the actual fall. Rabbit Creek has a nice one. There's a long, beautiful waterslide on Forney Creek. The cascades on Upper Hazel Creek and those on Ramsey Prong are worth lots of walking to see. Mill Creek Falls is the highest of nearly a straight drop I've seen in the park. Then there are Laurel Falls, Grotto Falls, and Rainbow Falls, all pretty. I still have Dome Falls, above Grotto on Roaring Fork, to see for the first time. And Bob Maher, the old broker-hiker-trouter, tells me I need to check out a waterfall on one of the prongs of Little River, on the north side of Clingmans Dome, and another higher on Mouse Creek than the one John and I saw.

Ordinarily, this thing on Gunter Fork probably is no prettier than some of those. But there was magic about it this particular time, the magic of a matchless combination of rock and ice and water and sunshine.

The sun—out of a sky that had no scrap of cloud all day—was aimed directly into the scene on the rocks. It sparkled every drop of water, every inch of ice.

The water made its final descent down the rock wall eight or ten feet in front of us. Most of the water was falling free from the right side of the wall. But a generous portion was sliding over the steeply sloped left side. And it was doing it under ice. Just the thinnest glaze of ice that followed the contours of the rock under it. And in that thin space beteen rock and ice hurried a thousand trickles of water. It was a psychedelic sight no drugs and lights could match.

I thought this thin ice crust would soon vanish—either melt under the direct sun rays or be washed down by the water trickles beneath it. But it was still there when we returned hours later. However, the sun had gone and taken the magic with it.

But, standing in the same spot on our return trip, we saw a less spectacular ice show an eighth of a mile nearly straight up the mountain, where the sun was still hitting. A rim of ice—solid at the top and spangling into icicles at the bottom—was suspended from a rock ledge. It was about twenty feet wide and three or four feet high. In the two minutes we watched it, two five-foot sections of it broke loose and came crashing down in mini-avalanches.

Two good shows from the same spot the same day really were more than we paid for.

When I walk in the mountains, I nearly always bring back something to keep. But this bright, cold day on Gunter Fork will keep longer than most. I will remember, among the minor things, that the ink in my ballpoint was frozen when we got back to the car and the thing wouldn't write a lick till the car heater had been going several minutes.

It doesn't matter much that we worked pretty hard on the eleventh mile to the top of the Balsam. Or that I burst a blister on my heel somewhere on the way back. Or that the bottoms of our feet felt like they'd been beaten with hammers. (That's what you get for jogging down a mountain.) In memory, these small unpleasantnesses diminish and the bright things last on alone.   —*11/14/76*

Azaleas on Gregory Bald

I went to Gregory Bald last Sunday to see the azaleas. Got rained on. Got my feet wet enough to do for the rest of the year. Saw lots of fog. Saw azaleas wrapped in fog. They're pretty good that way, but not as good as wrapped in sunshine.

Rain wasn't falling when I headed up the Forge Creek-Gregory Ridge Trail. But I'd heard Weatherman John Norton say on the radio that rain chances were seventy per cent for the day.

It had rained the previous night. Forge Creek was full and noisy. The rain had wiped the trail free of tracks, left it looking like the dirt yard of a mountain cabin freshly brushed with a broom. But there hadn't been enough rain to wash away the manure left by the horse which hadn't read the marker that said horses were not allowed.

Since there were no post-rain tracks on the trail, I knew I was the first hiker going up. I also had the honor of breaking the spider webs built across the trail.

Damp wilderness smells floated in the humid air. Not much wildlife was moving or speaking. Heard an occasional oven bird beeping away out there on the wet, wet ground. Once a pileated woodpecker ripped a raucous hole in the silence. Other birds spoke occasionally. But it was a quieter morning than usual in the woods.

A big fat slug glistened on the ground. A snail had parked his rig three feet up the trunk of a tulip poplar.

Biggest animal I saw from the trail was a gray squirrel. No panthers, bobcats, foxes, bears, rabbits, skunks, hogs, deer, mice, nor even a chipmunk.

Made the last crossing of Forge Creek before settling down to the long, tiring trek up Gregory Ridge. A few yards beyond the crossing was something new. A huge tree, a patriarch which had stood there at least 100 years before the first white human walked that trail, had come crashing down.

Trail maintenance workers had cleaned up the mess.

They had rolled a great trunk section to a resting place beside the trail. It is hollow. And as Gregory-bound hikers round a curve, that hollow looms ahead like a tunnel. Small people could walk through it. A half-dozen very close friends could spend a night in it. If it were off the trail, away from humans, a bear might winter in it. One may try it, anyway.

A few yards beyond the hollow trunk was something else new— Campsite A12. A blue-gray tent, as closed as a cocoon, rested there. The occupants apparently hadn't yet turned over the first time. Their supper dishes rested on a log. A small bag of something was suspended from a tree branch.

Though this is a new campsite, it already had commenced to have the look of a groundhog hole worn slick. When one of these places is heavily used, even for only a season, there is no way to keep it from becoming unsightly. No matter how good their intentions, campers trample and kill ground-cover vegetation, wear out the humus, then get down to bare earth, which they compact. This is one reason I go and come back the same day. But I know others enjoy overnight hikes. Or staying in the mountains days at a time. This wasn't much of a problem twenty years ago, when few did it. It is serious now.

Saw first flame azalea bloom half way up Gregory Ridge. Continued to see scattered ones along trail. Some azalea bushes had unopened bloom buds. Made me wonder whether many on top would be open.

I had been hurrying, hoping to get up and back down before the rain. But the first raindrops started pattering on the tree canopy when I was about a mile short of Rich Gap. But it wasn't a pouring-down rain and the canopy served as a pretty good umbrella for a time.

Met first humans of the day. A young man and woman, both carrying heavy packs, came down from the direction of the gap.

The rain settled down to serious business by the time I reached the gap, and I put on my poncho.

Up to that point, I'd seen no sign of the damage done by wild hogs, and I'd begun to wonder where all the hogs had gone. I soon found out.

The thinly wooded area on the north side of the trail between the gap and Gregory looked as through a crew with mattocks and spades had worked it over. I suspect the hogs rooted here for spring beauty corms. And I suspect there will be fewer spring beauty blooms next spring.

Started seeing more people. Met two young men who had spent the night at the Mollies Ridge Shelter. We compared the fragrance of some white azaleas growing on the left side of the trail with that of another clump growing on the right side.

You wouldn't think there'd be any difference. But there was. Those on the left side apparently had been in full sun (when it shone) and they were over-mature and not very fragrant. Those on the other side were shaded by a small oak. They were at their peak, and the fragrance was delightful.

Only the white wild azaleas are fragrant. Or maybe I should say they're the only ones I've sniffed that are. And they aren't numerous. Other places where I've seen them are beside Tellico River, in Monroe County, and beside North White Oak Creek, in Scott County.

Met two men and a woman on top of Gregory. They'd come up the shorter trail from Sams Gap, on the Parsons Branch Road.

Rain still fell and walking through the tall Gregory grass was about like walking in a creek. So I didn't get far enough off trail to review each azalea bloom separately. But from what I saw through the fog, I'd say this year's bloom is a little below average. Best blooms I saw up close were off the bald, down near the Moore Spring.   *—7/1/79*

4

The Down Side of Hiking

Trailing arbutus was beginning to bloom in the oak and pine litter on School House Gap Road last Sunday. Woodpeckers pecked. Little blue butterflies fluttered.

Down in Whiteoak Sink, an Eastern phoebe seemed interested in nest-building in some nook on the cliff above Blowhole Cave.

Spring beauties, bloodroot, toothwort, rue anemone, violets and hepaticas bloomed in the Sink. And wild hogs had plowed the flat area nearest the Blowhole.

The hog rooting was new, within the previous week. It hadn't been done a week earlier. I know, for I was there the past two Sundays.

Two Maryvillians, Bruce Watt and Dan Lawson, took another Maryvillian, John Stiles, and me into the Sink two Sundays ago. It was the first time for John and me.

Alberta and I decided that was where we'd take some friends who wanted to go hiking. They had to cancel, but Alberta and I were already leaning in that direction. So we went on alone.

The weather was perfect both Sundays, but the first Sunday was warmer. Warm enough for the air coming out of the Blowhole to feel cool. Dan and Bruce said you can cool yourself in the mouth of the cave in summer and get warm there in winter. The temperature was so near neutral last Sunday that I could feel neither hot nor cold air at the cave mouth.

Whiteoak Sink is a small, crazy kind of place in the extreme western end of Great Smoky Mountains National Park. You can follow a stream in it and it will vanish into the earth under your feet. You can watch another one fall about forty feet straight into a wide-mouthed cave.

When the four of us were there two weeks ago, we saw quite a bit of ice at one side of the waterfall cave entrance. And a piece of ice the size of a washtub remained there last Sunday, the first day of spring. The sun was making a mistbow there last Sunday.

People used to live in the Sink. People named Davis, McClannahan, Ledbetter, Emert and perhaps others. This is according to John Dunn, the Townsend postmaster, recommended by Dan Lawson as the best authority on the Sink.

They cultivated the flat land in the Sink. It's rich, dark soil. That plowed up by the hogs was loose and nearly black.

I assume that the National Park Service (NPS) would be just as happy if nobody went near Whiteoak Sink. For NPS maintains no trail into the place. Anyone going into it ought to go first with somebody familiar with it.

When people lived there forty or fifty years ago, they dug a narrow road for sleds and wagons. It curled down from School House Gap, following a small stream part of the way. This is still the best way to go. You may get your feet damp in the little stream that snakes down through the gloom of a rhododendron thicket. You may turn an ankle on a slippery log hidden six inches under a bed of leaves.

One reason NPS isn't particularly eager for visitors to go into the Sink is that it has had to rescue a few foolish spelunkers from the caves. Markers warn that nobody without a permit is supposed to enter the caves. Blowhole is a deep cave that goes straight down. Nobody but an experienced, well-equipped caver should go in.

After Dan, Bruce, John and I had seen the major sights, the Blowhole and the waterfall, we explored a little. Going through a thin strip of woodland, we came to another field. A spring rises on one side of this field, and a house probably sat somewhere near the spring. Somebody once piled lots of rock into a stone dry wall behind the spring. They had piled lots more rock into a long, low wall across a wide draw. We couldn't figure out the purpose, for the wall was too low for a fence. Maybe it was just a stretched-out rock pile.

We went back to the Blowhole and headed off in another direction, following the old wagon road. We lost it in a wide strip of woodland and found it again at the edge of a field on the other side of the woods. We followed it past an old home site, marked by a few rusting buckets and pots, and a long stone fence.

We heard a stream and went to it. We assumed we'd walked in a wide circle and come to the same stream we'd seen earlier falling into the cave. We figured we might as well follow it on down to the cave.

It didn't turn out quite that way. We followed the stream maybe 300 yards until it simply disappeared into the rocky streambed at our feet. There was no visible cave. The streambed continued, evidence that the creek did stay partly above ground during very heavy rains. We followed the streambed back into the area near the Blowhole. John Dunn later told me this creek runs into the Blowhole in wet weather.

Upon rereading some of this, I find I've mentioned "fields" and "strips of woodland." Maybe that's misleading. For it's all woodland now. But the trees are far fewer per acre in the fields that were cultivated a half-century ago. And the rich soil still produces a great crop of weeds in the old fields. Snow and wind of the past winter had laid the tall weed stalks flat, all turned in the same direction.

Something else a little misleading now is the name, Whiteoak Sink. For there aren't many white oaks down there in the flat land. The most numerous tree species there now is tulip poplar. Maybe white oaks will be dominant again in a climax forest there 250-300 years from now. A few really huge poplars probably will still stand there then.

More white oaks grow in the woodland strips, which were logged but never cultivated.

When Bruce first mentioned Whiteoak Sink to me several months ago, he said it was a great place for spring wildflowers. Only a few were blooming two weeks ago. There were lots more last Sunday, and we saw trillium, columbine, wild geranium and one or two small patches of either Dutchman's breeches or squirrel corn, all getting ready to bloom in a few days.

The only non-native flower Alberta and I saw was a forsythia, probably marking an old home site.

I'm not trying to lure anybody into Whiteoak Sink. For it's a place that can be quickly ruined by too many hogs or too many people. And I suspect unpleasant things could happen to one there. I'd guess at least 1000 copperheads live in those old stone fences and walls and half that many rattlers in Blowhole Cliff. With no markers to guide you and no maintained trails, you could get lost. And if you should venture into one of those caves, you might get lost for a long time.

If I were you, I wouldn't go near the place.   *—3/22/77*

Alberta and I one recent day hiked under arches of laurel bloom on the trail along Abrams Creek to Abrams Falls. Never saw the bloom so numerous so late in the season. (But the peak is passed there now. You have to climb a little higher to see good laurel.)

Abrams was running fairly full. Water was a trifle roily from organic matter washed out of the mountains by thunderstorms. Several picnickers were having lunch at the Falls. One young couple had a basset hound on a leash. They said he's a good hiker, except when he steps on an ear and trips.

In taking him to Abrams Falls, they fractured a park regulation. This trail is one of the places in the park where pets—even on a leash—are prohibited. But their infraction wasn't as serious as that of the owners of two big hunting hounds we saw running unleashed at the beginning of the trail. Chances are they'd been on an illegal hunt.

A repulsive sight at the Falls was a big pot hole half filled with litter. I've wondered about this hole. It's so straight, so nearly perfect, you wonder whether it is a completely natural result of stream scouring. Or did somebody lend a helping hand—Indians, maybe?

I've wondered, too, whether the Cherokees may have used it as a cook pot. They could have heated large stones and dumped them into the water in this stone pot and boiled lots of corn.

They didn't live there, but they sometimes had hunting camps in Cades Cove. Their closest town was Chilhowee, near where Abrams Creek entered the Little Tennessee (now Chilhowee Lake there).

I wouldn't want to eat any corn boiled in that pot hole this time. I didn't itemize all the gunk in it, but one of the things on top was a pair of underwear shorts.

(Park regulations now require hikers and campers to pack out everything—including underwear shorts. But these regulations often aren't enforced because funds are inadequate to hire enough rangers.)

Alberta and I walked back to the ledges at the top of the neck of the Abrams Creek Horseshoe to eat lunch. We settled down on a couple of rocks, and one of the first things I saw was another pair of underwear shorts somebody had left. This made two pairs of underwear in about two and a half miles of trail. If people are losing underwear at this rate along all six hundred miles of trails in the park, I think somebody is missing a bet in not getting a Ford Foundation grant to study behavior trends in national parks.   *—6/20/71*

Dangers of the Trail

Hypothermia.

That's what killed Mark Hanson, the Kentucky youth, up in the Great Smokies a few days ago. It almost certainly is what killed Geoff Hague, the Morristown Boy Scout, in February 1970.

It is a condition that strikes the wet, the cold and the exhausted. And the unprepared, or the inexperienced.

It is a "lowering of the body temperatures," according to Dr. Robert Lash, who helped in the search for the lost hiker and examined the body after it was found.

Hypothermia is the"usual mechanism of death for people who get lost in cold weather," Dr. Lash says.

"The usual story is that they start getting cold. If they're wet, that increases the heat loss. If they are fatigued and exhausted, this also increases the severity of the problem.

"As the body cools, various functions become impaired. Your motor power goes out, then your mental abilities go and you become unconscious. In a period of time, your brain and cardiac functions cease."

The symptoms:

"You start feeling cool. Then cold. Then fatigued. Then uncontrollable shivering, a reflex protective action to stir up heat by muscular exertion.

"Then your mind is already beginning to go."

As the body temperature drops to about 88 degrees, the shivering stops and muscular rigidity begins. The brain works less efficiently. As the body temperature sinks on down to about 85 degrees, the victim becomes irrational. He's unconscious at 80 degrees and death comes a few degrees lower.

Dr. Lash thinks hypothermia had started working on Mark before he and his companion, Ben Fish, separated east of Tri-Corner Knob on the Appalachian Trail (AT) late Sunday, March 9.

That Sunday probably will live in Ben Fish's memory as a nightmare as long as he lives. Ben and Mark and John Chidester, all Eastern Kentucky University students, had spent Saturday night at the AT shelter just inside the park, near Davenport Gap.

They ate breakfast, packed and headed southwestwardly along the AT. The first five miles are all uphill, up, up, up to Mt. Cammerer.

Ben and John had been Boy Scouts. Ben had hiked in the Great Smokies before. But, according to National Park Service officials, Mark had had little or no experience to prepare him for a hard day in the mountains, carrying a pack, hiking a long distance.

But it was John who dropped out first. His boots hurt his feet. He turned back at the end of two hours. Ben and Mark went on.

Snow was on the trail in the higher elevations, drifted deeply in places.

The going was hard for both men. Probably not much like what they'd imagined when they planned the trip.

They were among more than 100 overnight hikers in the Great Smokies that weekend. Most of the others were near the same age as these three. Even more came last weekend, and an estimated 250 of them are there this weekend, many from as far away as colleges and universities in Michigan.

These three started hiking at about 2500 feet above sea level. John probably turned back before reaching Mr. Cammerer, some 2500 feet higher and several degrees colder.

Then down they went to Low Gap at about 4242 feet, up again to Cosby Knob at more than 5000, down to Camel Gap at 4694, up to Camel Hump Knob at more than 5100 feet. Down to another gap and then up to Inadu Knob at 5918 feet.

They're getting into a long stretch of high country now. Trudging up Old Black, backs probably aching from the unaccustomed packs, they go above the 6000-foot level.

The snow is deep in places. Sleet and new snow start falling after the middle of the afternoon.

They climbed gradually higher, up to the 6300-foot mark where the AT passes Guyot Spring.

Mark was growing extremely tired. He took off the pack that hurt his back and shoulders and sapped his strength. And he left it beside the trail. This was a dreadful mistake. In that pack was his sleeping bag.

They were still trying for the AT shelter at Tri-Corner Knob, about twelve miles from where they'd started in the morning so long ago.

Night came. Even without his pack, Mark was nearing total exhaustion. He finally sat down in the snow. He told Ben he couldn't go any farther.

According to the statement Ben later gave NPS officials, he slapped Mark. Shouted at him. Pulled at him. Threatened him.

Mark said that no matter what Ben might do to him—shoot him, stab him, kill him—he just could not go on.

Dr. Lash's impression is that it was 9:30 or 10 that night when Ben finally left Mark and headed on toward the shelter. But he didn't make it. Not that night.

He, too, grew so tired he could not move another step. But he still had his pack. He unrolled his sleeping bag and crawled into it.

He got up the next morning and went on to the shelter. It was only five minutes from where he'd spent the night.

He found two other hikers at the shelter and they went back with him to look for Mark. They didn't find him.

It wasn't until a week later that searchers found his body. It was about a mile down the Tennessee side of the mountain from where Ben had left Mark. It was some ten feet from the cold waters of Buck Fork, one of the high headwater tributaries of Little Pigeon River's Middle Prong.

Of course, nobody knows exactly what Mark did, or what he thought after Ben left him.

With no sleeping bag to shield him from the sleet and snow, he must have been extremely cold. Dr. Lash quoted Ben as saying Mark's trouser legs were frozen from his feet to above his knees.

After he had rested a bit, Dr. Lash thinks, Mark may have become aware of the danger of his situation. And his "adrenalin started pumping," giving him strength to move again.

But he moved in the wrong direction, off the trail and down the mountain to disaster. Why?

Dr. Lash wonders whether there flickered across Mark's mind some memory of advice for a lost person to follow a water course. Was he lured by the lights of a car or lights in a house far down in Jones Cove or near Cosby?

When hypothermia starts working on you, what should you do?

Of course, the answer depends on the situation. If you know you're near shelter and your strength is sufficient to get you there, go.

But if you're in a wilderness and you're uncertain how far it is to shelter, stop. Conserve your energy, Dr. Lash advises.

"Try to find some means of getting warm again. And dry. Use

what's available." If a sleeping bag is all that's available, get in it. If there are two persons together, both should get into the same sleeping bag. Both naked.

"That's the best method on earth to start warming," he says.

Food helps, especially food high in carbohydrates and protein. These will help "replenish your body fires," Dr. Lash advises.

But the first treatment is prevention. Consider your equipment, your limitations. When you're out in the Great Smokies, "have some respect for what's up there."   *—3/20/75*

00000

I asked Dr. Robert Lash, head of the Poison Control Center here, whether a fellow going out alone in the mountains should not carry a shot of anti-snake venom. I thought it'd be nice just to give yourself a shot of the stuff, thumb your nose at the snake and walk out whistling.

But he said no. The danger, he said, is that you may be allergic to the anti-venom. If you're allergic to it and you get a shot of it in a hospital, somebody can do something to counteract it.

But he did have a few reassuring facts. No. 1 was that only one person in this country has ever died of a copperhead bite. This was a Crossville woman, several years ago, and she died not because the venom was all that powerful, but because she was allergic to it, the way some people are allergic to bee venom.

No. 2: Of the many people he's examined who were bitten by poisonous snakes, about a third needed no treatment because the snake failed to inject venom into the wound. Maybe he'd just used all his venom on a rabbit. Or he simply failed to contract his venom sack.

No. 3: None of his snakebite patients died or suffered tissue loss.

What would he do if he were alone, far up a trout stream, miles from his car, and a rattler nailed him?

Use a razor blade to make one small cut, one-eighth inch wide and one-eighth inch deep, across each fang puncture. Then with his mouth or a suction cup in a snakebite kit, suck out as much venom as possible. Tie some sort of band around the limb above the wound. But not tightly. Start walking out.   *—6/30/75*

5

The Hiker's High

With the ease that comes from long practice, Dr. A. Rufus Morgan lifts his jaunty red backpack, fits it to his broad shoulders and leads the group of about twenty-five hiking friends up the Trillium Gap Trail to Mt. Le Conte.

It is a special occasion, Dr. Morgan's annual birthday hike to Le Conte. This one celebrates his eighty-sixth birthday. It is his 122nd hike to Le Conte and his ninth this year.

Dr. Morgan is a mountaineer by heredity and choice. His maternal ancestors were Silers who came into Western North Carolina as pioneers and left their name on its geography. Silers Bald in the Great Smokies is one of three peaks named for them.

A retired Episcopal minister, Dr. Morgan lives at Cartoogechaye, a small North Carolina community in the shadow of the Nantahalas.

He is known to many hikers because he has hiked nearly every Western North Carolina mountain, as well as many in Tennessee. For years, he single-handedly maintained the fifty-five miles of the Appalachian Trail southward along the Nantahalas to the Georgia line. When too much age caught up with him for this task—which he performed while also fulfilling many other responsibilities—he formed the Nantahala Hiking Club. The club maintains this trail section now.

He is known to mountain craftsmen for several reasons. One of these is that he was one of those instrumental years ago in forming the Southern Highlands Handicraft Guild. He believes strongly that it is good for people to live in his rural mountain area. Promoting craft work has been one of his ways of helping them live in dignity, with pride in their skills and some money in their pockets.

And, of course, he is known for his long ministry in the Episcopal Church in many Western North Carolina mountain towns, as well as some in South Carolina. The church has honored him for his outstanding service.

Now, heading into his eighty-seventh year, Dr. Morgan wears the weathered, enduring look of a large old oak, or one of the big gray stones thrust out of the Great Smokies earth.

His hair is as white as a bald eagle's head, and he goes without a hat in nearly all weather. He started going hatless in a time when nearly everyone else in the mountains wore a hat. So attached were most mountain men to their hats that they wore them from the time they got up till they went to bed, indoors and out. Here is a story about Dr. Morgan, a hat and a moonshiner:

Officers raided a moonshine still in an area where Dr. Morgan was known. They missed the moonshiner at the still site, but they found his old black hat there. They concluded he'd heard them coming and had left in such a hurry he ran out from under his hat.

A few minutes later, the officers came upon a hatless mountaineer, and they were certain they had their moonshiner. They arrested him. He vowed he was innocent.

But they told him they knew he was the moonshiner whose still they had found. The hat was at the still, and here he was, hatless. There could be no other explanation, they said, for his being without his hat.

However, the man was not to be put down. He said there was another explanation. Obviously remembering Dr. Morgan's hatless habit, he told the officers, "I'm an Episcopalian."

Because of his advanced age and failing sight, Dr. Morgan has shed his official responsibilities. But he continues an amazing number of unofficial activities. One of these is hiking.

He has selected the route for his birthday hike. That is, he has suggested it. If a majority of the hikers prefer a different trail, it will be all right with him, he tells them. Nobody suggests a different one. It will be as he wants it—up the mountain by way of Trillium Gap, a 6.5-mile route, and down the next day by way of the Bullhead Trail, about seven miles.

Although Dr. Morgan has reached an age where most of those still living walk no farther than a few blocks, there is no doubt in the minds of his companions that the old man will reach the top. After all, it was only a few weeks earlier that he made his most recent hike up the same mountain. One more birthday will make little difference.

His stride is long and steady. The red pack stays near the head of the line of hikers. Obviously, some of those a good deal younger are having more trouble than Dr. Morgan.

But some of his friends worry about the chance that he might fall. His sight is so poor he might place a foot a little off center on a slippery rock at one of the numerous places where small streams cross the trail. One or two of the men stay close to him at these crossings.

He manages alone, though. His long, stout hiking staff helps compensate for the weak eyes. He plants it firmly and then goes ahead, even over the slipperiest places.

The hikers rest at Grotto Falls (where Roaring Fork plunges into a trailside pool) and some individuals occasionally pause a minute or two at other spots to catch their breath or to look at a plant. Several ask Dr. Morgan to identify plants. Looking at them as best he can and feeling them with his fingers, he identifies every one. He holds no botany degree but he is one of the best amateur botanists around.

At Trillium Gap, everyone takes off packs and gets out lunch. Asking the blessing, Dr. Morgan thanks God for the "beauties of October," the strength to hike, opportunities to rest, and congenial companions.

The "beauties of October" are particularly evident from the gap on up to the top. Birch trees provide plenty of yellow, and spindly witch hobble bushes wear leaves colored from pale yellow to dark wine.

A huge birthday cake, warm from the glow of many candles, rests on the Morgan table at dinner late in the afternoon in the Lodge.

After dinner, most of the hikers walk with Dr. Morgan to Cliff Top.

Cliff Top is a spectacular mass of rock, bare except for scattered mountain myrtle, stunted rhododendron and a few hardy kindred species. A southwestern outpost of Le Conte, it is a good place to go for a far-ranging view of the mountains. And, when the sky is clear, it is one of the world's best places to look at a sunset.

But the sky is not entirely clear this evening. A cloud ring rides the rim of the western horizon. The sun is out of sight. Either the hikers have arrived a minute late or the clouds hide the sun's last seconds above the mountains.

Below the bright sky, the scene darkens by degrees, mountain by mountain. The main range of the Smokies is darker than the sky, Sugarland Mountain is darker than the main range. The hues shade down through blue-gray, blue-purple to blue-black. Then dramatic change.

Rising out of the narrow upper valley of Little Pigeon River's West Prong is fog nearly as white as snow. It mushrooms up in humps and peaks like sheeted goblins. While the rest of the scene is as still as a painting on a wall, the fog moves, mostly upward but sometimes horizontally, in ghostly ballet against the dark bulk of the mountains.

Dr. Morgan sits on a ledge and watches. Some of the others are quiet, some talk.

A man sitting next to Dr. Morgan motions for silence.

The old man begins to recite long passages of poetry he obviously has loved for years. It is about mountains and people who love mountains. He writes good poetry himself, but this is not his.

As the light in the sky dims, Dr. Morgan lifts his voice in the old hymn, "Day Is Dying in the West." The others join him.

When the group starts back to the Lodge, the trail through the woods is dark enough for flashlights to be necessary, and the air much cooler.

It is much like watching exciting drama and then abruptly, after the last curtain call, walking out of the theater into the night. —*10/31/71*

0000

It is a sad day on Mt. Le Conte. Oct. 15, Dr. Rufus Morgan's ninety-fourth birthday.

This is his first birthday in more than most people remember that he has not celebrated by climbing lofty Le Conte and spending the night at Le Conte Lodge.

A priest of the Episcopal church, a prince of mountaineers, Rufus first climbed Le Conte in 1928. He climbed it the 174th time on his ninety-third birthday. This one was to be his 175th.

He made a reservation for himself and a dozen others late last year for this date.

They would shoulder their packs in the morning chill and start briskly up the trail. Nearly always, Rufus was in front or near the front. In recent years, a close friend or two made it a point never to be more than a step or two from him.

For his eyes, once nearly as far-seeing as an eagle's, had failed. He is nearly blind. He might stumble on a stone. It was not a fast hike up the mountain, not in these recent years, with Rufus in his nineties.

He was not nearly so swift afoot as he was when he began his ministry in 1914. He rode a horse between his churches then. Or if the weather was particularly bad, he walked.

He rarely stumbled on his hikes up Le Conte, no more than most others on the rocky, uneven trails. He had been over them so many times he knew what to expect. Though he could not see, he sometimes told his companions to look for certain wildflowers at particular spots on the trail. He remembered them there from earlier years.

After a long break for lunch more than half way to the top, the Morgan party would get going again and reach the Lodge near the middle of the afternoon or later. After a long rest, they would be refreshed for supper. Rufus would say grace. Then he'd blow out the candles on his birthday cake.

Other guests at the Lodge might wonder about the fuss over the old man. And if they asked, they learned that his life was bordering on legend.

Questioners might learn that he had been a pioneer educator. It was he who established Western North Carolina's school for mountain youngsters at Penland. And it was his sister Lucy who later joined him and established the crafts department for which the school gained fame.

After the birthday supper at the Lodge, the Morgan party and all others who wished to join them would walk out to Cliff Top to watch the day die gloriously in the western sky. Rufus would lead hymn singing. Then, as the last colors fled the sky, the group would get out flashlights and walk quietly back to the Lodge.

For some the day was a kind of celebration of God's blessings.

Last spring, Rufus suffered a back injury in a fall. He cancelled his October 15 reservation at the Lodge. But he said to keep the reservations in force for the others of his party. Word came last month to cancel all the reservations. The others did not want to make the hike without Rufus.   *—10/15/79*

Hiking Club Anniversary

Smoky Mountains Hiking Club is fifty years old and is celebrating that anniversary in Gatlinburg and on a trail or two in the high country.

No other adult organization in this region can be held responsible for so many aching muscles, blistered feet and storm-wet clothing.

Nor so many non-drug highs when the spirit ignores the sore feet and sweaty body and bounds like a deer, sings like a thrush and swoops like a falcon.

What is it about a trail to a mountaintop that will make some people work harder and endure more than they ever do willingly under other circumstances?

There aren't many simple straight-forward answers to questions like that. Most hikers reach for stories, for examples, in trying to answer. Marshall Wilson, who bears a good deal of the responsibility for getting this hiking club started, provides this illustration:

He and his wife Zelma, a daughter, son-in-law, and three grandchildren hiked to Rainbow Falls.

"At noon, as we reached the Falls, a sudden heavy rainstorm hit us and we were not prepared for it," Mr. Wilson said. "We crouched against a leaning rock ledge that afforded scant shelter and ate lunch, then started sloshing back down the trail."

There wasn't a dry thread on anyone, but nearly everybody was laughing. Mrs. Wilson was particularly amused at the rain streaming down the noses of her companions.

But six-year-old grandson Mike Eastridge was not a true believer. After trudging along in wet and miserable silence, he looked up at the laughing Mrs. Wilson and asked "Grandmother, is this fun?"

"The only response she could give," Mr. Wilson said, "was to laugh all the louder."

This is one of the stories Marshall Wilson tells in *Once Upon a Mountain*, some "recollections" the author put on paper for this fiftieth year of the club he helped form.

Mr. Wilson was a high school teacher in 1924 but he was working the summer of that year for the YMCA. In a ten-day period between job changes, he and his brother Willett went on a five-day hike in the Great Smokies.

Starting at Gatlinburg, they walked to Cherokee Orchard and

camped the first night. Then up Mill Creek (now Le Conte Creek) to Mt. Le Conte. Down Bear Pen Hollow they came to a campsite on the bank of Alum Cave Creek. The next day, they lunched with timber cruisers on brook trout and stewed ramps in white sauce and went to Alum Cave Bluff.

Up the old Will Thomas Road to Indian Gap they went the next day and on down to Smokemont and Ravensford. The final day was a rough one. They went back up the mountain to Indian Gap, then on down the north side of the Great Smokies to Gatlinburg. Then on to Pigeon Forge. From there, they hitched a ride to Sevierville but arrived there too late to catch the Sevierville & Eastern train (commonly known as the Knoxville Slow & Easy). They hiked on in darkness until they reached an empty railroad station near Catlettsburg. They slept there till morning and then caught a train to Knoxville. They had hiked more than forty miles the day before.

After that experience, Mr. Wilson helped others in the YMCA to establish a boys' camp and a hiking program. And he suggested that the Y also start a hiking program for adults.

However, as that idea was chewed on here and there in meetings and around campfires during the following months, it was decided that the program should stand alone, apart from the Y. One reason was that the Y might receive criticism for sponsoring a program that kept people from Sunday church. Thus, the Smoky Mountains Hiking Club was born.

But Marshall Wilson does not believe that a man walking a mountain trail on Sunday morning has missed a chance to worship.

"It is my belief that if the word 'worship' is liberally interpreted, many of us have worshipped from the moment we started a hike until we returned home; and all we missed was the preaching," he said. "And now, after fifty years of continuous experience, it is obvious in the Club's membership and behaviour that the wholesomeness, the sense of oneness with the universe engendered in the early years still prevails."

The stories hikers delight most in telling are those that involve the worst (or are they the best?) experiences. Mr. Wilson tells several good ones. But at this time of lowered thermostats, I like best this one about a hike he and the late Albert G. (Dutch) Roth made on New Year's Eve, 1928:

"Our objective was to scout a new trail from Elkmont up the Fish Camp Prong to Silers Bald, but we never reached that destination. Darkness was approaching by the time we reached a small clearing where, some years earlier, there had been a small sawmill, perhaps two or three miles below the bald, and in the clearing was a small one-room board shack having no door or window. In it there was a broken-down step stove with two small round lids and two joints of pipe which did not quite reach the roof."

Mr. Wilson said they put the stove and pipe all together and propped it up with rocks.

"The greatest disadvantage with that stove was that it could hold only small pieces of wood and replenishing it kept us hopping all night. But we managed to cook supper and make a large pot of coffee, and we spread our blankets on the floor.

"The temperature dropped lower and lower throughout the night. We stripped boards from the walls and floor and burned them. Eventually, we put our blankets together, two on the bottom and two on top, and snuggled between them to share our bodies' warmth. At daybreak the coffee in the pot on the stove was a solid block of ice."

The two weren't carrying a thermometer. But other campers who were at Mt. Le Conte the same night said twenty degrees below zero.

Another Wilson story is about a winter hike in snow up the old Thomas Road to Indian Gap and then westward along the mountain crest to Clingmans Dome. In the group beside Mr. Wilson were the late Edward J. Meeman, then editor of The News-Sentinel; John Moutoux, a News-Sentinel reporter; and Lucien Greene.

"En route, Lucien and John were talking almost incessantly about nothing in particular. Ed Meeman called for a halt and asked for a personal favor. He said, in effect, 'Let's see if we can be perfectly still, not say a word, for exactly five minutes . . . I want to listen to what these mountains have to say.' "

Smoky Mountains Hiking Club has been a strong force for environmental quality in this region. Its recent outstanding accomplishment was in getting the National Park Service to recommend a much larger wilderness for the Great Smokies than it originally suggested. The hiking club took the lead and deserves the largest slice of credit.

There's every reason to hope the club will provide the same strong leadership over the next fifty years.   *—12/1/74*

Hiking With West Barber

When you hike with West Barber he hooks his right forefinger into the belt loop just above your left hip, so lightly you soon forget it's there.

He adjusts his stride so that the two near feet, his right and your left, move in unison, so you don't trip each other on a narrow trail.

West hikes this way because he's blind. He's been totally blind since last December 4. He was working in the shop at his home, 3712 Timberlake Road, making Christmas presents.

A piece of wood spun from his lathe and buzzed like a malevolent insect at West's unprotected good eye. He'd lost the sight in his other eye as a result of a detached retina a few years earlier.

This tragedy hit West about a month before his eighty-fifth birthday. I had seen him a few weeks earlier, at the fiftieth anniversary celebration of Smoky Mountains Hiking Club. He's a past president of it. He was happy then, laughing, joking, playing a little game with himself and his friends. He was only sixty-five years old, he said. He'd been sixty-five ever since he retired from the architectural firm of Barber and McMurry. This was said in half seriousness. For West had decided when he retired that he would live his life in a manner that he could remain active, defy aging. He looked a lot more like sixty-five than middle eighties.

But it was a different man I saw a few weeks after the accident. West was wilted in body and spirit. His shoulders slumped and his chin drooped near his chest. He held a wadded, wet handkerchief. He did not smile and he told no stories.

That must have been near West's low period. But even then things were in the works to put his feet back on the trail and his spirit back near its normal high level.

Tom Duncan, an old friend and hiking buddy, was there, ready to guide West on a walk around the yard or the neighborhood. The close-knit Barber family—wife Carol, children, grandchildren and great-grandchildren—were rallying to the cause. For instance, grandson Doug Barber reads to West nearly every Thursday.

By the time West and Carol celebrated their golden wedding anniversary in early July, he was in good spirits again, a jovial fellow moving about among the guests. He and I then made a tentative date for a hike before snowfall.

By the time we got around to the hike a few days ago, West was in excellent physical condition. Such old friends as Tom Duncan, Guy Frizzell, Dick Bagwell and Bob Howes, along with members of the Barber family, had walked hundred of miles with West. He estimates he's walked 250 to 300 miles this year around his home, in the UT Farm area and in Sequoyah Hills. He's also been on some hikes in the Great Smokies. One of these, to Maddron Bald, is a ten-mile round trip.

For our hike, West decided we should hike from Rich Gap to Rich Mountain Tower, above Cades Cove. As we drove along, West wanted to be kept up-to-date on where we were. Had we passed McGhee Tyson Airport? Were we in Maryville yet? Townsend?

As we neared Cades Cove, it occurred to West that the gate might be closed on the old road leading up to the starting point of our hike. If it were closed, we could hike along the old Cooper Road, I suggested.

Though West has covered most of the trails in the Great Smokies, lots of them many times, he hadn't been on that old road that years ago linked the Cove to Maryville. He decided he'd rather hike the old road than the Rich Mountain trail.

A car ahead of us was stopped on the Cades Cove Loop Road and its occupants were watching a buck deer. The deer crossed the road just ahead of us, and I then saw three other deer a few yards back in the woods. I described all this to West.

"We've seen four deer," West said, smiling.

We reached the starting point of our hike and parked the car. Both of us put on day packs and West also took along the long, slender walking stick especially designed for blind persons.

It was a bright fall day. Lots of blue up above. Sunshine that warmed without burning. Lots of leaves both on the trees and on the trail.

I tried to keep West up-to-date on what kind of trees we were walking under and what kind of leaves we were walking on. Sometimes we walked under large white pines and on carpets of their needles.

We passed patches of trailing arbutus. West wanted to know whether next spring's bloom buds were set. They were. We crossed a ridge named Arbutus Ridge and a stream named Arbutus Branch.

We passed big clumps of galax, and West wanted to know had the leaves bronzed yet. Most of them had not.

We stopped for West to run his fingers gently over the blooms of gentians.

Were there goldenrod blooms along the trail, he asked. Yes. Lots of asters, too.

When we started walking, I did not set a very fast pace, for I hadn't hiked with West since he'd lost his sight, and I wasn't sure how fast he'd want to go. Perhaps he was a little leery of putting his feet down too fast on unfamiliar ground. After a half-mile of this, West said he'd like to move faster.

I warned him when we approached rocky sections of the trail. And when we were about to cross a fallen tree on the trail. He never fell once. In fact, I don't recall that he so much as stumbled more than once.

West talked at times about things related to his blindness. He likes the "talking" books and magazines (recordings) he receives in the mail from the state library for the blind. And he talked about his "visions."

West mentioned the face of a lovely child that appeared suddenly ten inches from his face as he lay in bed, tossing green trees seen through an opening in the ceiling, a landscape that appeared while he was riding with friends. Just as it was when he had sight in both eyes, a vision seen in one of his eyes differs a little from that which appears in the other eye. And one seen with both eyes has yet another appearance.

We stopped for lunch in a sun-warmed spot, and West ate the sandwich Carol had prepared for him. It's a meal by itself—whole wheat bread, cheese or peanut butter, lettuce, raisins, margarine and sometimes other items. West formerly made these for himself.

We hiked about five miles. West spoke of a "satisfying tiredness." Later, when we were talking about hiking, he mentioned "something of a spiritual benefit or satisfaction" he gets from walking. He mentioned his long-time love of the mountains, now become "part of me."

Does it matter that he no longer sees them?

"Of course it does," he said. But he had hiked so many of the trails during his years of sight that he knows pretty much what's out there on the trail beside him. Now, on unfamiliar trails, he enjoys it when somebody describes the scenes to him.

It was a good hike on a good day with a delightful companion.

—11/9/75

Brewer Hikes

Alberta and I hiked to Mt. Sterling last Tuesday, cold and clear under a blue sky in the morning but with afternoon clouds and a south wind hinting of the rain to come that night.

It was a good walk, starting from Mt. Sterling Gap, the point of a four-way intersection. North Carolina Highway 284, graveled, narrow, crooked and colorful, runs generally north and south. The ancient Asbury Trail, over which Bishop Francis Asbury brought Methodism into the mountains more than 150 years ago, runs off the east side of the road, and the three-mile Jeep trail to Mt. Sterling's fire tower climbs westerly from the road.

We took the Jeep trail. It's steep, with an altitude gain of 1954 feet from the gap (3888 feet) to the tower (5842 feet).

Thin snow lay on frozen north slopes, but the snow was gone from south slopes. Long masses of galax, from pink to copper bronze, grow along trail banks on the south slopes. So do patches of trailing arbutus and teaberry.

But the hike wasn't the only interesting thing about this trip. The route you drive to get there is a good deal more interesting—to me, at least—than any Interstate you're likely to travel.

I remembered the first time I was over that road. Then, as now, I thought it was about as crooked as any paved road you'll find in Tennessee. The only one that rivals it is U.S. 129, up the Little Tennessee Valley, along the southwestern boundary of Great Smoky Mountains National Park. But 32 is not as wide as 129.

That first time I drove over it, maybe fifteen years ago, I saw an excellent method of mountain garbage disposal. Her arms thrust out of the kitchen window, a housewife was scraping the dinner plates. Standing there on their hind legs, catching every crumb, were two hounds.

Tennessee 32 stops at the state line, at Davenport Gap. The road continues as North Carolina 284. But 284, though just as crooked and steep as 32, is unpaved. Riding on it can be pretty bouncy.

On that first trip, as I drove down 284 toward Big Creek, a big bobcat hustled across the road in front of the car.

On this trip last week, Alberta and I saw no bobcats and no hound-dog garbage disposal units. But we did see four handsome Redbone hounds. All four were in oil-drum doghouses and the drums were so situated that we were looking straight into these hound houses on our return trip.

I figured the hound owner was a bear hunter, and stopped to find out what kind of success he had the past bear season.

Not very good, said Hiram Leatherwood, a straight-backed, balding mountain hunter and farmer. Somebody poisoned his two best bear dogs, he said grimly. He got only one bear.

I'd guess the Leatherwoods have lived in that region since pioneer days. After we got home, I looked at the quad map of the area and noticed a Leatherwood Branch pretty close to where Hiram Leatherwood lives.   *—1/24/72*

00000

Made first trip of the season to the blackberry patch last Monday. Fine day, last Monday. Lots of clear blue up top, background for a few cottony clouds. The air was as dry as if it'd been wrung out. And there was a breeze.

Headed up a narrow dirt-and-stone-and-mud-puddle road, intending to drive as far as the Vega would go without dragging its belly on boulders.

Saw box turtle coming out of mud puddle at about same rate of speed the nuclear reactor pressure vessel has been traveling to Phipps Bend. His shell was wet and glistening. I waited for turtle to get out of the Vega's path.

About 100 yards beyond the turtle puddle, I came upon a real goodie. A hawk had just taken off with a heavy cargo dangling from its talons—a snake a foot to fifteen inches long, squirming its displeasure.

The hawk was flying straight up the road, trying mightily to gain altitude. It was maybe a yard off the ground when I first saw it. It required about fifteen seconds of flying the roadway for it to gain enough altitude to find an opening among the tree tops through which it disappeared to my left.

I'd heard of hawks catching snakes, but this was my first time to see one carrying a snake seconds after catching it. It was a good, good show. The only part of the hawk I could see clearly was the tail. It was fanned out, showing distinct black and white bands.

Later that day, I checked my favorite bird book, *Natural History of the Birds of Eastern and Central North America,* written a long, long time ago by Edward Howe Forbush, added to a long time ago by John Richard May, with the art work done by a promising young beginner named Roger Tory Peterson.

After reading what Forbush and May wrote about hawks and looking at what Peterson drew, I decided this snake-catcher had to be a broad-winged hawk. It's smaller than a red-tailed or red-shouldered hawk. It likes to nest in hilly, forested regions near streams. It likes snakes for lunch. And it has black and white tail bands.

Car dragged on a sandstone boulder. I parked and started walking. Came upon a grandson—not much bigger than a silver dollar—of the earlier-seen box turtle.

Found first blackberries. They were still red. Found a few ripe raspberries. Finally found some ripe blackberries.

Dry weather has cut the size of blackberries and the blackberry crop. And berries are not as juicy as they'd have been if four inches of rain had fallen in June.

Not many were ripe last Monday. Lots more should be ripe by today. I always figure July 4 to be the beginning of the season. I also found a few huckleberries. Within maybe an hour, I picked enough berries for Alberta to make a blackberry pie flavored with raspberries and huckleberries. I had enough surplus to scatter over my cereal for three mornings.

You'd think two box turtles, a snake-killing hawk and enough berries for a pie would be enough for a fellow to find on one blackberry-picking expedition.

But there were other small treats—songs of yellow-breasted chats and smaller warblers which dwell in a thicket which was clearcut five or six years ago. And a pair of blue-gray gnatcatchers.

I don't see many blue-gray gnatcatchers. For the benefit of non-birders, a blue-gray gnatcatcher is a pencil-thin, fidgety midget of a bird that looks like a miniature mockingbird. These two apparently were disturbed by a flicker which had got too close to their nest. And they were popping up and down like popcorn in a popper.

It was a great Monday.   —7/7/80

A small scene beside a trail in the Great Smokies:

The old hemlock log has been lying there maybe ten, maybe twenty years. It wears a blanket of moss, and from the moss grow violets in incredible abundance. They give the log something of the appearance of a casket blanketed with flowers.

These are sweet white violets *(Viola blanda)*, and, by actual count, more than 200 blooms transform the top of a five-yard section of the log into a garden.

A sweet white violet bloom is small and dainty, about the right size to hide behind a dime. It has two top petals that stick up like the ears of a miniature white rabbit. Two others stick down and out to either side, and these overlap the outer edges of the bottom petal. Delicate purple veins begin near the outer edge of the bottom petal and converge at its base, where there is a golden dot the size of a pinhead.

The leaves of the little plants are not as coarse in texture and not as large as the leaves of most other violets. Their delicacy matches that of the blooms.

They grow more thickly in one place—about two feet long by ten or eleven inches wide—than elsewhere on the log. They are so matted that they completely cover the surface and little else grows there.

Elsewhere, where the violets are not so all-covering, two or three small Virginia creeper vines crawl across the log, sinking roots through the moss into the softening shell of tree bark.

And here is a maple sprout—two tiny leaves extending opposite each other from a trunk an inch long.

Nearby is one of the youngest hemlocks in the forest. Nine short needles grow from a stem less than an inch long.

Stubby, hard little growths protrude from the old tree trunk in one square inch of space. Some kind of lichen, perhaps?

Moss, pale green and soft as velvet, covers most of the trunk, blurring lengthwise furrows that are the wrinkles of ancient hemlocks. But one furrow, probably a deformity in the trunk, is deeper and wider than the others. And in it are gathered hemlock needles, a few hemlock cones, and a few paper-thin last year's leaves.

A tiny black ant hurries northeastwardly across the field of moss and into the towering forest of violets. The only other visible creature on the log is a fly with a brown nose and hind legs longer than the front ones, jacking up his rear end like a jalopy with air shocks.

But there must be lots of invisible workers down there in the log, microorganisms working on the wood itself and on the litter that falls on the log.

Working closely with the rain that falls so abundantly in the Great Smokies, the microorganisms turn this dead stuff into a rich, moist gruel that's full of whatever it is that moss and violets need in their diets.

You can bury your nose deep in the cool violet bed and smell the mix of life and death while pondering the unceasing cycle of each into the other.

A nearby creek keeps singing over the old gray stones in its bed. A breeze tickles the little rabbit ears of the violet blooms.

And it is time to walk some more.   —*5/13/74*

Rainbow Falls in Ice

The snow was littered with diamonds.

Well, they looked like diamonds. Maybe lovelier than diamonds. Of course, it was the sun doing its magic on the crystals in the snow along the Rainbow Falls Trail to Mt. Le Conte.

This was last Monday, a cold, still day. From dawn till dusk, east, west, north and south, the sky was unblemished blue. Alberta and I took on a load of eggs and sausage and orange marmalade and toast and coffee, stuck lunch into a day pack, drove into Knoxville and picked up John Stiles, a fellow News-Sentinel reporter with whom I share Monday as a day off. We headed for Gatlinburg, Cherokee Orchard and the Rainbow Falls Trailhead.

Snow was nice and crunchy underfoot. Not crunchy like peanuts or cornflakes. Rather, it was a silky, whispery crunchy. Lots of feet headed for the Rainbow Falls icicle had packed it hard, but treaded boots had roughed up the snow enough to keep it from being slick.

Down in the deep hollow, Le Conte Creek trickled along between shining shoulders of ice. Ice crusted the pools of the little creek. It's running low now because nearly all the precipitation on Le Conte for the past six or seven weeks has come as snow, and much of the snow is still there. I'd guess that as much of it evaporates into the air as melts and finds its way to the creek.

We had decided the previous Saturday to walk the three miles up to Rainbow Falls to see the falls as a pillar of ice. This is a fairly rare occurrence, and I had missed it the few other times it has happened. And I figured I'd better not pass up this opportunity. After all, I'd hate to be run over by a tractor-trailer truck on one of its 70-mph lunges down an I-75 hill, without ever having seen the Rainbow Falls ice column.

I don't know how rare it is. It's bound to have been there sometime during the awful winter of 1917-18. Arthur Stupka, retired longtime chief naturalist of Great Smoky Mountains National Park, particularly remembers the one that formed in January 1940, the coldest month on record here. News-Sentinel photographer Dave Carter dug out a picture he made of the big icicle March 6, 1968. That probably was the most recent one until this bad winter spread itself all over the record books.

We were heavily dressed against the cold, and it was warm, pleasant walking. The diamond sparkles in the snow were extras we hadn't expected. Saw lots of tracks. Human tracks, mostly. But rabbit tracks, too. And tracks we thought were made by boomers, the little red squirrels of the Great Smokies high country. Saw some tiny tracks I guessed mice made.

Though it had been two days since the last snowfall there, the snow remained as brightly white in most areas as it was the minute it fell. It doesn't get dusty and dingy up there. Occasionally one comes upon a scattering of hemlock needles. Maybe a boomer knocked them down. Maybe the wind did it.

The snow was six or seven inches deep in places. It was all gone in others, the others being south slopes. Rhododendron leaves were tight green curls in shade, expanded to their natural width in sunshine. The sun ironed the wrinkles from red-pink galax leaves.

Rainbow Falls was a fine scene of snow and ice and rock. At about 4325 feet above sea level, it was cold as the dickens. I took off my gloves to make some pictures and my hands soon hurt.

The ice pillar is forty or forty-five feet high and perhaps twenty feet wide at the base, and it slims down to seven or eight feet wide at the top. This one doesn't look quite like the one Dave Carter photographed in 1968. It's not as pretty. Dave's pictures show an hourglass pillar, and that should be the natural look of the thing, I think. For I believe it starts forming at the bottom and at the top, and the upthrust icicle and the downthrust one meet a little above center. I don't know why this one doesn't have the hourglass look. Maybe it was crippled. Perhaps a section melted and broke and the cold returned and refroze it imperfectly.

I'd heard of the blue color of the ice and I was a little disappointed. I suppose the colors shift in angle and intensity with the changing sunlight through the day. When we were there, the color—aquamarine, I'd call it—was visible only from the left side, and faint.

Rainbow Falls probably provides the best winter scene within easy hiking distance in the Great Smokies. But I'd like to see another one not within such easy distance. This is Ramsey Cascades. In springtime this is one of the prettiest places in the park, a series of pools and waterfalls galloping steeply down a deep narrow valley, before plunging over the two-step (or is it three-step?) Ramsey Falls. I'd bet it's spectacular in ice and snow.   —*2/13/77*

00000

Dick Bagwell, the retired architect, and Carlos Campbell, the unretired insurance executive, are agreed on the reason the 1977 ice column at Rainbow Falls doesn't have the pretty hourglass figure some other years had. They say the weather has been so dry that the trickle of water coming off the top was not wide enough to form the wide top of the hourglass.

Dick and Carlos also are agreed on another thing about the Rainbow Falls ice column: the flow of the creek, such as it is, falls through a hollow center of the column. Stan Canter, Great Smokies chief naturalist, thinks so, too. This is what occurs at similar waterfalls in Yellowstone National Park, he said. But he's going to try to check out Rainbow before it melts this time.   —*2/27/77*

"Panther Hunt"

Alberta went panther hunting. I went with her.

But I didn't know she was panther hunting until we were walking along the Appalachian Trail last Sunday afternoon. Snow pellets were peppering the hoods of our windbreakers. Wind was moaning from low to loud through the balsams. Right out of the north it came, slanting the snow against the north sides of every twig and tree, leaving that side white and the other side untouched.

The snow pellets fell on deep moss beds, making a milk-and-mint color pattern one doesn't run into on just any Sunday afternoon. The air borne by the north wind was getting colder by the minute.

Prompted by exactly what I don't remember, Alberta suddenly informed me that she wasn't hiking. Instead, she was panther hunting. The message that came through was that hiking over those slippery exposed tree roots in the snow and cold wasn't something she'd be caught doing voluntarily. On the other hand, panther hunting was worth it.

Before we left home, I'd suggested that she bring her camera.

"We might see the panther," I said. It'd be a shame to see the panther and not get a picture of it to prove you weren't lying. I really didn't expect to see any panthers. And I'd forgotten about panthers by the time Alberta brought up the subject.

I refrained from telling her that the Great Smokies mama panther and two kittens probably were not so stupid as to be up there in that high-country cold where there was nothing to eat but people.

Besides who can be sure about cats? Wasn't it Hemingway who wrote of the leopard in the snow atop Kilimanjaro?

But this wasn't Kilimanjaro. And the only thing Alberta got out her camera for was the fog at Indian Gap. You've seen the fog produced by that machine for the witches' scene of "Macbeth" at Clarence Brown Theater? Well, some fellow sitting on a Tennessee cloud north of Indian Gap was operating a fog machine 1000 times as big and power-ful, and he was firing great, swift, ragged chunks of fog through the Gap at some target in North Carolina.

By the time we got back to Newfound Gap and headed down the mountain toward Gatlinburg, a park sand-spreader was spraying its load over the slippery highway.

Things got changed a bit overnight. By the time we'd eaten breakfast and left our motel and headed up the Jakes Creek Trail to Jakes Gap and Blanket Mountain, it didn't seem like the same mountain. Nor the same world.

No clouds. No fog. Little wind. The sky, the sun, the atmosphere had been bathed, scrubbed, rinsed, dried and polished.

The trail from Jakes Gap to the top of Blanket Mountain was one of the finest miles I ever walked. Blanket Mountain cannot quite decide whether it is forest or heath bald. Scattered scrub oaks, table mountain pines, maples and sourwoods grow there. But for each of these there are 1000 laurel and rhododendron bushes. We walked through a 100-yard rhododendron tunnel, with the branches from each side linking like crossed swords overhead.

Long stretches of trail are bordered by galax, red-bronze and brilliant in the sunshine. Mountain tea, trailing arbutus, ground cedar and ground pine share space with the galax.

Somebody ten or eleven million years ago thoughtfully placed two or three big grayback boulders along the trail. One can climb them and use them as observation platforms.

Farther south is Thunderhead Mountain, pointed at the sky.

And high on the north slope of Thunderhead and one or two other main-range peaks was the silvery glisten of hoar frost. This was the fog of yesterday afternoon and last night, captured and frozen to the trees. It was on Blanket Mountain, too. And it was melting. Under some frosted trees, there was a steady patter of particles of ice falling on the dry leaves.

Right on top of the mountain were the concrete footings of the fire tower that once stood there, along with a nearby stone chimney, the only remains of the fire lookout's cabin.

The mountaintop is relatively flat and carpeted with dead grass, speckled in places with the red-brown leaves of teaberry.

I wondered whether it was such a fine day as this that Return Jonathan Meigs, in about 1802, placed the blanket on this mountain and thus gave it its name. A foggy, cloudy day such as the one before just would not have suited Mr. Meigs' purposes.

For he and his helpers were surveying the line, agreed upon here in Knoxville at the Treaty of the Holston, to separate Cherokee lands from white settler lands.

The surveyors had plodded southeastwardly from Southwest Point (Kingston). When they reached Chilhowee Mountain, the rugged land was impassable by horses "and extremely difficult for foot men."

So, R.J. Meigs, as the story has been passed down, stood atop Chilhowee Mountain and picked out a prominent peak, apparently in line with the survey. He then climbed the peak and placed a brightly colored blanket on it. Then, by what route I do not know, he reached the crest of the Great Smokies and walked along it to a point where he could properly line up his surveying instruments with that blanket.

That point was on top of what now is called Mt. Collins. But some oldtimers call it Meigs Post, for Mr. Meigs drove a four-sided post into the ground as a marker.

In addition to Meigs Post, there are Meigs Mountain, immediately north of Blanket Mountain; Meigs Creek, a camera target of lots of tourists where it jumps down a bluff and then meanders into Little River, beside State Highway 73; and, finally, there is Meigs County. Few men left their names on so much Tennessee geography.

We saw a few robins and juncos. And, on our way back down the Jakes Creek Trail, we saw a large deer.

No panthers.　　　　　　　　　　　　　　　*—2/29/76*

∞∞

Autumn in the Great Smokies is a mad artist in a crazy hurry to splash on all his paint before he runs out of time and tree leaves.

It is a black bear, gorging on grapes, grubs and scarce acorns, hurrying to layer his back and belly with fat to fend off cold dreams as he snoozes winter away in a hollow tree.

The painter paints yellow pigment on the poplar leaves in Cosby Campground. A grove of straight-trunked yellow-plumed poplars lighted by a fiery sunset is a candelabrum unrivaled by the waxen torches of man.

Autumn is the aroma of tobacco curing in little gray barns on hillside farms above Cosby; the winey aroma of apples in the apple houses of Cocke County orchards, and the smell of country ham sizzling in the skillet in a farmhouse kitchen.

It's a blue woodsmoke curling out of a rock chimney into chill dawn air. And it's a cold houn'dog whining and scratching outside the door.

It's the scratchy, pleasant swish of fallen leaves under a hiker's feet on the Snake Den Trail out of Cosby Campground to Maddron Bald. And on the bald, it's the wine and purple hues of the leaves of teaberry, galax and blueberry bushes.

It's a pile of yellow pumpkins, their tops touched with frost, and it's the wind scratching noisily through a field of dry cornstalks.

Autumn is red and yellow leaves hurrying like little Chinese junks down the riffles of small mountain streams, congregating at the ends of pools and nearly halting the puny flow until the floods of winter purge the streambeds.

It is the first flight of evening grosbeaks arriving from the North, to get their fill of handouts of sunflower seeds at feeders and to pluck seeds from the tops of poplars in mountain coves.

It is a monarch butterfly, fluttering southward above the treetops, daring to fly 1000 miles on those fragile wings of gold and black. It is a fat groundhog making one of his last foraging trips in a Cades Cove meadow before denning for the winter. It is a 'possum up a persimmon tree, a country boy collecting papaws, robins stuffing themselves with wild grapes.

Autumn is a hiker loading up on eggs and sausage and biscuits and coffee, then walking mile after mile in sunshine and shadow, uphill and down; getting tired and thin-bellied; dropping a pack and stretching out on a ground cover of bright leaves, looking up at an old red-tailed hawk circling against a blue sky.

It is a season that sends melancholy thoughts back to the Cherokees, who believed creation was in autumn and paid homage to their gods in ceremonies that lasted through the long, starry night in towns along the Oconaluftee, the Tuckasegee and the Little Tennessee.

It is an old timber rattler stretched in a lazy line across a rock in the noon sunshine, soaking up all the warmth he can get before winter numbs and stiffens him.

It is the shortened days dropping off the calendar, the wind whistling faster, colder, carrying the last leaves in spinning patterns. It is the first sleet peppering the windows of Mt. Cammerer tower.

And then it is winter.   *—10/17/80*

6

Elusive Trout

Lucinda Ogle of Gatlinburg was reminiscing the other day about trout fishing in the Great Smokies way back when lots of folks couldn't afford fishhooks, much less fancy trout rods and dry flies that cost more than a dollar apiece.

And she was especially remembering Fishing John Ramsey, who was the maternal grandpa of her late husband, Earnest Ogle.

"When we were little shavers, and long before I married Earnest, his grandpa Ramsey was known to be the best trout fisherman in all the mountains," Lucinda said. "He would walk fifteen or twenty miles to fish a stream.

"Sometimes he would come up our Le Conte Creek and catch most of our fish. After a rain, when the water was a little milky looking, was the best fishing time. So we would be watching for John and run ahead of him, rocking the big fishing holes."

(If you know nothing at all about trout, you may not understand that throwing rocks into the pools scares the dickens out of the fish, so they would not be likely to take any bait Fishing John offered them.)

Lucinda said all the children on Le Conte Creek were cousins. "So one child would run by the road to tell the kids, 'Here comes Fishing John up the creek,' so they could get to work."

Lucinda said Fishing John had a habit of saying "By God." It wasn't exactly a cuss word, not the way Fishing John used it, Lucinda said. At least that was the view of the children, who admired Fishing John, even though they rocked his fishing holes. "But our dyed-in-the-wool Baptist parents thought it was.

"One day, about a half-dozen of us cousins were fishing near Dad's sister Florence's house. The fish weren't cooperating with us. We had heard why John was such a good fisherman. He would spit on his bait and say, 'This is John Ramsey. Bite, by God.'

". . . So we all started spitting on our crooked-pin hooks and yelling real loud, 'Bite, by God,' when down the trail came Aunt Florence with her big switch and gave us all several licks on our legs . . . So there was no more cussing from us. And no more fishing that day."

Lucinda said that at a recent reunion of former Le Conte Creek residents, some of them got to talking about methods of fishing they used when they couldn't afford fishhooks.

"My cousin Rockford Oakley said, 'Don't you remember how we used to Indian fish in winter time? First, prop a sorta flat rock against another at the lower end of a big hole of water, leaving the biggest and strongest kid holding as big a rock as he can hold to drop on this leaning rock. Then the other kids take long sticks and thrash the water up in the swift part where trout . . . are always hid. When (a fish) darts to the shelter of the leaning rock, drop the rock from above, and it will addle the fish, so it floats to the top. Then the rock-dropper grabs it.'

". . . Some other ways we fished was with a bent pin tied with a flour-poke thread, an earthworm strung on the hook. This took fast jerking. But it took faster jerking when we just tied the worm in the middle with the flour-poke thread. As quick as you saw the fish shut his mouth on the worm, you jerked . . .

"In summer, we would do what we called 'granny them out.' (We) would wade the stream, running our hands together from each side of a rock, catching them by hand. Sometimes we would bring out a waterdog, or lots of times a watersnake. We would let loose of these real quick."

What Lucinda calls "grannying" is called "grabbling" in some quarters. I once watched one of my cousins grabble a whole string of fish out of Stoney Fork Creek.   *—12/3/79*

Hurting for Clay Harts

If my first day out was any indication of things to come, this looks like an awful trout season for me. We Great Smokies trouters are hobbled with nine-inch and twelve-inch limits this season. And this trouter is hurting from a lack of Clay Harts. I will explain about Clay Harts presently.

Last fall, Alberta and I had a most pleasant day walking through the fallen leaves on the Rough Creek Trail, off Little River and up to the spine of Sugarland Mountain. We saw several small trout snatching flies from the surface of Rough Creek pools, and I decided this would be a good place to open the 1975 season.

But when the the National Park Service (NPS) a few weeks ago upped the keeper limit to nine inches, I figured we weren't going to bring home many Rough Creek trout, for those we'd seen had been smaller.

We decided to go to Rough Creek, anyway. It had been such a good fall hike, we wanted to see what it was like in spring.

Well, it was like acres of white phacelia blooms, looking like snow sprinkled with mint. The best show was just above the parking area at the end of the motor road up Little River.

And it was like silverbell trees crowned with bloom. And thousands of white trillium. More of violets, blue, white and yellow.

It was a Louisiana water-thrush bobbing its behind along the creek. And it was birdsong spilling down out of the treetops, tinkling waterfalls of sound.

But, more than anything else, it was ramp-harvest time. I mistook the first ramp hunter I saw for Alberta.

Alberta is a non-trouter. She was staying on the trail, carrying a camera and our lunch, while I was down in the creek. I happened to decide it was time for lunch at a place where the creek and the trail were 150 yards or so apart. I saw a woman in a blue windbreaker, similar to one Alberta was wearing. And I whistled. She didn't respond quite right. Then I saw a man with her, and I realized I didn't know these folks and that I might get a knot on my head for whistling at the wrong woman.

But this couple was in no mood to hit anybody in the head. They were middle-age, I'd guess. The man was a Great Smokies oldtimer, but I gathered from his conversation that this was the first time he'd been back in a long time to this particular section. He said his father had helped build a Little River Lumber Co. logging railroad up Rough Creek, and he asked whether I'd seen any remains of the old road. I had not, except for the roadbed farther down the creek.

They had seen Alberta, who had sent word that she was waiting down the trail for me. They didn't tell me that they were hunting ramps. But Alberta saw them again later and they had a pretty good load of ramps. They recommended pouring hot grease over them and then frying eggs with them in the same grease. I don't think I'm going to be able to persuade Alberta to try the recipe.

I also saw two other parties of ramp hunters. One consisted of two women who were in the middle of a ramp bed when I saw them. The other party consisted of three young men who carried bags for ramps, but they were resting when I saw them.

As far as I know, a ramp is the only plant that grows in the Great Smokies that a person can pull up by the roots with no worry that a ranger will arrest him for doing it. It is a concession NPS makes to oldtimers of the mountains, but I doubt that they check credentials to make certain all ramp harvesters are oldtimers. Possibly they figure that not many except oldtimers will want ramps.

I suppose the annual ramp harvest is not great, for the ramp doesn't appear to be an endangered species in the park. I saw lots of them along the creek.

Compared with last fall, when we saw nobody else in Rough Creek Valley, the place was crawling with people this time. In addition to all those ramp gatherers, there was even another fisherman. I'd guess he wasn't far from home. For he was using equipment and technique that mountain trouters have used effectively for a long time.

No fancy store-bought fishing rod. No reel. Just a long pole—and in this case, a rather crooked pole—with a short length of line tied to the tip.

The fisherman was down beside the creek, paying close attention to what he was doing. He didn't hear us come up behind him on the trail, a few yards away. We stopped and watched, for this fellow was practiced at what he was doing.

Half crawling, half kneeling, he inched quietly along the creek bank. Not too close to the creek, for he didn't have to be close.

With that long pole, he can stand far back and dabble the lure in the water. Time after time, he dipped his lure into the water that hurried down a V-shaped stone channel into a pool. He moved the lure downstream at about the same speed as the water, covering seven or eight feet at a sweep. A fisherman can't cover much water this way, but he doesn't have to cover much in streams the size of Rough Creek.

"Is he using an illegal lure?" Alberta whispered.

I was wondering the same thing, for the masters of this form of trouting have been known once in a while to use everything from worms and grasshoppers to strips of fishtail for bait. But this was unfair to the fellow. For those who fish with the long pole also can use dry flies, wet flies, nymphs and streamers.

I could not say positively what this man was using. But it wasn't a dry fly. Nor was it a worm or grasshopper.

He finally saw us and we exchanged bad news. He said he had caught no fish at all. I had caught none nine inches long.

Before we leave the subject of the nine-inch limit, I'd better make it clear that I'm not objecting to it. Maybe some of those little fellows I caught and released will be nine inches long the next time I catch them. That's the theory on which the limit was imposed, anyway. We'll see whether it works.

If I'd had a Clay Hart, maybe I'd have caught a nine-incher, anyway. For there must be at least a half-dozen fish that big in Rough Creek. And a Clay Hart is pretty hard for a big trout to resist.

A Clay Hart, for all those millions who don't know, is some white chicken feather, a little snatch of fur from the tail of a fox squirrel, a long-shanked hook, and some thread and glue to tie it all together.

I should mention, also, that considerable skill goes into the tying-it-all-together. The first man to use his skill on this particular lure was, as you might guess, named Clay Hart.

But Mr. Hart is dead. He died a year or two ago. Maybe longer. I didn't know him well, but those who did say he was a fine trouter. He came to see me once, to talk about some subject I've long ago forgotten. He was one of those people, who, after they're gone, you wish you'd had time and opportunity to know better. I recall that he was an entertaining talker, and that, beside being a tyer of Clay Harts, he was the creator of some good meat sauces. He sold some of the sauces commercially.

Clyde Ward, who used to sell me Clay Harts at the Athletic House, said Mr. Hart stopped tying them several years before he died. Maybe his fingers grew unsteady, as old fingers sometimes are inclined to do.

A few others tied Clay Harts for a time. But as far as Clyde and I know, nobody has tied them to sell for a year or longer.

The scarce component of the Clay Hart is the squirrel tail fur. Fox squirrels are not common around here. But during the last squirrel season and with the help of Sam Venable, News-Sentinel outdoor editor, Clyde obtained a squirrel tail or two.

And he thought he had a fellow lined up to tie Clay Harts. But that man just kept on not tying them. He has not tied one yet. Not for Clyde, anyway.

But Clyde still has the squirrel tails. And he has something which has become far rarer: a Clay Hart. As far as we know, it's the only one left. It'll serve as a model for any fly tyer who wants to start tying them.

Surely, in this time of unemployment and underemployment, somebody with good eyes and fingers would like to make a few bucks tying Clay Harts.

Maybe I left the impression that Clay Harts are only for trout fishing. Not so. On this handsome streamer I've caught bass—both largemouth and smallmouth, plus rock bass—crappies and bluegills. I believe a carp once attacked a Clay Hart I was using. I've never put one to the test on whales or sea monsters.   —*4/27/75*

Brookies and Rainbows

I sometimes think I always get to the right creek at the wrong time.

It must have been at least ten years ago, one morning when I was fishing Middle Prong of Little River, that I decided to test Spruce Flats Branch for brook trout. I didn't know then that an old logging road led to the branch from farther up Middle Prong. I climbed up beside the waterfall that spills Spruce Flats waters down the into Middle Prong.

It was the waterfall that made me think there might be brook trout in the stream. For the exotic rainbow trout down in Middle Prong couldn't get over that waterfall to bother the native brook trout, providing brook trout were there.

Back then, nearly any time I found a waterfall on a stream reasonably high in the Great Smokies, I checked above it for brook trout. I once caught rainbows from a pool at the foot of a waterfall in Indian Flats Branch. Then I went above the waterfall and caught nothing but brook trout. I went back there once or twice a year for two or three years. The brook trout fishing was great, well worth the three-mile walk from the confluence of Lynn Camp and Thunderhead Prongs.

Then the National Park Service opened the road up Lynn Camp to within a half-mile of the brookie waters. Lots of people who'd been too lazy to walk three miles were not too lazy to walk a half-mile. Too many fished the little stream, and the quality of the fishing dropped from great to poor.

I drew blanks on most streams I checked—for instance, Meadow Branch above the cliff it plunges over to get to West Prong, and Roaring Fork above Grotto Falls. No brookies in either.

And it was the same in Spruce Flats. Nothing there but some small fish which I now know were blacknose dace.

The reason I know they were blacknose dace is that Doug Harned says they are. Doug, now with the TVA Division of Forestry, Fish and Wildlife Development, wrote his master's thesis on a project he did back in 1974-75 on Spruce Flats Branch.

What he did was put brook trout in it and then not tell me about it until the National Park Service (NPS) banned all fishing for brookies in the park. Doug's work is entitled "Comparison of Wild and Hatchery Brook Trout in Spruce Flats Branch . . . " And it is Management Report No. 8 of the Uplands Field Research Laboratory.

Into this small 2.5-mile troutless stream Doug released two batches of fingerling brookies. One batch was offspring of Great Smokies brookies, the other of hatchery trout whose ancestors were New England fish.

Doug wanted to learn which did better in Spruce Flats Branch. The results were mixed. Those of New England ancestry had better growth rates, but those of Great Smokies ancestry had better survival rates.

Another objective of the project was to learn the value of stocking brook trout in some of the troutless streams. This is a longer-range thing, and the results aren't in yet.

Doug's project is part of the overall NPS effort to save the brook trout from extinction in the Great Smokies. The most drastic action taken so far for this purpose is to ban fishing for brookies. Presumably, the current ban is temporary.

But Jerry Eubanks, assistant park superintendent, and Mike Myers, resource management specialist, say a study is in progress to get the final answer on whether the Southern Appalachian brook trout is a distinct sub-species. If it turns out that he is, he may go on the endangered species list. And if this should happen, I presume there'd be no more fishing for him, in the Great Smokies or elsewhere. Perhaps in a few years, brookie population would increase, like alligators in Louisiana, and the fishing ban could be lifted.

According to Doug Harned and others, brook trout in the Great Smokies have suffered from logging operations, introduction of rainbows and brown trout into brook trout waters, and heavy and illegal fishing.

Doug says Spruce Flats Branch is believed to have been the last section logged in the park. Little River Lumber Co. finished logging there in 1938.

The logging and attendant railroad building in the Great Smokies silted the streams and removed the trees that shaded and cooled them. Brookies don't prosper in warm, dirty water. Rainbows and browns can survive in waters unfit for brookies. Of course, some Great Smokies streams, generally those below about 2000 foot elevation, never had brook trout. Abrams Creek is the major example.

After logging ruined lots of the brookie streams, sportsmen in this area proceeded to stock rainbows in them. I have listened to Karl Steinmetz, that fine old lawyer-sportsman, tell about this. Puffing his old crooked-stem pipe and speaking in his Pennsylvania Dutch accent, Karl told of carrying those rainbow fingerlings. They were in lard cans half full of water and kept cool with chunks of ice. Karl and his buddies also carried in fertilized rainbow eggs, planting them in the streams.

Karl also helped the trout fishing fraternity in other ways. For instance, he drafted the legislation establishing Tellico Wildlife Management Area. For all these things, Karl is remembered in the minds of old trouters, as well as in bronze. After his death in 1959, the Tennessee Conservation League honored his memory with a bronze plaque affixed to a big natural stone, a few yards from North River, where Karl liked to drift dry flies.

Time has a way of changing things. It has healed the scars of those logging operations of decades past. The forest is back. The streams are cool and shaded again. And brook trout could live in many of them again—if it weren't for those rainbows introduced so long ago. Brook trout don't do too well competing with rainbows. Most the brookies left are in the little headwater streams, where Karl Steinmetz and others didn't plant rainbows. Many of the surviving brookies are separated from the rainbows by natural barriers, such as waterfalls. *—5/1/77*

CCCCO

There I was, in the Middle of the Raven Fork of Oconaluftee River, trying to stay upright as I crossed. Then this trout had to go and complicate things. Raven Fork heads up on the southern (North Carolina) slope of Mt. Guyot, hit by a cloudburst that earlier this month washed out a bridge on Ramsey Prong, on the Tennessee side.

The lures I used that day on Raven Fork didn't work very well. Most of the time I used a weighted nymph, but it wasn't heavy enough to sink far in the fast water.

The Raven Fork was crotch deep and traveling triple the speed limit. The rocks on which I was trying to travel were big and slippery and sharply angled. I was giving lots of attention to where I was putting my feet and little attention to the nymph that was whipping about down there in the hurrying water five or ten yards below me. Suddenly I realized I had on a fish.

I set the hook. The trout took line downstream at such a rate you'd have thought his mama had just called him to supper. I started paying more attention to the fish and less to my feet. That's when my feet went downstream and my head upstream, and the fish and I were down there under the surface together. We kept each other hooked.

When all the foolishness was over, the fish turned out to be a good rainbow, brilliantly colored. If he was a stocker, he'd been stocked a long time ago. For they don't come out of the tank truck with a complexion like that. *—8/24/78*

A Good Trouter Never Gets His Feet Wet

My knees ache. My thighs hurt. Two of my typing fingers are ailing. And my vanity is bruised in a place or two. But I expect to be recovered by the time you read this.

What brought on all these wounds to body and psyche was a return to mountain trout fishing after a three-year lay-off. Not since the medical people repaired a spinal disc three years ago had I given their job a real test. For that matter, the rest of the aging body hadn't had much of a test since then, either.

It seemed that this spring was the now-or-never time to find out whether I was fit for the mountain trouting deal. I'm not talking about the kind of trouting you do when you drive along a highway beside a stream and get out and do a little fishing and then get back into the car.

There is this small stream in the Great Smokies which is more than four miles beyond the point where you can go in an automobile. You walk this distance up and down steep ridges, knowing you're going to walk back in the afternoon when you're more tired than you are now while the dew is still on the grass.

I do not intend to mention the name of the creek, for there probably are a few other foolish fishermen who would use it. I might meet one of them on it sometime and it would ruin my day. I used to fish it once or twice a season, and I've never seen another human in it or on the trail to it.

But a few others fish it. I've seen evidence of this, but not much. You don't see the worn places in the moss on the rocks where people have stepped, nor the discarded sardine can where somebody has eaten lunch.

In addition to the solitude this creek offers, it has a couple of other things going for it that I appreciate. One is that I usually can catch a few fish in it, though I'm not a skilled trouter.

It's my theory that if you're going to seek trout with a flyrod, you ought to start learning when you're fifteen or sixteen. It's like driving a car. Learn in your youth, and doing the right things comes automatically. A man skilled in using a flyrod is beautiful to see. He also can stand poised and cool on rocks slippery as ice as a torrent tugs at his legs. He can cast a dry fly in the face of a hurricane in a thicket of rhododendron and other entanglements and never snag it.

Well, I didn't start early. I must have been thirty or thirty-one when I bought my first flyrod. I soon became so disgusted with the thing that I sold it back to the man who sold it to me. However, I later bought another, and then another.

I never achieved the skill and grace I admired in some others. Nor could I tell any of those stories about catching one-hundred and five and releasing all except five. But after years of awkward effort, I reached the stage where I usually could keep a promise to bring home trout for supper. And I mean without use of corn, worms, crickets, grasshoppers, stickbait or doughballs. I also mean wild trout, hatched in the stream, not those unloaded two days earlier from the hatchery truck.

My best day among the trout was when I rounded the Abrams Creek Horseshoe without losing a lure and without falling once. Abrams has the slickest rocks in the mountains.

I've heard some say that a good trouter never gets his feet wet. This is fine if you can manage it. And you can on some small streams supplied with large boulders. You step from boulder to boulder. It's easier to catch fish in these, too, for you can use the boulders for cover, casting over them to the pools above. Fishing them is a delight. In fact, rock-hopping them is a pleasure, whether you fish or not.

But this favorite creek of mine is not one of these. Sometimes you can step on dry boulders in it. In a few places you can walk the bank. But there's a lot of it that has to be waded.

Well, the walk over the ridges was fine. Thrushes and warblers were singing, flowers were blooming and my breakfast was lasting well. Saw the first laurel bloom of the season, as well as a sample or two of flame azalea, about a million violets of purple, blue, yellow and white, along with star grass, Catesby's trillium, sweet shrub, and gay wings.

At the creek, I switched from hiking boots to felt-soled shoes and shivered a little at first feel of the cold water.

Right away, the rocks seemed slicker and the water deeper than I remembered. The fly didn't go where I aimed it. I caught 325 rhododendron leaves, broke a leader tip twice on hemlock branches overhead, and hooked and released twenty-eight submerged snags.

Between hooking all this flora, I caught a few small trout which probably were en route to nursery school. After maybe a half-hour of fishing, I felt a stronger tug at the nymph I was using. The tugger was a lovely rainbow with the deep crimson markings typical of wild Great Smokies trout. I debated about keeping him. He was about ten inches long. I'd half-way promised myself to keep nothing smaller than eleven or twelve inches. But I hadn't seen any of these. So I kept this one, telling myself I wouldn't keep another so small.

Shortly later, as I was drifting a lure down a beautiful run of fast, deep water, the line changed directions suddenly, the way it does when an eager fish has grabbed the lure. I set the hook and felt a good jolt of resistance. Then nothing. The leader tip had broken. It wasn't the fish's fault. He wasn't that strong. It was my fault. The leader was weakened from having been sawed about on hemlock, rhododendron and dog hobble snags, and I hadn't taken enough time to change it.

Things got worse. I began mouthing cuss words stronger than I'd tasted in years. The rocks that weren't slippery were unstable. Step on them and they immediately tilted in the wrong direction. I fell, going down with all the grace of an elderly horse. I was lucky. No broken back. Only a stove-up left little finger resulted from the fall. After that, I snagged a hook in the finger next to it.

When I wasn't falling I was stumbling, making too much commotion in the water. That's not the way to catch trout. Little fish start racing around like junior-grade Paul Reveres, telling everybody with fins that a catastrophe is coming up the creek.

After I'd slipped and slid and twisted and turned and stumbled and fallen in the cold water for about three hours, my knees started aching. To make the pain worse, no twelve-inch fish would associate with me. No eleven-inch ones either. I finally kept three more in the nine to ten-inch range. But I was determined to finish my limit with a bigger one. However, no bigger one ever offered himself.

After about five hours and a round-trip of three or four stream miles, I climbed out of that creek and onto the trail, with only the four trout, rocks in my shoes and pain in my knees to show for it. Measured by how tired it can make you, a mile in a creek like that is equivalent to about four on a trail.

After I threw away the rocks in my shoes and put on dry socks, I began to con myself into the notion that it really hadn't been such a bad new beginning after a three-year layoff.

I consulted my watch to see how much time I had to cross the ridges and get back to the car and then to a phone. I was to phone my wife by a certain time. Otherwise, she'd have half the rangers in the park out combing the creek for a demented white-haired old man. She looks with disfavor upon my taking such jaunts alone.

Actually, it probably isn't a wise thing to do, considered only from the standpoint of safety. But there are other factors to consider.

I had about an hour and a half to do the four miles-plus of ridge-hopping back to the car, allowing for a five-minute rest at the top of the highest ridge. It was a superbly satisfying five minutes.

You have to be pretty tired to appreciate the luxury of having the whole unsheeted world to lie upon while you stretch and take deep breaths of decent air and look at the sky.   —*5/7/72*

7

The Uncharted

Granville Calhoun was the fellow responsible for digging those prospecting holes for copper on Silers Bald way back in 1905. And he can still tell you about it.

This subject came up here in a discussion of Paul Fink's book, *Backpacking Was the Only Way.* He mentioned the "prospect pits" on Silers in connection with a 1922 hike.

Later, Bob Laurence, of the U.S. Geological Survey office here, sent me a copy of a page from an old report which said in part:

"Some prospecting was done at Silers Bald...on the crest of the Smokies by Mr. Calhoun and others about 1905. A shallow pit in a sandstone outcrop along the trail at the southeast end of a meadow disclosed small quartz veins, as much as three inches wide, and tiny stringers and disseminations of galena and chalcopyrite. On the headwaters of Jonas Creek to the northeast, about 500 feet vertically below the summit, a shallow opencut and two tunnels were dug to prospect a similar mineralized zone in sandstone . . . "

Granville would have been about thirty when he was up there on Silers looking for copper. He's 101 now. He and a widowed daughter, Mrs. Pauline Kindley, and a son Seymour, live together in Bryson City, N.C. Seymour will be eighty his next birthday.

Alberta and I stopped by the Calhoun home when we were roaming around that section on vacation a few weeks ago. We learned Granville had had a stroke since the last time I was there, and this had left his speech impaired. I had trouble understanding him at first, but the situation improved as I grew accustomed to him. Meanwhile, Seymour translated the difficult parts. Except for the speech impairment,

Mr. Calhoun has bounced back from the stroke in pretty good shape for a 101-year-old fellow. His mind and memory are good, and pretty soon he was telling a bear story I hadn't heard before.

This was about the bear that ran over him. He and some other fellows had just started a hunt one cold morning more than fifty years ago. The wind was whistling out of North Carolina into Tennessee.

Some of the hunters had started a bear drive up the Carolina slopes. Granville was on his stand at the Hall Cabin (named for his father-in-law, Crate Hall), atop the mountain near Derrick Knob.

Granville had moved down from the crest a few feet onto the Tennessee side, to get out of the worst of the wind, and was hunkered down building a fire.

The drivers' efforts were successful sooner than Granville had expected. Here came this frightened bear up out of North Carolina, hotfooting it across the crest, down into Tennessee and right over the top of Granville.

Chalk up one bear that Granville did not get. But he got lots more. He hunted bear more than forty years in the Great Smokies. In fact, there wasn't much that mountain men did that Granville didn't do and do well. Except make moonshine. He never did that, and he did not drink it. He didn't smoke cigarets or chew tobacco, either.

In the days of his youth and young manhood, he was a walker, a mountain roamer. He could walk all day, up hill and down, at the same pace. Sometimes he walked from his home in Hazel Creek Valley, up the Bone Valley Fork of Hazel, then up over Jenkins Trail Ridge, to Haw Gap, to Spence Field and then down into Cades Cove, in Tennessee. He sometimes walked more than thirty miles to Bryson City in a day, spent the night there and walked back the next day. He could have ridden one of his father's horses on these trips. Or he could have ridden a train part of the way. But it cost money to do that.

Granville also was a cattle herder in the mountains when he was a young man. In later years, he leased from the owners (mostly lumber companies) much of the mountain from Clingmans Dome about sixteen miles west to the Hall Cabin, for grazing. By then, he had herders working for him.

Granville and the herdsmen from the Cades Cove area once got together to estimate as closely as possible the number of cattle then grazing in the western half of the Great Smokies. Their figure: 1600.

From his herding, hunting and just plain roaming around the mountains, Granville came to know nearly every hill, hollow, bald and gap in the western half of the range. Lumber companies prized his services as a guide. He guided timber cruisers for companies in North Carolina and for Little River Lumber Company in Tennessee.

A man who spent so much time out in the mountains had to eat whenever he got hungry. So Granville became a camp cook whose offerings were prized by anybody lucky enough to share them.

Granville recommends this method of cooking a wild turkey if one finds himself out in the mountains with a turkey but no pots and pans: Prop the dead bird up on its feet with sticks near your camp cook fire. Suspend above it a strip of bacon on a sharpened stick. Let the bacon grease drip slowly on the cooking turkey. Turn turkey from time to time, so it gets done evenly all around. Prop open the breast cavity.

"You can tell when it gets done, for the meat starts breaking loose from the bones," Granville said.

But he didn't use that method of cooking on one memorable hunt. He and his father-in-law once went into the mountains to look for some straggler cattle one cool fall day. Like most mountain men, they just happened to have their guns and dogs along. They happened to meet four Carolina men and six Tennesseans who were hunting. So they forgot about cattle and started hunting.

At the end of that day, the twelve had eleven wild turkeys, a spike-buck deer, one bear, one groundhog, one or two coons, several gray squirrels, a boomer and a ruffed grouse.

Granville said he used some of the meat from all that game in two ten-quart buckets—one from Tennessee and one from Carolina—cooked it over a log fire, made dumplin's with a half-sack of flour, had five gallons of coffee, and ate far into the night. One thing about cooking and eating a turkey in the spring in the Great Smokies, according to Granvile, is that you better eat ramps with him. For the turkey eats ramps and the meat won't taste good unless you're eating ramps, too.

When Granville was growing up on Hazel Creek, there was no tradition about eating turkey for Christmas dinner. Families prepared whatever meat they liked and happened to have on hand. His favorite was pork. Not country ham or tenderloin, but pork ribs.

Back in the days before electricity and electric refrigerators came to the region, people used various methods of preserving food. Granville remembered this unusual one for butter:

Into a large earthen jar one would pour a layer of salt, then a layer of butter, another of salt, another butter, and so on until the jar was filled. Then the jar could be kept in the smokehouse.

Schooling was different then, too. Granville's first "book" was a wooden paddle on which father had pasted the letters of the alphabet he had cut from newspapers.

Sometimes when I'm at Silers Bald with enough time to do some hunting, I'm going to try to find the tunnel Granville had dug down at the headwater of Jonas Creek. (Jonas is a tributary of Forney Creek.)

Seymour quoted his father as saying there was pretty good copper ore there, enough that Granville got an option on it for W.S. Adams, for whom he worked in the copper business. Mr. Adams bought it.

But the Silers Bald copper was never mined because of one of the longest lawsuits in North Carolina history. The firm headed by Adams and one headed by G. R. Westfeldt clashed over ownership of copper land in Hazel Creek Valley. The lawsuit raged off and on in the courts for twenty-six years. Granville was in it from beginning to end. He has a stack of books, the bound volumes of all the testimony and pleadings.

But the Silers Bald copper stayed in the ground.   —*5/30/76*

00000

A long, strong link with the past snapped last Sunday with the death of Granville Calhoun in his home at Bryson City, N.C., at the age of 103.

Granville was more than half as old as the nation. He was one of the few who lived through both the country's Centennial celebration and its Bicentennial. But he was a bit young to fully appreciate the first and a little too old to kick up his heels much for the second one.

Besides, the really active parts of Granville's life occurred between those big national celebrations. In his long life on the south side of the Great Smokies, he did nearly everything a mountain man can do, except make liquor.

Granville was a man people came to see. He was a leader who would get done what needed to be done. He was a fountain of lore and information about the mountains. And he gave of it freely. Granville was the first man any author visited if he intended to write about the south side of the Smokies.

The first writer who came to see Granville probably was Horace Kephart, from St. Louis. That was in the fall of 1902. Granville did more than provide information for Kephart. He may have saved his life. For Kephart then was sickly, suffering from too much alcohol. He was so sick and weak he could hardly ride the mule to the Calhoun home.

I'll try not to belabor the old story of Granville and Mrs. Calhoun nursing Kephart back to health with strawberry wine, milk, chicken and speckled trout.

Kephart became healthy enough to live on in the Great Smokies for many years. He wrote *Our Southern Highlanders*, generally acclaimed as the best book ever written about the people of the Southern mountains. Kephart was one of the early backers of national park status for the Great Smokies. Mt. Kephart and Kephart Prong bear his name. Granville's name appears many times in the Kephart book, and one of the best chapters deals with a bear hunt the author made with Granville and some of his friends.

Michael Frome went to see Granville when Frome was gathering information for *Strangers in High Places*, his history of the Great Smokies. I suppose John Parris of The Asheville Citizen has written a couple of hundred yards of copy on Granville.

I made my own pilgrimage to Granville's home when Alberta and I were doing the research for *Valley So Wild*, our book on the Little Tennessee River. It was in 1969 or 1970. Granville, in his middle nineties, was a tall old man, lean as a rail. He was completely dressed. Suit with vest, white shirt, red tie with white dots. And, though he was in the house, he wore his hat. Like many other mountain men of his time, Granville put on his hat when he put on his other clothes in the morning and kept it on till he undressed at night.

I'm looking at my notes from that interview, trying to find some stories I haven't written before.

Here's one that indicates the bounty of Great Smokies streams more than seventy-five years ago: Granville's double brother-in-law, Judd Hall, challenged Granville to a fishing contest one Saturday morning. They covered a mile and a half of Proctor Creek in four and a half hours. Granville said he had to quit because "my arm wore out." When they reached home and poured out and counted their fish, the total was 476 brook trout, six to ten inches long. Granville caught two more than Judd.

On dog care: "Mountain men liked to have their dogs with them in the mountains, whether they were hunting, herding or just roaming." Granville said he built dog stalls onto the outside of one of the Hall Cabins (a cabin used by herders and hunters on the mountain crest). This was necessary, or at least desirable, because weather on the mountaintop sometimes was extremely cold. Granville remembers one dog, owned by another man, which had to be carried into the cabin, wrapped in a tow sack and thawed out in front of the fire. Granville said he once fixed a bed in a downed hollow buckeye tree for one of his own dogs.

On sheep-raising in the Great Smokies: "A few Hazel Creek people tried to raise sheep." But Granville said the lambs had too many enemies—dogs, eagles, wildcats and a few panthers . . . He remembers an old panther which raised a litter of cubs on a cliff above Hazel Creek.

On wearing shoes: "Kephart wrote of some mountaineers who went all winter without shoes." Granville says, though, that he can recall no one who didn't own a pair of shoes. He said some didn't wear them on mild winter days, but they owned them.

Granville said that day that he wanted to live to be 100. He said he'd been drunk only once in his life—when he and some other boys fifteen or sixteen years old attended a Confederate veterans reunion. He says he "never smoked a cigaret in my life and . . . never chewed a chew of tobacco in my life." He said he didn't eat or drink anything "to excess."

Unlike many mountain men of his time, Granville lived a peaceful life. The life of a good citizen. And he died peacefully, as he slept.

—*5/14/78*

Painter of the Smokies

At a time when most people walking the unmarked trails of the Great Smoky Mountains carried rifles, Charles Christopher Krutch carried a sketching pad.

Nobody living now can say with certainty when the gentle son of German immigrants began his tramps in the mountains. William J. McCoy, Jr. probably can come as close as anyone. For when he was eleven, Bill McCoy began going with the old man. He listened to him talk about earlier trips and he stayed with him in the mountain homes of families with whom Mr. Krutch obviously had been staying off and on for years. Bill is pretty certain that Charlie Krutch began painting his watercolor landscapes (he later also did many oils) of the Great Smokies before 1900. Probably a long time before then.

Nor does anyone today know how many Great Smokies landscapes Mr. Krutch painted. Sixty of them were exhibited at once at Dulin Gallery, and these probably are only a fraction of total production.

One reason so little is known about him is that he was shy, not given to saying or writing much about himself. Another is that he had no wife or children to keep tab of his achievements.

A nephew, the late Joseph Wood Krutch, author, naturalist, philosopher and critic, wrote affectionately of "Uncle Charlie" in his autobiography, *More Lives Than One*. But a reader gets the impression that the famous nephew's affection for Uncle Charlie may have been blended with a drop of condescension for his paintings. For he wrote:

"Every summer he (Uncle Charlie) disappeared for a month or more into the Smokies where he lived with a family of mountaineers in one of the isolated valleys far beyond the reach of the logging train which alone connected what is now the Appalachian National Park with the outside world. There he shared his hosts' beans and bacon and, I have no doubt, partook moderately of their moonshine. From these expeditions he returned with sketches to be elaborated into vistas and peaks and clouds of which he must have painted a hundred or more. His technique was limited and his reputation never got beyond East Tennessee but he did have a feeling for his subject and there was hardly a Knoxville family with any pretensions to smartness which did not own at least one of his productions."

Maybe that's a proper assessment of Uncle Charlie's painting. On the other hand, maybe it's off target just a little, like Joseph Wood Krutch's name for that national park back home.

Bill McCoy has a higher opinion of the Krutch technique. Limited, maybe, but "sufficient for the use he made of it, even sophisticated for his time," Bill says. Charlie Krutch specialized. Landscapes. That was it. No studies of Will Cole, or Joe Cole, or Davis Bracken, or any of his other mountain friends. No painting of a tree all by itself. But he comes close to this by featuring a tree in a handsome red-brown landscape, one of those exhibited.

Mr. McCoy said the red-brown one is as similar as anything Mr. Krutch ever did to the work of Corot. (Mr. Krutch sometimes was called the "Corot of the South.")

Mr. Krutch's work had some faults, all right. One reason is that he did not always have the money to buy the best paints, and he sometimes spread inferior paint thinly. One reason Bill knows about this is that he has restored some Krutches. In fact, he got into painting himself from restoring Krutch paintings. (But his major vocation is engineering, not art.)

Mr. Krutch was part of Bill's life as far back as he can remember till the old man died in 1934, when Bill was six. He called Mr. Krutch "Uncle Charlie" and actually thought for a year or two that he was blood kin.

One of young Bill's favorite places was Mr. Krutch's room in Bill's father's photography shop at 313 S. Gay St. Mr. Krutch was a retoucher. He deftly removed some of the blemishes from the pictures of the McCoy photographic customers. He'd had some photographic training in Atlanta. But none as a painter.

However, sometime before Bill was born, Mr. Krutch had taught himself to paint. Some early Krutch landscapes were of the general area where First Creek entered the Tennessee River.

The Krutch home was near there, at 914 E. Hill Ave. In his last years, after other members of the family died or moved away, he shared the home with his spinster sister, Miss Lou, as she was called. Her death followed his by a year.

He walked from home to the McCoy studio. He did what retouching needed doing and spent the rest of his time there painting. Bill doubts that he ever sold a painting for more than $300, though some of them now bring up to $1500.

He painted mostly from sketches he'd made in the mountains. Bill McCoy remembers with admiration the old man's sketching technique. "He sketched more rapidly than anybody else I ever saw. It looked like it just flowed out of the end of his pencil," Bill said.

Though he completed a few paintings in the mountains, he ordinarily brought back only sketches and his memory for the painting.

Canvas sometimes was an unnecessary luxury for him. One of the Krutches exhibited at Dulin is "Thunderhead's Rhapsody in Blue," painted on a circle of cardboard twelve inches in diameter.

Bill, who now owns the painting, knows its history from the beginning. One day Mr. Krutch was cutting a circular hole through a cardboard film drying cabinet for an exhaust fan. When the circle of cardboard fell to the floor, he picked it up and said, "I know where there's a frame that fits this."

Somebody's doodling is visible through the paint of another Krutch-on-cardboard when the light strikes it at a certain angle.

The most cardboard Krutches probably were the miniatures he did on penny postcards. He painted one side, addressed the other and mailed them. The painting was the message.

I think my favorite of the paintings at Dulin is one not much larger than a postcard—a watercolor waterfall nestled in a black shadowbox frame. Bill thinks it's of Abrams Falls. Maybe. But if it is, the artist positioned himself in his imagination where he could not have done so in reality—downstream from the falls but above them in altitude.

Bill and Stuart McCroskey, who owns Holston Printing Co., where Bill rents office space, found this little painting in a box which also contained other personal items of Irvin S. Saxton, an elderly former Knoxville lawyer who now lives at the VA hospital at Mountain Home. Mr. Saxton had left the box at the printing company years earlier, when the company was under different ownership. He had forgotten them. Bill wrote him that Great Smoky Mountains Natural History Association was in the market for Krutch paintings. So Mr. Saxton gave it to the Association. It's one of the seven Krutches which the association has acquired in the past year. All were in the exhibit.

Joseph Wood Krutch was not quite correct in saying his uncle's reputation never got beyond East Tennessee. For some wealthy Easterners, early visitors to the new Great Smokies park, bought Krutch paintings to take back to New York with them.   —*10/5/75*

Making the Maps

Bicentennially speaking, there wasn't much action around here in mid-summer 1775.

To be sure, Richard Henderson a few months earlier had pulled off one of the biggest real estate deals in this or any other region. He bought "Kentucky," which really wasn't Kentucky as it is on the map today. It was twenty million acres of land in what are now parts of Tennessee and Kentucky. But that deal was made way up in upper East Tennessee, at Sycamore Shoals of the Watauga River.

It was about eleven years before James White would grind the first grain of corn in his tubmill here and plant Knoxville's first turnip seed.

Yet, circumstances boring in from different directions dictate that we discuss matters historical today.

One circumstance is a copy of an old surveyor's boundary line and notes passed on to me recently by William J. McCoy Jr., president of Tennessee Associates Inc.

Another is a conversation with John Morrell about Andy Gregory and Blanket Mountain and Meigs Post. Meigs Post is a fascinating subject for oldtimers and historians of the Great Smokies.

Still another circumstance is that John Stiles, a fellow News-Sentinel reporter, and I floated the Little Tennessee River Monday and saw what to us was a new dig by the archeologists investigating the old Indian town sites along the river.

I wondered whether the diggers at this dig were looking for Tuskegee.

Tuskegee has been a problem for the archeologists. They can't find it. Not for sure, anyway.

Though I'm willing to be corrected by any competent historian, I suspect the reason the remains of Tuskegee are hard to find is that the Cherokees didn't live there long enough to leave many remains. Not nearly as many as at Chota, Citico, Toqua, Tomotley and others.

When the English built Fort Loudoun, the builders wrote of it being a mile and a half downstream from Tomotley. No mention of Tuskegee. That was in 1756.

But historians say one of the greatest Cherokees, Sequoyah, blacksmith, silversmith and inventor of the Cherokee syllabary, was born at Tuskegee in 1760, the year Fort Loudoun fell.

So 200 years ago, Sequoyah, son of an Indian mother and a white father, was a fifteen-year-old boy rambling along the banks of the Little T, probably having no idea he would become one of the ninteenth century's greatest Americans, no idea that the world's largest trees, TVA's second nuclear power plant, and a fashionable Knoxville residential area some day would bear his name.

Henry Timberlake saw Tuskegee when he lived with the Cherokees along the river a few months during the winter of 1761-62. He shows it on his famous map as the nearest Cherokee town to the old fort, perhaps only a half-mile upstream.

It was at Tuskegee that eighteen-year-old James Moore was burned at the stake 199 years ago this summer. A rebel chief named Dragging Canoe and other young chiefs who were unhappy with the deal Richard Henderson had pressed on their elders brought back the Moore youth and other prisoners from a raid on the English settlements in Upper East Tennessee.

An avenging army of whites burned Tuskegee and several other Cherokee towns a few months later, and Tuskegee may never have been rebuilt, for the Cherokees began abandoning towns along the Little T the next year and moving south to the Chattanooga area.

So it may be that Tuskegee existed fewer than twenty years, not long enough to leave many remains.

Incidentally, Dr. Alfred K. Guthe, director of UT's McClung Museum and boss of the digs along the Tellico, said the dig John and I saw was not Tuskegee. At that particular dig, they've found much older stuff, going back 8000 or 9000 years. He does think—but he's not positive—that they may have found Tuskegee farther back from the river. A little bit of Indian stuff is there, not enough to indicate long occupation.

The fortunes of the Cherokees continued downward. In treaty after treaty they gave up more and more land to the hard-pressing white folks.

And that brings us to the Treaty of the Holston, held near where Knoxville's First Creek enters the river, in 1791, and to Bill McCoy's map and to Meigs Post.

The new boundary line between whites and Cherokees set by the Treaty of the Holston was from Southwest Point (Kingston) southeastward in a straight line to a crossing of the Holston (now Tennessee) River at the dividing ridge between the Little Tennessee and Little Rivers. And it was to continue from there in a straight line to the North Carolina line.

But they didn't get around to surveying the line until 1797. Benjamin Hawkins was in charge of the survey.

Bill McCoy's map that the surveyors made as they moved along starts "on the Clinch, one-fourth mile above the ferry in view of S. W. Point."

At the starting point, the surveyors marked "U.S." on the north side of a Spanish oak and on the south side of the same oak, they marked "C" for Cherokee. Mile after mile, as they moved southeastward, they marked trees in that fashion. They took the line near Maryville and on to Chilhowee Mountain.

In a note on the map they wrote, "From Holston (now Tennessee) to Chilhowee Mountain there are many intruders on Indian lands . . ."

They got into the Great Smokies foothills and their last note on the map reads, "This line terminates at the 30th mile from Holston, in the midst of mountains which cannot be passed by horses and is extremely difficult for foot men."

Jonathan Meigs finished the survey in 1802. According to John Morrell, who has retired after a fruitful career with the National Park Service, Meigs stood atop Chilhowee Mountain and picked out a prominent Great Smokies peak that lined up well with the boundary survey. Then he climbed it and placed a brightly colored blanket on it. That mountain has since been called Blanket Mountain.

Meigs then made his way to the state-line crest of the Great Smokies and walked along the crest till he could properly line up with the blanket on the survey line. He planted a square wooden post in the ground where he stood (on top of what later was named Mt. Collins, the first high peak west of Indian Gap). And the post has since been called Meigs Post.

Indian boundary lines became lines for state grants, property lines between individuals, between companies. Those old frontier boundary lines always were subjects of hot debate. Making matters worse with this one was the War of 1812. When the British burned Washington, the last two or three pages of Meigs' notes were so charred they were unreadable.

Somehow or other, in about 1912 or 1913, according to John, Meigs

Post was moved all the way west from Mt. Collins to the top of Miry Ridge. Since it then was the beginning of the dividing line in Tennessee between property of Little River Lumber Co., on the east, and Appalachian Lumber Co., on the west, this brought on a lawsuit. Little River lost.

John thinks it was Andy Gregory who years later took Meigs Post (certainly not the original one) back to its rightful place on Mt. Collins.

Still later, in the 1950s, John Morrell himself substituted a concrete Meigs Post, with a metal marker on top, for the decayed wooden one.

So if you draw a straight line on a map between Mt. Collins and Kingston, you'll be looking at one of the most controversial boundary lines this region ever had.   *—7/6/75*

00000

I'm losing faith in cartographers and gaining faith in people like Bob Barker, John Morrell and Claude Hyde.

Some loose ends were left dangling here and there in a piece about the hike John Stiles and I made to that Western North Carolina country that includes Hangover Mountain, the Naked Ground, and Stratton Bald. How the Naked Ground and Stratton Bald came to be so named were a couple of the loose ends.

Two other mysteries were Hudson Deaden Branch, on the Tapoco quadrangle map, and Goldie Deaden, on the Santeetlah quad.

"Who were the Deadens who left the name on this wild geography?" I asked.

John Morrell was first to reply. John, who lives up above Pigeon Forge, is retired from the staff of Great Smoky Mountains National Park. He's a lawyer, surveyor, and he knows a lot of the history of the Great Smokies.

"I hereby offer this theory as to the 'Hudson Deaden Branch' and the 'Goldie Deaden,' " John wrote.

"Deaden is not a family name, but is a corruptive of the term 'deadening.' I never saw a cartographer who could spell."

John went on to explain that "deadening" refers "to the old mountain practice of deadening trees by girdling them with an axe in the spring of the year, preparatory to the clearing of 'new ground' the following spring, at which time the previously deadened trees were cut down, piled up and burnt. It is extremely difficult to burn green logs."

And I believe I'm right in adding that a man could plant a crop of corn that first spring and cultivate it and harvest it in that ghost forest. Having no leaves, the dead trees did not make enough shade to hamper growth of the corn very much. But back to John, who said:

"The practice of killing trees by deadening (or girdling) them was used also to encourage the growth of grass for summer pasture, and to enlarge the areas of the grassy balds...

"Incidentally, one of the tributaries of Fighting Creek (the third branch above Hickory Flats Branch) is known as the 'Bill Deadening Branch.' Evidently the custom was to name the deadenings after the given name of the man who did the work.

"Selective deadening of trees (species not desirable for timber sales) is still practiced by the U.S. Forest Service, and is done by cutting a few hacks into the sapwood and inserting salt or some chemical compound that kills the tree."

Bob Barker, Andrews, N.C., agrees with John on how the "deadens" got their names, but he says he doesn't know about the Goldie Deaden and Hudson Deaden Branch. He does, however, know about the John Deaden. It was named for "old man John Deputy, from Monroe County, who lived on, or almost on, the state line on the old Forty Mountain Indian Trail . . .

"Charlie Denton said John Deputy deadened several acres of timber to cultivate and later plant corn, but as time went by, John Deputy made more money blockading and forgot to finish the clearing job. The place became known locally as the John Deaden."

Claude Hyde, Robbinsville, N.C., says a family by the name of Hudson lived on Bear Creek and deadened a patch of timber on what became known as Hudson Deaden Branch. And a man named Goldie deadened a patch of trees for a cabin site on Horse Cove Ridge.

Someone—I've forgotten who—several days ago asked me how Patrick Meadows got its name in Graham County, N.C. His answer is in this paragraph coming up from Mr. Hyde:

"(The) King family cleared King Meadows. Sim Hooper cleared a small meadow we call Sim Meadows. Patrick Hooper cleared and fenced the Patrick Meadows on the head of Huffman Creek."

It is over "Bob Bald" and "Stratton Bald" that I have my biggest fuss with the map-makers. You may recall that I mentioned Stratton Meadow and said it was named for John Stratton who settled there. And I said Bob Bald was named for John's son Bob, but that I didn't know for whom Stratton Bald was named.

On the Tapoco map, the cartographers put "Stratton Bald" down in the southwestern corner. On the adjoining Santeetlah map, apparently about a mile from Stratton Bald, they put "Bob Bald."

The first fellow to set me straight on "Bob Bald" and "Stratton Bald" was a Stratton descendant, Eugene Stratton, 1414 Cornelia Street. He said it's only one place, not two, but that people call it by both names. I think he prefers "Bob Bald." Claude Hyde and Bob Barker said much the same thing.

Claude and Bob also reported on the Naked Ground. It now is only a wooded gap on the divide between Slickrock and Little Santeetlah Creeks. Most of the trees there are beech, and they look to be twenty or more years old. And I've been trying to find out how it came to have such a colorful name, Obviously, it once looked other than it does now.

Mr. Hyde said the Naked Ground "used to be just that."

Well, to me, that means it was bare earth or earth and rocks. No grass, no trees, no weeds or shrubs.

John Morrell guessed something like that, too. John, who has never been to the Naked Ground, asked whether there was any evidence of rock outcropping there.

Then he recalled that when Tom Sparks was herding cattle on the Spence Field (on the main ridge of the Great Smokies) he used "depressions in the rocks on the Rocky Top of Thunderhead as receptacles for salt, and as it was leached out by rains or scattered by cattle, the immediate area became 'naked.' The same thing sometimes occurred around the 'lick-logs' in which cattle salt was placed. Another possibility is that the ground might have become 'naked' as the result of fire."

Then along comes Bob Barker and says:

"I was there (the Naked Ground)—twice—twenty-four years ago with Victor Denton, then a Wildlife protector . . . Paid jointly by the state and the U.S. Forest Service. It was bare and naked then—just a grass spot in a low gap—on the top of the mountain."

So I gather that, when Bob saw it, it was merely another grassy mountain meadow—similar to Stratton Meadow, or Spence Field, or Gregory Bald. So why would those mountain herdsmen have given it a name completely unlike the other names they commonly used for such a grassy spot surrounded by forest? I wonder whether, at some time much earlier, it wasn't more like John Morrell imagined it to be—and maybe for one of the reasons he mentioned.

Bob also supplied more enlightenment on John Big Fat and Sally Big Fat, whose nickname lives in Big Fat Gap, that notch in Hangover Lead.

John and Sally (Big Fat) Conseen lived near the gap, and they got their nicknames because they were a bit hefty.

Bob sent copies of some 100-year-old court records concerning John and Sally. Sometimes they were referred to only as John and Sally Big Fat; sometimes their real name, Conseen, was used. The case involved the theft of ten hogs from them.

Sally Big Fat must have lived up into the 1890's. For I remember hearing the late Harriet Swan Ledgerwood speak of her. When Harriet Swan was a little girl, she was a bit plump, and she was teasingly called Sally Big Fat.

She and her parents and two brothers then lived at another of those grassy mountain meadows, this one appropriately called Swan Meadow. Years later, when she was living in Oak Ridge, she went to Joyce Kilmer Memorial Forest on one of the hikes The News-Sentinel and Smoky Mountains Hiking Club used to sponsor. I remember she told stories of visiting the family of John Denton, the only family ever to live in what's now Joyce Kilmer Memorial Forest.

Mr. Hyde says the Swans and others in the mountains lost most of their cattle when a heavy spring snowstorm hit the mountains early in this century. He said one of the few survivors was "one old white cow owned by John Denton." She managed to get out of the deep snow of the high country and down to food and warmer weather in the lowlands.   —*3/31/74*

8

Those Big, Beautiful Trees

Last Sunday dawned the unlovely gray of a bowl of oysters somebody forgot to eat the night before. Number one wife Miss Alberta and I decided it would do us both good to go up unto the hills and walk. And sweat. And breathe a little hard. And get tired.

The particular hill we decided to walk unto is Cove Mountain, on top of which stands a crippled fire tower. Cove Mountain is kind of a northern annex to the main range of the Great Smokies.

Before the fire tower was crippled, a fellow could hike up there, climb the tower and enjoy a great view of the main range of the Great Smokies. The Brewer hiking book has a chapter on this hike, and much of it is devoted to what one can see from that tower. So, since the tower is a cripple now and one isn't supposed to climb it, that chapter has to be rewritten for a new printing of the book sometime soon. So we went to refresh our memories on what can be seen on that hike besides a view from the tower.

Drove to Fighting Creek Gap, on the Little River Road. Nearly a dozen cars were already parked there. The first leg of this hike takes one to Laurel Falls. That short trip is so popular the National Park Service (NPS) has had to pave the trail.

From gap to waterfall, one walks through second-growth forest of mostly pines and oaks. Lots of hardy, tough-leaved galax, teaberry and trailing arbutus grow along the first part of the trail. Galax leaves, which grew last year, are as smooth and tough as polished leather and colored all the way from green to smoky red.

Searched for an arbutus bloom, just one sign that the plants up here knew spring had arrived three days earlier. The best I could find was an unopened bud that was pink at the tip. Made note to check it on return trip.

Lots of water poured down split-level Laurel Falls. Several people were there, looking, making pictures. That was the turnaround place for most of them. We temporarily ran out of people after we left the falls and headed on up the trail, ascending the slightly curving Chinquapin Ridge leading to Cove Mountain.

Far down to our right, Tanager Branch, tributary to Laurel Branch, splashed along in youthful merriment.

Less than a mile above the waterfall, we entered a forest that has intrigued me the previous times I've been there. It has the look of virgin forest. Grandpa tulip poplars and hemlocks stand there in the massive, straight-trunked grandeur that inspires some people to break out in poetry or prayer. Occasional silverbell trees grow among the hemlocks and poplars. They'll bloom in late April and May. Now, last year's papery four-veined seed husks cling to some trees and litter parts of the trail.

After walking up out of the hemlocks and poplars, we were among oaks again. But not pines. The oaks—whiteoaks, Northern reds, scarlets—have lots of maples for company here. To me, this forest doesn't look virgin. Most of the trees aren't nearly as large as the hemlocks and poplars below. Yet, one sees an occasional very large whiteoak. (You understand, I am not expert in these matters.)

Up along the crest of Chinquapin Ridge, we came upon a disturbed area. It had the look of a place where wild hogs had rooted for acorns. I hadn't heard of European wild boars reaching this northern outpost of the park. And I suppose the disturbance could have been caused by something else, but I don't know what.

Up near the top, we met Knoxville landscape architect Bill Oliphant and his son, Paul, coming down.

By now, the sun was out. Blue was up there where gray had been. Buzzards, one hawk, crows, a few juncos and a solitary phoebe were on the wing. Pileated woodpeckers were noisy but out of sight.

On top, somebody had rigged a makeshift ladder to substitute for the first flight of steps up the tower. I don't recommend using the makeshift ladder. An unsteady person could fall and break something.

On the way back down, Alberta and I stopped and sat on the trunk of a downed silverbell. Just below us was the moist, decaying trunk of one of those old grandpa trees. Its top side was moss-covered. Also growing out of it were two moose maple saplings, a yearling hemlock, several ferns, toothwort, wood sorrel and spring beauties. The toothwort and spring beauties should be in bloom soon, maybe now.

Scattered in artistic haphazardness on the winter-brown forest floor were the trunks of scores of these long-dead grandpa trees, strikingly marked by their green tops of moss.

What quirk of circumstance caused this small piece of forest to escape untouched by the loggers? We decided John Morrell might know. I would phone him later.

Meanwhile, we hurried on back. I found that the sunshine had coaxed open that morning's pink-tipped arbutus bud. The sky was graying again. We went home before the rain started.

I phoned John Morrell two days later. John is a combination lawyer-surveyor-historian who worked for the park from the beginning and until he retired several years ago.

Why is that virgin forest up there above Laurel Falls?

John dug into his memory and said that old Abraham Millsaps received a grant of 2000 acres of land a long time ago. It stretched from Little River on the west across the ridge and down into the headwaters of Fighting Creek.

John said W. B. Townsend once tried to buy the land from the Millsaps heirs for his Little River Lumber Co. He wanted to cut the big trees up there in the forest. The heirs wouldn't sell. Later, though, they decided to log the land themselves. And they wanted to haul out the logs on Townsend's Little River Railroad. Remembering their refusal to sell to him, Townsend refused to haul for them.

Later, the Millsaps heirs did sell to someone else. And still later, somebody did log some of it. John is uncertain about these details.

I phoned Ed Trout, park historian. Ed looked at his maps and records and also talked with Glenn Cardwell, park technician who is a native of the area and knows something about nearly everything up there.

Ed proved me not to be a likely candidate for a degree in forestry. He said the top section, where the oaks and maples grow, also is virgin forest. The oaks and maples simply don't grow as large at their altitude and in their poorer soil as the hemlocks and poplars grow down there in their richer soil.

Ed said Glenn thinks that when logging finally did get started on that ridge, the loggers decided the land up there where the big trees still grow was too rough for horses to pull logs.   *—3/30/80*

Tree-Cutting Days

A few days ago, I asked Bob Barker to explain that old logging term, "ball-hooting." Here's what he wrote:

"When I was a kid—fourteen years old—I got a job, no questions asked, 'bumping knots' and clearing right-of-way on the Norwood Lumber Co.'s operation at Forney Creek, getting out spruce, high above the hardwood timber. Some huge hemlocks were cut, too.

"Timber was cut with double-bitted Sager-Plumb axes and Disston cross-cut saws. No power saws then. Pay twenty cents per hour. Board forty cents per day in logging camps, usually held in place against the side of a steep mountain with cables, since level land was rare.

"A narrow gauge railroad came up to get the logs, with powerful Shay and Climax steam engines. A self-propelled steam loader stayed at the log-landing, to load the logs on log cars . . . Logs were skidded down to the log-landing from high above by teams; no tractors then.

"When the teams had collected a bunch of logs in the skid row, a big hemlock would always be in front, with its nose sharpened by axes to a point, so it would not foul against stumps in the run to the landing far down below. This big hemlock had a jay grab driven into it at the front, just like a big thumb sticking up. All other logs behind would be grabbed to the hemlock, by grabs driven into each at the end, notched in deep, so as not to break loose in the run to the landing. Sometimes as many as sixty or seventy logs were grabbed together.

"When all was ready, water would be turned into the skid log road, like a creek, to get it slick. Then one or two—most of the time just one—team would be hooked to the lead log by the spread, which had a hook held onto the jay grab by pressure alone. Once the logs started, the teamster would leap on the big hemlock and whip the horses into a gallop, then 'jay' them to the right, in a cleared place. The spread would fall off. The logs would slide by, gaining speed by the second. And a lookout on a high stump below would holler, 'BALL HOOT!'"

This was to warn the crew working on the landing far below "to run for their lives and back the loader . . . out of the way, since many logs tore up the railroad track daily, and it had to be rebuilt again and again.

"Sometimes the lookout would shoot a shotgun or ring a cowbell. And at one point, where he could not be seen, he ran up a red flag on a pole . . . and shot a cannon cracker.

"The logs ran so fast and furious (that) friction against a stump would set it on fire and sometimes the grabs would break the chains or pull out and three or four sets of logs would be headed for the landing, usually in a deep hollow.

"It was dangerous and some men got killed and injured, but that always happened on logging jobs . . . "

J. H. Evans, who used to live at Hartford, in Cocke County, and now lives at Oak Ridge, is another who remembers ball-hooting. He describes it much the same as Bob Barker does. But he adds a bit about the horses.

He said an experienced horse always was placed on the outside. When the teamster yelled, "Jay," that horse would, if necessary, bump the other horse to the side and away from the speeding logs. Sometimes, "jay holes" were dug into the side of the road bank, and the horses dodged into these when the jay hook uncoupled.

There was still another method of transporting logs in rugged sections of the mountains where mules and horses—and steers—could not go. (I mention steers because the people at Keller Foundry recently sent me a pair of steelshoes of the type worn by oxen used in logging.) This other method—or contraption—was the skidder. As best I can understand it, the skidder was an elaborate block and tackle which could drag logs on the ground or carry them through the air for hundreds of yards.

"My father operated one of the overhead skidders for Little River Co." says Charles E. Cope, Rockford. "And I have heard him talk of hauling in trees—water oak and tulip poplar—that measured twelve feet in diameter.

"These men were a hardy bunch. They worked in almost all kinds of weather—rain, sleet, and snow. I've seen my father pull off overalls that were so frozen they would stand up alone."   —4/7/74

Hobo Jack was a Redbone hound who had the reputation in and around Robbinsville, N.C., of being a good bear and boar dog.

How he came to have such a name is a story that old Graham County storyteller, Claude Hyde, has for us.

Hobo Jack is dead now. So is Cecil Rice, the man who owned him, according to Mr. Hyde.

When the dog was young and able to hunt, he and Cecil Rice would catch a Bemis Lumber Co. logging train out of Robbinsville and they'd ride the train to lumber camps high up in the Snowbird Creek watershed. Hobo Jack and Mr. Rice then would go bear hunting, but they used the logging camps as headquarters while they were out on extended hunts.

Hobo Jack liked loggers. He also liked the excellent and plentiful grub dished out at logging camps.

After hunting season was over, Hobo Jack would stay around Robbinsville for as long as he could stand the traffic and the noise. After he was fed up with life in town, he'd take off for a logging camp.

But this time he'd go alone.

"He'd head for the log train, jump on a car and pull out for the mountains," Mr. Hyde says.

"He had to switch trains at Big Snowbird, where the wide-gauge track ended and the narrow-gauge took over, to get to the camp."

He'd stay a few weeks, long enough to "get real fat on the good grub." Then he'd catch the train back to Robbinsville.

Mr. Rice once took Hobo Jack on a hunt in Pisgah National Forest, in Buncombe County. The dog and his owner became separated, and Mr. Rice went back to Robbinsville without him.

But someone found Hobo Jack and put him on a Southern Railway freight train to Topton. He waited there for the Bemis train and rode it back to Robbinsville.

"I was running a cafe in Robbinsville during World War II," Mr. Hyde said. "Hobo Jack would come to the back of the cafe and bark a time or two. I would toss him a few hamburgers. He would eat them and go on his way.

"He learned lots of tricks. For instance, he'd go three or four miles out of town. He'd watch for a car coming back. He'd pretend to be crippled, so they would stop and pick him up and haul him back to town. Everyone knew him and most of his tricks.

"He lived to be eighteen years old and he is buried just below Chief Junaluska's grave on the ridge overlooking Robbinsville. He has a marker on his grave. If you ever visit the chief's grave, you can visit Hobo Jack's at the same time."

Well, Mr. Hyde, I have visited Chief Junaluska's grave up there on the hill, but I didn't know about Hobo Jack then and I didn't happen to notice his grave. Maybe his does not have a nice iron fence around it, as does Junaluska's.

I don't know quite what to do about Mr. Hyde and Bob Barker. They disagree on the logging term, "ball hoot." Bob, you may remember, lives over in Andrews, which is in Cherokee County, a mountain or two south of Robbinsville. But he knows and is known by a great many people in Graham and Swain Counties, plus Blount, Monroe and Knox, in Tennessee.

Claude Hyde also is well known in all those Western North Carolina counties, and he probably is pretty well known in some of the mountain counties out West, where he did some logging in his younger days.

[Bob Barker's opinion is in the article just preceding.]

Now here's part of what Claude says:

"I find myself in disagreement with friend Bob Barker over the term 'ball hoot.' This is one of my nicknames. The Swedes and Norwegians had never heard this until I set back in two feet of snow in the Cascade Mountains and hollered, 'BALL HOOT!' as the logs ran out of the chokers and went flying off the mountain."

(I looked up "choker" for us. In this context it means "a noose of wire rope for hauling a log.")

"Ball hooting was 100 per cent hand work," Mr. Hyde said, "done by a crew with axes and peavies." It was "running the logs off steep slopes, where horses and steers could not get. This was the hardest work ever undertaken. You had to peel the run of the logs, bump all the limbs and knots off, and nose the logs so they would not tear the poles out of the skidding roads . . .

"I can't tell you what we called the boy who greased the skid roads. It is unprintable.

"But when a Swede hook tender asked me how much a 'right smart' was, I promptly told him it was a damned sight more than 'quite a bit,' which is the expression used by the people in the Northwest . . ."

Turning to the subject of jaying, Mr. Hyde said he's seen steers that learned to jay just like horses. But he says he's seen both steers and horses fail to jay when they are supposed to and get their legs cut off for the failure.

Horses or steers are hooked to a front log of a line of several logs hooked together. The particular hook used between the first log and the horses is a "jay hook." The jay hook remains hooked only as long as the horses are pulling and causing tension on the hook. On the yell "JAY!" the team darts out of the path of the speeding logs. Without tension, the "jay hook" becomes uncoupled. And the teamster jumps off the log.

Mr. Hyde was one of fifteen young Western North Carolina men who took off to Washington State to get logging jobs in 1934, in the middle of the Great Depression. Most of them were killed or crippled. Mr. Hyde was one of the crippled, but he recovered enough to do lots of bear hunting when he got back to the Carolina mountains. But a train accident and then arthritis finally got to him.

This didn't stop Mr. Hyde, but it changed his hunting methods.

"After I became disabled, I could only go out in the woods, sit down and be still," he says. But he says he sees more game that way than he ever saw when he was moving around in the woods.

"Just hide behind a big rock or tree and let the game find you," he advises. "Never try to find it."

"I seen four bear and eight deer, using this system one fall when there was beech mast. Several hogs—one sow and five small pigs—walked within five feet of me. (I would never kill a sow with pigs or a bear with cubs.) I have seen cottontail rabbits get so excited when fast dogs were about to catch them, they would jump right into a man's arms.

"I have caught young deer with spots on them, petted them, let them nurse my finger. They would follow me just like I was their mother . . .

"To hunt wild turkeys when they were plentiful, all you had to do was find a hollow chestnut tree close to an open place or meadow. Turkeys would walk right by you. I have had them so close I could touch them with the gun barrel."

But now, Mr. Hyde, you have another problem. Hollow chestnut trees are scarcer than turkeys.   *—8/16/74*

I hope New England loggers and Western North Carolina loggers never have to work together, for they don't speak the same language.

This I learned when I got to puzzling around with "jillpoke." "Jillpoke" is a word John Gould, New England columnist and author, casually slid into a letter to me, as though any normal human would know the meaning of it.

I could find it in no dictionary, and we have a couple of very large ones here in The News-Sentinel office. But after I publicly displayed my ignorance, Claude Hyde, the Robbinsville, N.C., former logger, bear hunter and storyteller came to my aid. A few weeks ago he said a jillpoke was simply a pry pole, something a destitute logger might use if he couldn't afford either a cant hook or a peavey.

Mr. Hyde gave the matter more thought after he wrote that letter, and then he wrote another one. In it he said, the term "jillpoke" was used for several different things.

" . . . If a car was not in the clear on a side track, they set a pole between engine and car, and shoved car in the clear. Called this jillpoking. Kept from going back to switch and pulling in on side track to move car in clear."

He went on to explain that most flat cars used in logging trains "had a cast iron plate on end of car, like a socket, to set jillpoke in. Kept it from slipping when shoving a car on a side track."

Fine—until we heard again from John Gould. Quoting from one of his books, *Bildads, Boiled Owls, and Wazzats, Maine Lingo*, Mr. Gould said a jillpoke is "a long log on a river drive which gets one end stuck somehow and swings to start a jam. Thus, an awkward person likely to do something foolish or start trouble. A real gormy person is a jillpoke." Incidentally, I wonder whether Mr. Gould knows what a logger is talking about when he mentions a "dead man." This is one Mr. Hyde threw in for free. He says it was a "log you planted in the ground on angle to hook a tackle block on in an open field where there was no stump or tree to hang the block on. A team would just pull it deeper into the ground instead of pulling it up. This was for logs so large a team could not pull without a tackle and block."

Another one he mentions is a "whip and luff." This thing consisted of "three blocks . . . one on a stump, the other on the log, and the third block was what they called the running block between stump and log." —*10/10/74*

U.S. Champion Trees

People down in Mississippi and Louisiana aren't going to like it very much if an East Tennessee pecan tree turns out to be the biggest one in the country. But it's beginning to look as though this may happen, whether they like it or not.

This pecan grows in the rich, moist farmland of Pigeon River, on land owned by Knoxvillians Mr. and Mrs. W. K. Remine, 940 Irwin St.

Tennessee state forester Bill Korn, who is trying mightily to find the biggest tree of every species growing in the country, says it is not yet official that the Cocke County pecan tree is the nation's largest. What is certain, he says, is that it is bigger than the current champion registered by the American Forestry Association.

The official champ, Bill says, has a trunk girth of nineteen feet, seven inches, is one hundred twenty-four feet tall and has a crown spread of one hundred three feet. It grows in Louisiana.

But this big pecan beside the Pigeon, which Bill hopes will be the new champ, has a trunk girth of nineteen feet, three inches. It is one hundred forty-three feet tall and has a crown spread of one hundred fifteen feet.

Since the Louisiana tree has greater trunk girth and the Pigeon River tree greater height and crown spread, how do you decide which is the larger?

According to Bill Korn, you count one point for each inch of trunk girth, one for each foot of tree height and one for each four feet of crown spread.

This system gives the Pigeon River tree 403 points, compared with 385 for the Louisiana tree.

I was looking at a list of champions the American Forestry Association published in 1973, and I found that the pecan champ then was a Tennessee tree, one over in Natchez Trace State Park. A little irony connected with that tree was that Arthur Stupka nominated it.

Now, Art Stupka, as lots of you know, lives in Sevier County, outside Gatlinburg, and is the former chief naturalist of Great Smoky Mountains National Park. The irony is that Art nominated this tree in Southwest Tennessee, while a larger pecan tree was in a county next door to Sevier. Of course, the reason is that he saw the tree in the state park, but nobody ever told him about the one in Cocke County.

Another irony in this story is that the apparent new champion, growing up here outside the natural range of pecan trees, is bigger— as far as we know now—than any pecan in the tree's natural range. The tree's natural range includes West Tennessee, Western Kentucky, Louisiana, Mississippi, and portions of Missouri, Texas, Illinois, Arkansas and Iowa.

Mrs. Remine gives this history of the Cocke County pecan:

James Allen built a house in the Newport vicinity between 1830 and 1840. Sometime later—but not much later—his daughter Lillie married a Mississippi man named Crawley.

It is believed, Mrs. Remine says, that Crawley brought this seedling pecan from his home soil of Mississippi and planted it beside the Pigeon on family land of his bride. It grew and grew in that rich Pigeon River bottom until it very likely is the largest pecan tree on earth.

So much for pecan trees. How about American elms? Now that the Trigonia elm is dying, what elm will take its place as the largest in the state?

Korn says it looks like a tie between a Knox County tree on the French Broad River and a Blount County tree on Little River.

The Knox elm stands on property of Dr. Fred Hufstedler in Kimberlin Heights. It has a trunk circumference of twenty-three feet. It is ninety-one feet tall and has an eighty-foot crown spread.

The other one is in Wildwood, on property of L. H. Shields. Its trunk girth is twenty-two feet and four inches. It is ninety-four feet tall and has a crown spread of 100 feet.

If you run these statistics through the point system, you'll come up with 387 points for each elm.

Korn says Tennessee apparently will have a new national champion Carolina silverbell. Ken Johnson nominated it. Ken, in case you've forgotten, was one of Dr. Mike Pelton's UT students studying bears in Great Smoky Mountains National Park.

Ken's first interest in the big silverbell, in the valley of the West Prong of Little River, was that it would be a good den tree for a bear. It was big enough, and it had an opening for a bear to get into it. But no bear lived there.

The trunk is thirteen feet, six inches in circumference. The tree is eighty-six feet tall and has a crown spread of twenty-nine feet. This gives it 255 points.

The current champion silverbell, growing near Wyndmoor, Pennsylvania, has a trunk girth of eleven feet, one inch. It is fifty feet high and has a crown spread of fifty-two feet. So it has only 196 points.

Bill Korn is trying to find all of Tennessee's champion trees. But he hasn't had any suggestions for several species. Here is the list of species for which there have been no nominations:

Alder, hophornbeam, American hornbeam (ironwood), river birch, yellow birch, box elder, Northern white cedar, Chinese chestnut, crabapple, rock elm, September elm, Fraser fir, shagbark hickory, huckleberry, Kentucky coffee tree, sweetbay, striped maple, blackjack oak, peach, pear, plum, redbud, rhododendron, smoketree, red spruce, poison sumac, smooth sumac, staghorn sumac, winged sumac, witchhazel, yellowwood, bur oak, swamp white oak, basset oak, shingle oak, common privet, blackhaw, balm-of-Gilead, bald cyprus, Hercules-club (devil's walking stick), horse chestnut and mountain ash.

Can American Chestnuts Return?

Somebody again is trying to undo the catastrophe that befell the Appalachians when the blight killed the chestnut trees.

Well, not all of them, really, but nearly all of them. A very few still live. And it is partly on these that the National Parks and Conservation Association (NPCA) pins its hopes of developing a strain of sweet American chestnuts that can resist the blight.

There is also some hope that chestnut sprouts may be helpful to researchers. There are lots of sprouts. The blight didn't kill the root systems of many trees. Sprouts continue to rise from these.

Let's read a bit in the NPCA magazine for September:

"At first the sprouts were stricken in their first year. But after the first wave of the epidemic had passed through an area, the sprouts began to live longer and grow bigger before succumbing. This process is continuing today, and some sprouts reach heights of twenty-five feet or more with diameters of ten or twelve inches before the fungus hits them. Some even bear a crop of nuts, though not in great quantities.

"The more optimistic observers point to this as evidence that our chestnut is developing some resistance to the disease and may eventually attain it to a high degree . . .

"Most foresters and botanists, however, don't go along with this line of reasoning. They believe that the reason the sprouts live longer now is because there are fewer spores of the blight flying around in the air than there were when the epidemic was raging."

NPCA is asking citizens to send chestnuts in the husk from old trees or sprouts. NPCA officials believe that any tree or sprout producing nuts today has some degree of immunity. Seeds sent to NPCA will be planted in a nursery in Maryland. The seedlings will be replanted in a larger area.

"With time and luck we hope to produce disease-resistant trees by crossbreeding the most disease-resistant selections," NPCA says.

I suppose it's too late for anyone around here to help them this fall, though somebody just might have some chestnuts left. But I've been checking on a few trees known to remain in this region.

When Herrick Brown and I came down from Mt. LeConte Creek a few weeks ago, we checked the two large chestnuts that still live in the valley of that small stream. They are barely alive. The blight has killed most of the bark around the trunks. But some bark remains and a few branches remain alive on the same sides of the trees as the bark. Herrick said this was the first fall he gathered no chestnuts under the trees. But he saw chestnut burrs high in the trees. So they did produce.

Glenn Cardwell, park technician in the Great Smokies, says a smaller chestnut bears nuts in the eastern end of the park, near Cosby.

A recent issue of The Cherokee One Feather, the Indian newspaper at Cherokee, N.C., carried a story about a chestnut tree approximately 100 years old which still bears chestnuts. It's on Thomas Ridge, inside the park. *—12/12/74*

One of the things I found on my desk when I had to go back to working for a living was a box from Mrs. Reba Swicegood, Rt. 1, Rockwood.

In it were three or four chestnut burrs and one American chestnut. No, the chestnut wasn't for me to eat. Mrs. Swicegood wanted me to forward the burrs and chestnut to the National Parks and Conservation magazine.

I had mentioned that the magazine was trying to find American chestnut trees and tree sprouts that bear chestnuts. Few are left. But officials of the magazine apparently think these that have survived so long may have developed a degree of immunity to the chestnut blight. And using them, perhaps they can develop a blight-resistant American chestnut that will again provide bounty to bears, squirrels, hogs, turkeys, deer, mice and men.

This reminded me to ask Herrick Brown whether those two chestnut trees in the LeConte Creek watershed of the Great Smokies are still living.

They are, Herrick said. One bore chestnuts again. Herrick found empty burrs under the tree but no chestnuts. Some critter beat him to the nuts. Herrick thinks, from the size of their seats inside the burrs, some of the chestnuts were large ones.

He found neither nuts nor burrs under the other tree, but he said it looks healthier than the one that produced.

These two are large, mature trees; not sprouts. The blight has been working on both of them, but it has not succeeded in killing them.

Herrick also said he'd seen burrs on a chestnut sprout growing near U.S. 441, in the vicinity of Trout Branch, also in the Great Smokies.

I believe Mrs. Swicegood's burrs and chestnut came from a sprout.

All this also reminded me that Ken Seigworth, one of my Norris neighbors, passed along to me the Sept. 12 issue of Science magazine which contains an article about a new approach to the chestnut blight problem. The authors, N.K. Van Alfen, R.A. Jaynes, S.L. Anagnostakis and P.R. Day, say in effect that there hasn't been much success so far in producing a blight-resistant strain of chestnut. So they move in the other direction—to fence out the blight itself.

This thing is pretty technical and I don't pretend to understand every word of it. However, I think I understand the main idea of it and I'll try to boil it down to understandable English.

The chestnut blight is caused by a fungus, *Endothia barasitica.*

Somebody found in Italy some years ago a weak strain of this fungus. It does not kill the trees.

The same weak strain later was found in France. And it also was discovered there the weak strain somehow prevents the strong strain from severely damaging the trees. Maybe it's a little like finding a friendly dog to protect you from a vicious one.

However, when the weaker form of the virus was brought here it seemed not to protect against the strong American form. But scientists have continued to work with this idea and they think that a weak form of the fungus may be developed as a control for the disease in this country. *—11/3/75*

OOOOO

"It now appears certain that the American chestnut tree can be restored to the American people."

That is the opening paragraph of a Page One story in the July issue of News and Views, a publication of the American Horticultural Society. Dr. Robert W. Harris sent me his copy.

To more than half the Americans alive today, the return of the American chestnut may not seem to be a matter of great importance. For they never tasted an American chestnut. A chestnut, to them, is a nut grown on some exotic chestnut tree planted here since a fungus disease from the Orient killed virtually all our native chestnuts between about 1900 and 1940. Most of the killing here in East Tennessee was between 1925 and 1940.

I remember gathering chestnuts in Hancock County when I was five or ten years old. And I particularly remember a chestnut tree on Grandpa Brewer's farm. Its branches were as large as ordinary trees. And because it stood alone in a pasture, uncrowded by other trees, the branches spread far out. And about the time of first frost, we gathered chestnuts in a wide, wide circle under this old tree.

They weren't as large as most of the exotic chestnuts we have now, but they were far sweeter.

Then the fungus, commonly called the chestnut blight, began killing the chestnut trees. It probably was the worst, the most far-reaching natural disaster ever to hit the Appalachian region.

Now, according to News and Views, a new strain of the fungus has come upon the scene. Dr. Richard A. Jaynes, associate geneticist at the Connecticut Agricultural Experiment Station, learned some European chestnuts infected and dying because of the disease were making a come-back in France.

Research indicated a new and weaker strain of the fungus was inhibiting the Asiatic strain. So the infected trees were getting well.

Dr. Jaynes brought the new strain to this country. He found it worked on our chestnuts, too. But there was a major worry. The chestnut blight fungus lives on oak trees, too, but doesn't hurt them. But would this new strain also be harmless to oaks?

Before the question about the oaks was resolved, nature took a hand. A woman cross-country skiing near her Michigan home noticed that blighted American chestnut sprouts appeared to be healing. She sent bark samples to the Connecticut Agricultural Experiment Station.

Laboratory studies there showed a Michigan strain of the fungus, similar to the European strain, was causing the healing.

This all sounds too good to be true, and I don't guarantee it is. But the American Horticultural Society, I presume, is a reputable organization which would not be spreading this story if it were false.

We've got lots of chestnut sprouts in East Tennessee, just waiting to grow into big chestnut trees. Trouble is, they nearly always die before they get big enough to bear chestnuts. Now, maybe if we can get some of this new and finer fungus down here, they'll stop dying.

—*8/1/77*

00000

In a Cumberland Plateau ravine, a few miles east of Sparta, in White County, grows an American chestnut tree.

It is about thirty years old, nearly eighty feet tall and at least seventeen inches in diameter at breast height. For the past few years, it has been producing a crop of sweet American chestnuts each year.

"It has been growing like a house afire the last five or six years," says Dr. Eyvind Thor, professor of forestry at UT.

Thor says this is one of perhaps as many as two dozen American chestnut trees in the Eastern U.S. which once were sick and now are healed. They suffered from the blight brought to this country from the Orient early in this century. It killed nearly all the American chestnuts.

But it did not kill their root systems. The roots keep sending up sprouts. The sprouts grow for a few years and then are attacked by the blight. Only rarely do sprouts live long enough and grow large enough to produce a few chestnuts.

Thor says the Cumberland Plateau chestnut one was afflicted with the blight like all the other chestnut sprouts.

"It was infected very heavily with the fungus," he said. "It had fifteen or twenty big cankers on it."

But those blight-caused cankers are covered with healthy new bark. It is healed, as if by a miracle. As far as is known, it is the only large Tennessee American chestnut completely free of the blight.

Thor said it also is the only known tree this far South that once suffered from the blight but now is free of it. The others are farther north. Most of them are in West Virginia and Pennsylvania.

Nature did it. What nature did this time was use a virus to attack the chestnut blight fungus. In this particular tree, what had been a healthy fungus, sapping the life of this chestnut sprout, became a sick, weak fungus. One that the tree was able to withstand.

This "cure" that has come to a handful of American chestnuts came earlier to many more Italian chestnut trees.

But first, some blight history:

The blight was brought to this country from China very early in this century. It did not bother Chinese chestnut trees, probably because they had developed a resistance to it over thousands of years. But this country's trees had no natural resistance. So one of the most valuable tree species in Eastern North America became little more than a memory in a period of about forty years.

The blight took another trip in about 1917. It went from the United States to Italy in a cargo of chestnut mine timbers.

For some reason, the virus—or a similar one—that only now is attacking the fungus in American chestnuts much earlier began attacking the fungus in the Italian chestnuts.

Europeans didn't know at first what was causing the "cure" in the Italian trees. But a French scientist, Jean Grente, who had been working on the blight because the French feared it would spread from Italy into France, figured it out.

Grente also found ways to help nature with her work. He managed to infect the healthy fungus, that was killing the trees, with the sick fungus. France's chestnut trees are doing well.

Grente has been working with American scientists on the problem here, according to Thor. But progress here has not been nearly as swift as it was in Italy and France. The virus attacking the fungus in France rarely can be transmitted to the healthy fungus here.

But it may be only a matter of time before nature herself speeds up the work here. And it also may not be long until scientists working here score a breakthrough similar to Grente's in France.

Thor says the reason Grente's system is not working as well here is that America has so many more strains of the fungus.

But he said five PhDs, with a large staff, are working on the problem at an experiment station in Connecticut. He sent samples from the Cumberland Plateau tree to the Connecticut group, and they verified that this tree was saved because the fungus working on it became sick and weak after a virus attacked it.

Thor's own major work on the chestnut is of a different nature. He is trying to develop strains of American chestnut that have natural resistance to the blight. By starting with trees that appear to have more than normal resistance, he is attempting to develop successive generations that are more and more resistant.

He thinks the two different approaches may work well together—a tree with a high degree of resistance bothered only by a sickly blight ought to survive and produce a lot of chestnuts.

If all this comes to pass, it will be a modern miracle produced by man and nature working together. And a lot of humans and even more animals will be thankful. If the American chestnut makes a comeback in the same century it nearly suffered a knockout, it would be the biggest blessing that's come to Eastern forests.

The American chestnut grows larger than its cousins anywhere else. Its nuts are sweeter. Deer, turkeys, bears, wolves, mice and countless other animals feed upon them. Acorns, used since the downfall of chestnuts, have been poor substitutes.   *—7/29/79*

9

Native and Exotic

Anybody except a gold-plated optimist looking at this Bicentennial year and into the second 200 might be tempted to try to turn around and go back. For the main thing one sees up ahead is more and more of us trying to get by on less and less.

When the Founding Fathers got this thing going 200 years ago, we were a nation of about 2.5 million people. A fellow wanting a new house had only to sharpen his ax and go out a few yards into the woods and cut some trees and call in some friends and neighbors to build it.

Today we are a nation of 215 million, and there are far fewer trees to cut. The price of houses has gone up a bit. Typically, you'll have to work the equivalent of six years of your life just to pay for a house. That is one measure of how much things have changed in 200 years.

We hadn't got hooked on oil 200 years ago. As far as I know, we depended on candles, pine torches and the open fireplace for household illumination back then. But somebody discovered how to dig an oil well in 1859, and we have since become so dependent on the stuff that lots of us can't get to the job, the grocery, the church, the liquor store, or go fishing without it. We also wear clothes made out of it, drink coffee out of oil-based cups, use it in making fertilizer. As far back as 1947, we in this country started using more oil than the country produced.

Nobody knows for sure how much oil there is left in the world. But one of the nation's most respected petroleum geologists, M. King Hubbert, predicts we will have used most of it by 2050. Lots of young folks around today will still be around then to see whether he was right. And to suffer the consequences if he was.

I know. There is all this talk about extracting oil from coal, but we've so far got lots more words than oil out of it. This probably will be done some day. But at considerable cost. Dollar cost. Environmental cost. And when you load onto coal all the jobs now done by oil, plus what's already done with coal, we could run out of coal before we struggle through the next 200 years.

Running completely out of this that and the other is only part of the story. What's going to make it rough on people and pocketbooks is that, generally speaking, each ton of coal, barrel of oil, ounce of gold, costs more to obtain than the one before it. That's because we got the easiest first. Sinking an oil well 100 miles out in the Gulf of Mexico costs a lot more than drilling one in the middle of Texas.

And when oil costs more, so will food. For the American agriculture that feeds us and lots of others around the world depends on oil—to operate the combines and all the other oil-drinking machinery of a modern American farm.

However, there are a few intelligent worriers who see what some of the problems are and have some ideas that may be helpful. One of these is A.J. (Jack) Sharp, UT professor emeritus. So, for this occasion, I've been hoarding some remarks Jack made on this general subject within recent months. Let's start with this one:

"It may be startling to some of you, as earlier it certainly was to me, to realize that every time one has more than the average amount of food, clothing, or other necessities, one or more persons somewhere must have less than the average."

Ponder that before you buy the car that drinks lots of gasoline. Or before you build a house larger than you need. Or before you grow obese on more food than you need.

Jack thinks the "problem of too many people is the most fundamental and serious" one we face. But he said the "unwise use of resources" and use of them in "unwarranted amounts . . . can multiply the effects of over-population. It may be surprising," he said, that "each of us has at least twenty times the impact on the environment as the average Asiatic Indian. It is the consumption of resources to which the deleterious effects on the environment are related: The strip-mined soils, the destruction of ozone by freon, the polluted air and water, the production of waste and garbage. The Indian does not have the materials available to consume."

Jack also said that a common reaction to the problems faced today is to "cop-out, through the use of alcohol, or drugs, or blaming others." He said the "cop-out" not only increases the problems for the individual but also for society. "I will not suggest that all dreams are destructive," he said, "for the best features of all cultures arise out of dreams."

Observing that many defend the "cop-out" with violent criticism of the work ethic, Jack said he agrees that "work done strictly for personal profit, or self-aggrandizement, or ease, at the expense of others, does nothing for our humaneness. However, problems were never solved without effort."

Comparing man to lemmings, Jack said man is "heading for the far bank of the river. Suicide is not his intention." But Jack wonders whether we have the intelligence to turn back.

"Up to now (man) has lived in a self-optimizing environment. Natural processes have kept him supplied with oxygen and water, with fertile soil, space to move, and even esthetic pleasures, without the necessity of intervention or forethought on his part. He has reached the point where those autonomous natural processes can no longer cope with his demands. So it is not a question of whether he wants to assume control; he is obliged to."

Man will have to decide many things in the future that nature decided for him in the past—how clean his air and water, how fertile his soil, even how high his disease and death rates, Jack thinks.

I don't think he's saying we'll have to sacrifice so much that we'll suffer. Rather, he's saying we may suffer if we don't sacrifice.

There's hope, he says. But the outcome will depend on "self-discipline and not on the other fellow. Some say our youth understands the problem of survival," Jack said, "but I hear them discuss waste disposal and recycling in one breath and insist on increasing consumption of many products with the next. I hear adults almost with tears in their eyes discuss malnutrition and starvation and in the next moment guzzle a beer or smoke tobacco. Who is willing to give up 'spray-on' gadgets in order that our grandchildren will not fry?

"You and I may survive (our normal life span) if we do little or nothing, because of our ages, but our descendants will not," Jack said. "For their survival, we must adjust to the universe, not try to adjust it to us; this it will not do.

"And this, in reality, is a religious matter," Jack said.   —*1/4/76*

Native Americans Beleaguered

At about this time in the summer of 1776, Chief Cornstalk of the Shawnees led a delegation of more than a dozen chiefs of the Northern tribes down across the Little Tennessee River to talk with leaders of the Cherokee at Chota.

Their purpose: To form a solid Indian alliance against the white settlers who were pressing westward into lands the Indians considered their own.

Seventy days they'd been on the trails, they said. Once they had detoured many miles to avoid discovery by whites. They said they'd seen large numbers of white people in new fortifications, at salt springs and near the buffalo grounds.

A Mohawk spokesman said white people had come into Mohawk villages and killed some of his people.

"What is the case of my people one day may be the case of any nation another day," he said. "My people the Mohawks are fighting the Long Knives (whites). They have sent me to secure the friendship of all nations of Indians, for the interests of all red men are one. The red men must forget their quarrels among themselves and turn their eyes and thoughts one way. I now offer you this belt, and if my brothers the Cherokees agree with what I have said, let them take it."

They probably were meeting in the town-house at Chota, a major city of the Overhill Cherokees and capital of the entire Cherokee nation. Leaders of Cherokee towns from the mountains of North Carolina, South Carolina and Georgia probably were there.

Lt. Henry Timberlake, who was there fifteen years earlier, described the town-house as being "raised with wood and covered with earth," and as having the appearance of a "small mountain at a little distance. It is built in the form of a sugar loaf, and large enough to contain 500 persons . . . Within, it has the appearance of an ancient amphitheater, the seats being raised one above the other, having an area in the middle, in the center of which stands the fire; the seats of the head warriors are nearest it."

When the writers of the Declaration of Independence were picking out their words, the most populous area of what is now Tennessee was the broad bottomland of the Little Tennessee where lived several thousand Cherokees in nearly a dozen towns.

Nobody knows for sure how long the Cherokees had lived there. But more of them probably lived there then than during any year since. For this was the beginning of a long period of adversity for the Cherokees. Now, 200 years later, another change is coming to the bottomlands where so much history happened. Barring a stop order by the U.S. Sixth Circuit Court of Appeals in the snail darter lawsuit, the waters of TVA's Tellico Lake will start rising over many of the old Cherokee town sites early next year.

[The snail darter lawsuit delayed the dam's closure until November, 1979.]

With much ceremony—for the Indians loved ceremony—the other Northern chiefs offered their symbolic belts to the Cherokee chiefs. A Cherokee who accepted a belt thereby joined the cause of the one offering it.

Cornstalk was the last to speak. "In a few years," he said, "the Shawnees, from being a great nation, have been reduced to a handful. They once possessed land almost to the seashore, but now have hardly enough ground to stand upon.

"The lands where the Shawnees have but lately hunted are covered with forts and armed men. When a fort appears, you may depend upon it, there will soon be towns and settlements of white men. It is plain that the white people intend to extirpate the Indians. It is better for the red men to die like warriors than to diminish away by inches. The cause of the red men is just, and I hope that the Great Spirit who governs everything will favor us..."

After more such talk, Cornstalk produced a purple war belt nine feet long and six inches wide. Over it he poured vermilion, symbolizing blood. One of the first to accept it was Dragging Canoe, a young Cherokee chief who was unhappy with the older chiefs who he thought had not resisted strongly enough the efforts of land-seeking whites.

Some other young Cherokees joined the Northern visitors in wild enthusiasm. But two old men did not join. One of these was Oconostota, the nation's war chief for more than twenty years. It was he who had led the Cherokees sixteen years earlier in defeating 1500 troops under English Col. Archibald Montgomery in North Carolina. Montgomery was en route to break the Cherokee siege of Fort Loudoun. It was one of the rare occasions when Indians defeated white troops in battle. And the fall of Fort Loudoun shortly later marked the first and only time a garrisoned English fort fell to Indian attackers.

The other old chief who did not accept the belts of the Northern Indians was Attakullakulla, chief diplomat of the Cherokees for more than forty years. He had dined with King George II in 1730, had made countless trips to Charleston to bargain with colonial governors, had been captured by the French and held for a time in Canada as an honored guest, and had helped fashion countless treaties between Indians and whites.

Perhaps Attakullakulla and Oconostota were remembering earlier conflicts with whites. Generally, the Cherokees had not fared well. Even those victories over Montgomery and at Fort Loudoun had been avenged in double measure. Lack of a sustained supply of ammunition was one of the reasons the Cherokees, though winning a few skirmishes and a battle or two, never won a war against the white soldiers.

Another reason was lack of sustained, united purpose among the Cherokees. A war chief could take with him only those warriors he could persuade. The Cherokee tolerated extreme differences of opinion and action among themselves. Attakullakulla visited his white friends at Fort Loudoun while it was under siege by his people. Cherokee women defied the chiefs and took food to their white soldier husbands and sweethearts inside the fort.

Shortly after Cornstalk's delegation departed, Dragging Canoe and other young chiefs planned attacks on settlers in Georgia, North Carolina, Virginia and what is now East Tennessee. The Overhills were to make surprise attacks in Virginia and East Tennessee.

But the settlers weren't surprised. Among those who had warned them was Nancy Ward. It was another instance of conflicting actions. Nancy Ward was the Cherokees' Ghi-ga-u, or Beloved Woman, a rank bestowed upon her more than twenty years earlier after she took up the rifle of her slain husband Kingfisher and continued firing in a battle with the Creeks. She later married white trader Brian Ward.

The whites met and defeated Dragging Canoe's forces at Island Flats July 20, 1776. Most of the Indian attacks in other sections met with little success. But the Indians did bring a few prisoners and eighteen white scalps back to the towns of the Little Tennessee.

They burned eighteen-year-old James Moore at the stake at Tuskegee. Another prisoner was Mrs. William Bean whose husband later set up shop at Bean Station. She was tied to a stake atop Toqua Mound and a fire was lighted at her feet. One of the rights of a Beloved Woman was to free prisoners. Nancy Ward raced to the mound and freed Mrs. Bean.

Because she warned the settlers and saved Mrs. Bean, Nancy Ward has always been a heroine to Tennessee whites. At the same time, she apparently never was considered a traitor to her own people. She held high office in the Cherokee nation more than 150 years before white women in this country could vote. She spoke for her nation at at least two treaty conferences.

Georgians, Virginians, North Carolinians and East Tennessee settlers quickly retaliated for the Indian attacks. In fact, some historians say the colonists had been planning attacks against the Indians before the Indians attacked them. A white army burned five Indian towns along the lower Little Tennessee. The next year, Dragging Canoe and his followers left the Little Tennessee and settled near Chattanooga. Nearly half the towns along the Little Tennessee were abandoned.

Most of the Cherokees were gone from the Little Tennessee bottoms before Nancy Ward died in 1824. Nancy, regarded by many as one of the great women of the region's history, spent her last years peacefully as an innkeeper at Womankiller Ford on the Ocoee River.

—7/4/76

What Makes a "Native"?

Can a foreign species, such as the European wild boar, hang around long enough to acquire kind of a squatters-rights nativity?

Dr. Bob Hines, the Cleveland, Tennessee dentist and hunter of the wild boar, brought up this and some other interesting questions.

"Does one have to have one's origin here to be native?" he asked. "If so, then we—the whites—in these United States are 'furriners.' When does a species become a native—fifty years—sixty years? Does the park intend to rid itself of rainbow trout? Brown trout and other exotic species? Then why the wild boar?"

(Before we go further I'd better tell newcomers to this argument that Dr. Hines and I do not agree on it. He wants the hogs to be permitted to stay in Great Smoky Mountains National Park. Though I think Dr. Hines is a fine gentleman, whose views on nearly anything deserve respectful consideration, I want the hogs out of the park.)

Dr. Hines, I have to agree with you—white folks here aren't native. Not as a species, that is. And strictly speaking, neither are the Indians. The first Indians here weren't born here. The people who specialize in such matters tell us that our first Indians came from Asia several thousand years ago. So, as a species, they're old settlers, not natives.

But while that may be correct, it's not practical. As far as the practicality of the hog matter is concerned, those wild boars might be considered naturalized citizens after they have done all the damage they can do to the other plant and animal species in the park. By then they would be living in some sort of on-going equilibrium with the other things up there.

How long would that take?

I guessed 500 to 1000 years. But I thought I'd better ask Dr. Jack Sharp. Jack, the UT emeritus Alumni Distinguished Service professor, has such expertise in these matters that what he says is more of an estimate than a guess. He said 200 to 300 years.

So far, the wild hogs have been in the park less than thirty-five years. More important, they have not been there in large numbers more than ten or fifteen years. They very likely haven't reached their population peak. Nor their peak of destructiveness.

Some of the hogs defenders say they don't hurt the park.

Nuts!

They obviously hurt the park. Anybody who says differently isn't thinking of what the park is supposed to be. Maybe they still measure it in terms of how many board feet it would produce if it were logged.

But it's not going to be logged. It is there for people to enjoy. It is there for them to experience the beauty of its wildflowers, forest, streams, birds, bears. It also is there as a big chunk of natural land for scientists to study. And it is there for the protection and preservation of native wild animals and plants.

If wildflower fans go to a spot where they saw spring beauties blooming last year and find that the hogs have rooted up the place this year, then the hogs have defeated one of the purposes of the park.

If a park visitor hikes to some small stream, expecting to enjoy the sight of clear mountain water, and finds it murky with silt from hog-wallowing, the hogs have scored again against a park purpose.

I haven't seen the murky water yet this spring, but I saw the wildflowers rooted up a few Sundays ago in Whiteoak Sink. There are hundreds of areas where the hogs repeat the performance. In normal springs, the beech gaps along the mountaincrest, where trillium, spring beauties and trout lilies grow, are some of their favorite rooting sites. Researchers suspect but cannot prove that the hogs may exterminate other plant species from the park.

One of these might be a big lovely lily, the Turk's cap. It grows mostly along the mountaintop. Dr. Susan Bratton, of the Uplands Field Research Laboratory in the park, said in 1974 that the hogs the year before had eliminated most of these lilies between Clingmans Dome and Silers Bald.

In some areas where the hogs like to root, Susan found they rooted up ninety-five per cent of the area. They apparently like to eat some of what they root up—the corms of spring beauties, for instance. They inadvertently kill other plants simply by rooting them out of the ground.   —*4/17/77*

00000

From the way some North Carolinians have been talking, one might think the European wild boar is an endangered species clinging to the biosphere by a fragile thread.

Actually, it's about as endangered as crabgrass, cockroaches and carp. It's been about sixty-five years since George Gordon Moore imported a dozen of the things from Europe and plopped them down inside a stout, high fence in the vicinity of Hooper Bald, Graham County, N.C.

Almost immediately, some of them ripped through the fence and started expanding their range, and they've been expanding ever since.

Moore also imported other species, including bison, elk and some bears that weren't like the black bears in this region. Not one of the other species lasted very long in the North Carolina mountains. Only that wild hog.

Back in the 1940s or 1950s—nobody knows exactly when—the

hogs crossed the Little Tennessee River and got into Great Smoky Mountains National Park. In the thirty-odd years since they first poked their snouts inside the Great Smokies, their number has grown to an estimated 2000.

In contrast, the population of the native black bear, which has lived in these same mountains for millions of years, now is estimated at 500 to 600.

When officials of the National Park Service (NPS) got serious about killing the hogs in the Great Smokies, some North Carolina hog hunters started screaming. And NPS, temporarily at least, stopped killing hogs.

At a meeting several days ago in Robbinsville one woman boar hunter said she wanted those hogs left alone in the Great Smokies "so we won't have to tell our grandchildren what one looks like."

A man said that if the hogs "are wiped out, it's going to get into our pocketbooks around here."

Maybe these hog hunters can be excused for overstating their case. But back in late September, the attorney general of North Carolina, Rufus Edmisten, said in part:

"The wild boar is a very valuable resource not only to North Carolina but to the entire United States. I sincerely hope that we will be able to reach a solution that will preserve the future of the wild boar in North Carolina's mountains."

The message that comes across in all these quotes is that if NPS is able to eliminate the hogs from the national park, that's the end of the hogs in North Carolina.

Hogwash!

The only thing that will even dent the hog population in the North Carolina mountains, outside the Great Smokies, is those overeager hunters who are hollering.

According to Ben Sanders, wildlife biologist for national forests in North Carolina, there are an estimated 850 European wild boar in the Cheoah, Tusquitee and Wayah Districts of Nantahala National Forest, in North Carolina.

And how many black bear are there in these same three districts? An estimated 165.

Because of hunting pressure, the populations of both bear and boar are thinner in the national forest than in the park.

What the Carolina boar hunters want is a reservoir of hogs inside the park. A boar doesn't know park boundary lines. They often leave the park and go outside, where hunters can kill them legally. So the hunters want them left in the park. And they want it at the expense of the damages hogs do to wildflowers and other animals in the park.

Does the Forest Service want the hog range expanded?

No, not according to Mr. Sanders.

"We're basically not interested in having them spread all over the area," he said. They compete with native animals for food—with wild turkeys, bear, squirrels, grouse, quail. Another reason is that they root up trails and recreation areas.

The hogs pay no attention to the North Carolina-Tennessee boundary. Dick Conley, a wildlife biologist for the Tennessee Wildlife Resources Agency, says the hogs inhabit a good portion of the nearly 300,000 acres of the Ocoee, Hiwassee and Tellico Districts of Cherokee National Forest in Tennessee. The hogs also were stocked several years ago in the 80,000-acre Catoosa Wildlife Management Area in Morgan and Cumberland Counties.

In 1971, West Virginia wildlife biologists got thirty hogs from Tennessee for release in Boone County. They put them in pens to allow them to adjust to their new surroundings before release. Just as their ancestors did on Hooper Bald, these fellows broke out of their pens and started traveling. They now live in a territory of about forty-five square miles.

Another false issue raised by the hunters is that hog carcasses sometimes are left to rot in the Great Smokies backcountry. According to the hunters, the meat should be carried out for the needy.

There is about as much reason to bring out every oak and poplar that falls in the park and take it to a sawmill to make lumber to build homes for the needy. If a hog is killed within a mile of an automobile road, it's all right to see that the meat is taken out and used.

But let's consider a 150-pound hog killed fifteen miles from the nearest motor road. Getting him to that road will take most of a day for two men. I'd guess the pay for two men for a day would approach $100. The NPS surely can find better use for $100.

In my opinion, the welfare of the park will be best served if NPS quickly puts this North Carolina hunter hubbub behind it and rids the park of those hogs the quickest way possible.   *—10/23/77*

Panthers in the Smokies?

Gatlinburg (Special)—An official of the National Park Service has confirmed a panther sighting in Great Smoky Mountains National Park.

Gilbert Calhoun, assistant park superintendent, said four park employes—Walter Laws, Emmett Wiggins, Horace Cunningham, and Lee Cochran—saw the animal in the Cataloochee area about 9 p.m. July 23.

A few private individuals have told The News-Sentinel about seeing panthers in the Great Smokies and neighboring mountains over the past few years. But this is the first time that employes of the Park Service have made such a report.

Calhoun said park officials had heard rumors of panthers in the park and had encouraged members of the staff to report any such sightings. He said the sighting in Cataloochee is "the first report to date."

The four described the animal as "large, dark gray, (with) extremely long tail, (making) long leaps and bounds, appeared to have been chasing a young deer."

They said they found "large and small cat tracks" in mud, indicating the presence of a kitten with the adult panther.

The Park Service also reported that a camper reported seeing a panther on a paved road in the Cataloochee area about three weeks earlier. There was a further report of someone hearing a panther scream in the same area in June.

The Cataloochee area is in the remote southeastern section of the park, in North Carolina.   —8/6/75

00000

Nothing, and I mean nothing, has done so much to perk up my summer as the news the other day of a genuine U.S. Government panther in Cataloochee Valley of Great Smoky Mountains National Park.

For fifteen years I've been writing about panthers. And for fifteen years people have been snickering at me.

"Brewer," somebody would say, "I see you're pushing that wampus cat story again. Haw, haw, haw!"

The unbelievers seemed to be about evenly divided among:

1. Those who thought somebody has sold old gullible Brewer another bill of goods.

2. Those who thought there's that sly old Brewer trying to peddle that old panther tale to some more gullible readers.

I wrote about panthers in the Norris Lake area, panthers in the Great Smokies, panthers on the Blue Ridge Parkway. And I seem to recall one story about a panther somewhere in Cherokee National Forest.

Some people saw panther tracks. Others heard panthers scream. Some owned dogs which were worked over by panthers. A few people saw panthers.

The trouble was that no hunter ever walked out the woods with a dead panther slung over his shoulder. (And I never wanted this to happen, anyway.)

Nobody brought me a picture of a panther to go with the story.

And no game management official or park official ever confirmed one of the panther reports. On the contrary, they just smiled, a little indulgently, somewhat superiorly.

But all that changed last week when Gil Calhoun, assistant superintendent of the Great Smokies, passed along the report of a panther sighting by four park employes in Cataloochee.

There were some good reliable sightings earlier. They just didn't have the U.S. Government stamp of approval. And no cat previously was reported by a committee of four. I think the best previous ones were:

1. Dr. William T. Smith, retired UT chemistry professor, and Mrs. Smith saw a panther bound across the Blue Ridge Parkway fifty to seventy-five feet in front of their car, in broad daylight, in 1972. This was in the vicinity of Crabtree Meadows. They saw the cat in profile, including the long tail. (The tail is important. Otherwise, the animal could be an over-grown bobcat.)

2. Murl Brown of Maryville and his son Charles saw a panther near the Gregory Bald Trail, within a mile of the Moores Spring Shelter, in June 1962, when they were hiking up to see the flame azaleas. They also got a good look. The animal was standing on a large rock about 100 feet from them, long curved tail almost touching the rock.

Claude Hyde of Robbinsville, N.C., sent me a copy of a story from his state's conservation magazine about a hunter seeing a panther chasing a deer in the Carolina coastal section.

Mr. Hyde also wrote me about a man near Robbinsville who thinks a panther killed one of his hogs. I thought I could find that letter again, but it must be hiding somewhere in the mess on my desk.

The part of last week's report that was most encouraging was that there also were tracks in the mud of a U.S. Government panther kitten. So there must be at least three panthers up there.

Now, let us pray that no lout feels the need to prove his manhood by shouldering a rifle and going panther poaching.   *—8/11/75*

00000

Nicole Culbertson thinks there's a good possibility that the panther never has been extinct in Great Smoky Mountains National Park.

Nicole, working with the Uplands Field Research Laboratory in Great Smoky Mountains National Park, used some of this space to ask for reports from people who have seen mountain lions in or near the park.

Lots of people crawled out of the woodwork and told her what they'd been embarassed to tell nearly anybody else: They had seen panthers. But when they mentioned it to others all they got back was laughter or sort of a pitying, condescending look. I know. Though I never told anybody I'd seen a panther (which I have not), I have quoted several who said they saw them. And I caught some of the snickers, too. Seeing panthers was like seeing the Loch Ness Monster, or pink elephants.

One of those who talked with Nicole was Glen Branam. Glen's a Great Smokies employee now, a dispatcher. But what he told her about happened a long time ago, in 1941, when he was sixteen years old.

Glen and a friend about the same age, James Barnes, now dead, were hunting in the Greenbrier section, near the park. They killed a young panther, a kitten that weighed about twenty pounds. Two or three days later, they killed another kitten the same size. The two obviously were of the same litter.

Now, thirty-six or thirty-seven years later, Glen says he's always regretted killing the kittens. (It probably was not illegal to kill them then. But it is now, for the mountain lion is an endangered species now.)

After Glen finished his World War II service, he began working for the park. And several times in 1946 or 47, he saw an adult panther inside the park, about a half-mile up the Greenbrier Road from State Highway 73. He saw it at night, and at about the same time each night, near ten o'clock. Glen told some park officials about it. They didn't believe him, would not go with him to look for themselves.

Nicole received information on 140 different lion or lion track sightings in or near the park. She interviewed 100 of those who said they had seen panthers or their tracks. She judged forty-eight of these to be reliable.

That is, the persons making the reports had good views of the animals or their tracks, had seen them in good light, and the persons appear to be reliable. For instance, Nicole put a slight bit more faith in reports by park employes, for they know the area and its animals and would be less likely to mistake a bobcat or dog for a lion.

Some other reliable reports:

J.R. Buchanon, a park employee, in 1956 or 1957, saw lion tracks around Bunker Hill Tower, in the western end of the park. Then he found the carcass of an animal the lion apparently had killed and covered with leaves and debris. He and Arthur Whitehead stayed and watched the carcass until a panther returned to it.

Jim Garland (now dead), another park employee, in 1955, was in Bunker Hill Tower and saw a lion approaching some deer. The deer saw the lion and ran away.

Nicole received reports of the most lion sightings in 1975, a total of eleven reliable ones inside or near the park. She believes that at least three lions, and possibly as many as six, lived in the park in 1975.

—1/5/78

Panthers Challenged

One of the pillars of my faith is bending, buckling, nearly breaking.

Not faith in a conventional deity; rather, a faith in East Tennessee wildness—Great Smokies primeval forest, fat ole timber rattlers, bears, brook trout and panthers.

It's the panther pillar that's being tested, challenged; shaken like a smart old farm dog shakes a copperhead.

Gray-bearded readers will recall that I started writing about panthers when only the late Jim DuBose and I believed in them. And I wasn't always sure about Jim, the charming, story-telling operator of Andersonville Boat Dock.

Jim periodically heard a panther screaming around what then were the lonely shores of Norris Lake, near the Anderson-Union County line. This would have been in the 1950s and early '60s. Two or three people said they actually saw the Norris Lake panther.

In the years since Jim DuBose broke the ice and first talked of panthers, dozens of people have told panther stories in East Tennessee and Western North Carolina.

Most people snickered at these stories and some snickered at me for writing them. So I was overjoyed in 1975 when the people who run Great Smoky Mountains National Park took official notice of a panther, until then officially believed extinct in this region.

They said four park employees—Walter Laws, Emmett Wiggins, Horace Cunningham and Lee Cochran—saw a panther in the Cataloochee area of the park. A year or two later, Kent Higgins, a respected park ranger who keeps things in order in the Cades Cove area, was "98 per cent" certain an animal he saw bound across the Laurel Creek was a panther.

Another report I put great faith in came from Dr. and Mrs. William T. Smith. He's a retired UT chemistry professor. Driving on the Blue Ridge Parkway in 1972, these two saw a large long-tailed cat bound down an embankment and across the pavement fifty to seventy-five feet in front of them. They had a good look, in broad daylight and at close range. They were 100 per cent sure it was a panther.

In the latter half of the 1970s, Nicole Culbertson, working out of Uplands Field Research Laboratory in the Great Smokies, interviewed one hundred persons who had heard or seen panthers in the vicinity of the Great Smokies.

Nicole found one man, a park employee, who told her he and another youth had killed two panther kittens, weighing about twenty pounds each, in 1941, in the Greenbrier area near the park.

Based on all these sightings by reliable persons, the National Park Service (NPS) started treating the panther (cougar, mountain lion, puma) as an established citizen of the Great Smokies. In various reports, NPS officials discussed maintaining the desired habitat for this big cat.

But now, in spite of all those sightings and the NPS official embrace of the reality of panthers, there is growing doubt that the panther is real anywhere in Eastern America, except Florida. In moving away from a belief in panthers, the NPS people are leaving me hanging, vulnerable again to the snickering multitude.

Stu Coleman and Bill Cook, two NPS gentlemen versed in wildlife management, aren't saying these fellows didn't kill two panther kittens thirty-nine years ago. They say only that they cannot now find conclusive evidence that this largest North American cat lives in the Great Smokies or any other nearby place.

Part of the doubts of Bill and Stu are based on the findings of a U.S. Fish and Wildlife Service man, Bob Downing. Or, rather on the non-findings of Bob. Bob about two years ago was given the job of finding where the panther lives in Eastern America. He has failed to find him, except in Florida, and he's looked pretty hard.

Well, exactly what are Bob and Bill and Stu looking for?

They're looking for something a panther left—a fluff of hair, a pawprint, scat (droppings). They have searched the mountains with snow on the ground and failed to find a panther track. They've put out sandboxes and baited them with scents that ought to smell alluring to panthers. But not one pawprint did a panther leave. No hair. No scat.

What about those "panther" screams that people have heard from the Great Smokies and the Chilhowees to the shores of Norris Lake?

Bill says he and Stu have the recorded screams of panthers and bobcats, and it's pretty difficult to distinguish one from the other.

Well, a bobcat doesn't have a long tail. What about those big long-tailed cats the Smiths, Kent Higgins and others saw?

True, a bobcat has no long tail, Bill says. But a big Redbone hound has a long tail, and a Redbone is near the color of a panther.

Bill and Stu don't say positively that all those folks were mistaken, that they heard bobcats screaming and saw hounds crossing roads. They just say that, if the panthers aren't here, it's possible that the people saw and heard those other animals. Bill and Stu are still looking for panthers, but they have grave doubts.

As a long-time believer in panthers, I don't give up just because of a lack of pawprints and scat.

I thought I'd call somebody at the new National Environmental Research Park at Oak Ridge. Some of the previous panther sightings I've reported were there.

And when that park was dedicated a few days ago, I reminded Dr. Stan Auerbach, director of Environmental Sciences at Oak Ridge National Laboratory, that the park was the second big wish of his that had come true in recent years. (The first was the beautiful new office-laboratory building that houses Stan and his staff and their experiments.)

What else would it take to make him happy?

"A picture of a cougar," he said.

He meant a picture of a cougar somewhere in his 13,000-acre park. He said I should phone Tom Kitchings and Jay Story, wildlife research men who keep track of wild animals in the park. Stan said they had recent panther reports.

He couldn't have known how recent. We talked Oct. 2. The most recent panther report was the next day. Tom Kitchings said two guards saw the animal cross a road fifty yards ahead of them. No, they said when questioned, it was not a dog. It was a big cat. It was the fourth 1980 sighting on the Oak Ridge reservation.

The sighting Jay believes in most was in 1976. He was the sighter. He was using a powerful light for counting deer. His light picked out a reddish animal, about the color of deer in summer, twenty-five yards distant, in the edge of a woods. He watched it move out of the light into the woods. The tip of its long tail was dark. It walked on the leaves, left no tracks. The panther the guards saw walked on grass and left no tracks.

I'm not going to grieve much over the absence of scat. That doesn't necessarily indicate all these panthers are ghosts. They just do a good job of covering.   *—10/12/80*

Beaver Comeback

If beavers make a significant comeback in the Great Smokies region, Cades Cove would be the best home for them.

This seems to be the conclusion of Francis J. (Frank) Singer, David LaBrode and Lorrie Sprague, who recently did a paper entitled "Reinvasion of Beaver and the Otter Niche in Great Smoky Mountains National Park."

One hundred years ago, according to the Singer-LaBrode-Sprague paper, beaver were extinct in East Tennessee and were found in small numbers only in a few counties of West Tennessee.

In the past few decades, beaver were transplanted back into some East Tennessee and North Carolina counties.

By 1966, ole Brother Beaver was back in the Great Smokies, chewing birch and dogwood and yellow poplars and lots of other trees. But these particular beavers are not believed to have been among those stocked in either North Carolina or Tennessee. Though no one seems to be absolutely positive about this, the belief is that they came up out of Georgia into North Carolina. They got into the North Carolina side of the park first. Hazel Creek was one of their early streams.

They later came into the Tennessee side and were seen on Little River, in the Metcalf Bottoms area. They got into the Greenbrier section in 1978 and into Panther Creek last year.

Panther is a tributary to Abrams Creek, but it enters Abrams far down toward where Abrams enters Chilhowee Lake. No beaver has been reported so far along Abrams in Cades Cove, which is believed to be the best spot in the park for beaver.

Why is it the best?

Because it's a relatively slow stream winding along the relatively flat lands of the cove. Here a beaver colony can chew down trees and build dams that will back up small lakes.

Most streams in the Great Smokies plunge down steep stream beds and are too fast for beavers to dam.

And if beavers find a home along Abrams Creek, in the Cove, it could be that otters will join them. Otters and beavers sometimes go together. They like the same slow-moving streams.

The last otters were reported in the Great Smokies in 1936. If otters come back, the park alone doesn't have enought suitable habitat for their survival, according to Singer, LaBrode and Sprague. But it could be part of a wider area that could support an otter comeback.

A few otter sightings have been reported in East Tennessee in recent years—along the Little Tennessee River, for instance. But Frank Singer says he's not positive of these. He says the closest otters he's sure of live in the Hatchie, Tuscumbia, Buffalo and Duck Rivers. But he won't say for sure that a few are not in East Tennessee.   *—4/13/80*

Snake Questions

Are snakes particularly ill-tempered during Dogdays because they are shedding?

Do copperheads and rattlers have peculiar odors?

Those were a couple of the questions I asked Harry W. Green when I went over to UT to see him and his snakes recently.

Harry, a pleasant young Texan with dark red hair and mustache, is working on his PhD here and he's studying snake behavior.

Snakes shed several times a year, not just during Dogdays, Harry says. They may be more irritable when they're shedding.

Harry says copperheads and cottonmouth moccasins have scent glands, and they sometimes smell a little like cucumbers.

Harry likes snakes, and he knows quite a bit more about them than most of us. He's a defender of snakes. After I wrote something about snakes a few weeks ago, here came a letter from Harry, in which he said in part:

". . . I think fear of these creatures is largely a matter of ignorance or carelessness. First, most of the snakes in the Smokies are harmless (the same is true almost everywhere in the world, except Australia). Second, the two venomous species in our area can be avoided if a few common sense precautions are taken:

"Watch where you walk, and carry a light at night. Never step over or sit down on a rock or log without first looking on the other side. Don't put your hands into holes or up onto ledges where you cannot see. Don't pick up any snake unless you are positive it is harmless.

Don't pick up venomous snakes, even dead ones, with your hands. All of the venomous snake bites I am familiar with resulted from carelessness, and they often involved a person actually handling a live snake."

(He later told me he was bitten by a copperhead when he was in high school, and he has known ever since that it's "stupid" to pick up a poisonous snake.)   Harry says snakes are worth having around for two reasons.

"They are members of the webs of predator-prey relationships that make up living communities; many kinds eat mostly rodents and can thus even be of economic value. Snakes are also survivors of the great wilderness that was America before man's arrival, and as such are part of the esthetic outdoor experience.

"The next time you encounter a snake, pause a while to contemplate the marvelous way its colors promote survival—either by camouflage (copperheads are good examples of this) or by optical illusions (try to keep your eyes on a fast moving black racer in the grass). And recall that this reptile manages to locate, subdue, and swallow relatively large prey 'in one piece' without benefit of legs or hands. If the snake is a pit viper (or a boa or python at the zoo), consider the fact that the heat receptors on each side of its head can detect tiny amounts of infrared radiation in just a fraction of the time required by a sensitive man-made instrument. Truly beautiful and amazing animals!

"I hope that as people become more and more educated about nature," Harry continued, "they will even come to appreciate reptiles, but we've got a way to go. While it is reasonable to remove venomous snakes from around houses, especially where small children live, even rattlesnakes and copperheads should be protected in national parks."   *—7/27/75*

Rare Mushroom

A month or so ago we were discussing rare plant species and the need for preserving them, and today we'll chew around a bit on the rarest one I've heard about. It's *Gloeocantharellus purpurascens*.

Maybe we'd better not chew on it literally. For it's a mushroom. It may be poisonous. Besides, I don't think the people most interested in it would appreciate our chewing on it.

I asked Dr. Ronald H. Petersen of the UT Botany Department whether it is safe to eat. He didn't know.

"It's been too precious to eat," was his response.

Then it must be pretty rare. In how large an area does it grow?

In a place approximately ten square yards in size. This is on the North Carolina side of Great Smoky Mountains National Park. I'll not be more specific. For although the great majority of people would like that something so rare be preserved, there are a few barbarians abroad in the land who might take delight in destroying it.

The first person to mention the mushroom to me was Mrs. Bill (Jean) Allen, a UT student from Norris. One of Jean's school projects is to get this mushroom on the Department of the Interior's official endangered species list. If she and Dr. Petersen succeed in this effort, *Gloeocantharellus* probably will be the first mushroom to make it. For the endangered species listers had not had an earlier request on a moss, alga, liverwort or mushroom.

The discoverer of *Gloeocantharellus purpurascens* was Dr. L.R. Hesler, that remarkable gentleman who retired as UT's dean of liberal arts in 1958 but continues to work at his office nearly every day.

Now one of the world's leading authorities on mushrooms, Dr. Hesler became interested in them in 1924. It was a muggy, moist summer, and mushrooms were popping out of the ground all over the Knoxville area. Housewives were calling the UT Botany Department, asking which mushrooms were safe to gather and cook. So Dr. Hesler, then head of the department, began trying to find answers for the callers. He's been trying to learn more about mushrooms ever since and he may have got to the point where he knows more than anybody else.

On the phone the other day, I asked him when he first found *Gloeocantharellus*. He guessed about twenty-five years ago. Then with a hint of a chuckle in his voice, he said that, at his age (eighty-seven), he's been known to be in error on such guesses, and if I wanted to know exactly, he'd better look it up. He did, and his guess was off a bit. He found that mushroom thirty-five years ago this past Aug. 11.

He found it in a pine woods. There are lots of other such pine woods in the Great Smokies, places where the moisture, shade and soil types are similar. It may grow in some other such place. But Dr. Hesler has not found it in any of them. Nor, as far as he knows, has anyone else.

In a world containing millions and millions of acres of pine woods, why does *Gloeocantharellus* grow only in a space the size of a kitchen floor?

Dr. Hesler didn't know. But he has a theory. He said some mushrooms are found pretty much all over the world, others only in small local areas. His theory is that those in the small areas evolved later than the others and have not had time to spread. So *Gloeocantharellus* probably is "relatively recent in terms of eons."

Its future as a species is fragile and chancy. Within a matter of seconds, a bulldozer could shove it into history's botanical graveyard. In dry weather, someone careless with a match might start a small fire which would char the humus it needs for survival. Too many feet tramping the area could destroy the same humus.

Yet, *Gloeocantharellus* has survived for at least thirty-five years and probably lots longer. It'll be interesting to see how it makes out in the future. —*8/31/75*

[Dr. Hesler died on November 20, 1977. The rare mushroom was not placed on the endangered species list.]

Fraser Fir: Doomed?

For all practical purposes, the Fraser fir tree likely is doomed in Great Smoky Mountains National Park, a victim of the balsam woolly aphid.

This is a conclusion reached after studying a report by Dr. Ronald L. Hay, associate professor in UT's Department of Forestry, Wildlife and Fisheries. Ron Hay, with help of two of his graduate students, C. Christopher Eagar and Kristine D. Johnson, has been studying the woolly aphid-fir situation in the park since early 1976.

Mt. Le Conte, which has few trees except firs, probably will be nearly deforested when the firs die.

And when will they die?

They're dying now. By New Year's Eve, 1988, they may be all dead. It could take a little longer. On the other hand, it may not take that long.

Fraser fir is one of the two evergreen species that clothes the summits of the highest sections of the Great Smokies. The higher the altitude, the more nearly pure is the stand of fir. The summits of Clingmans Dome, Mt. Guyot and Le Conte are places where this beautiful tree predominates almost to the exclusion of others.

About 4000 feet is the lowest elevation the tree has grown in the park. And the one stand that low, on the Tennessee side, near U.S. 441, is already dead. The tree ordinarily doesn't grow below 4500 feet in the park.

Starting in the eastern section of the park, the fir grows from Mt. Sterling and Cosby Knob westward to a point two or three miles west of Clingmans Dome.

The other high-elevation evergreen in the park is red spruce. Most people regard the fir as the lovelier of the two. It's the one whose tiny cones stand upright. It is the one with the aromatic needles and it is the one with blisters on the bark. Some oldtime mountain "doctors" used the clear, sticky liquid from these blisters as a treatment for many ailments.

Oldtimers called Fraser fir "balsam." But true balsam fir grows much farther north.

Fraser fir grows only in the highlands of the Southern Appalachians. It is in North Carolina's Plott Balsams, on Mt. Mitchell, Roan Mountain, Grandfather Mountain, Mt. Rogers and in the Great Smokies.

The stand in the Great Smokies is far larger than any of the others. The only stand not under aphid attack is the tiny one on Mt. Rogers, in Virginia's Jefferson National Forest.

Like two other destructive agents in the park, the chestnut blight and the European wild boar, the balsam woolly aphid is an exotic, brought to this country through ignorance or carelessness.

The woolly aphid was brought here from Europe, on nursery stock, sometime before 1908, when it was found on balsam fir in Canada. The first infestation of Fraser fir was found on Mt. Mitchell in 1957. Though it was found then, by that time it had done so much damage that it obviously had been there several years. For 11,000 trees were already dead.

The aphid was first discovered in the Great Smokies in 1963. By then, it had killed forty-five trees on Mt. Sterling, just north of the summit. But evidence indicated the tiny insect had been working on some of those trees for at least five years, or since 1958. Wind is believed to have carried the aphids from Mitchell to Sterling.

Now, twenty years after the first aphid is believed to have reached the park, they have spread to nearly every area where fir grows in the park. Ron said every mature fir except two were dead on Mt. Sterling by the end of 1977. One of the two died this year and the other is dying.

Generally, the aphids have been moving from east to west in the park and from lower elevations to high ones. They start at the lowest point where fir grows and move upslope.

Ron says the distribution of woolly aphids in the park "expanded alarmingly" this year. Some peaks which have been infested longest "are almost void of fir. In all cases, established aphid infestations have increased in size, primarily upslope."

The summit of Clingmans Dome is the only place in the park where fir grows that remains free of aphids. But Ron says the insects have reached trees near the eastern end of the parking area below the Dome.

"I expect to see infested fir on the summit of the Dome by late summer, 1979," he said.

He predicts the aphids will kill the mature firs on Mt. Guyot within three to five years, on Le Conte in five to ten years, and on the Dome within ten to fifteen years.

He is not saying that every Fraser fir will be dead. Only the mature ones. What will happen to young firs is not clear yet. Somewhat like chestnut sprouts, they may be around a long time. But not as sprouts, for aphid-killed firs don't sprout.

But Ron says aphids don't kill lots of young firs until they reach trunk diameter of five to six inches. He thinks this is at least partly because young firs have smooth bark, and the aphids need rough bark to latch onto and do their dirty work. By the time a fir gets that large, it begins to produce a few cones. So young firs may produce younger ones and keep the species alive in the park.

But it seems more likely that yellow birch and red spruce will move in and eventually reforest the areas now clothed mostly in fir.

Can anything be done to turn the tide against the exotic insects?

Apparently not. Ron says there is no practical way to do it. "Lindane is effective in killing the balsam aphid," he wrote, "but it must be applied until run-off occurs along the entire bole and branches. To further compound the difficulty of this procedure, spraying must be done from the ground. Silvicultural control has involved complete removal of the host species."

The National Park Service tried removal when the aphids were first found on Mt. Sterling. They cut all the trees on which they found aphids. But they apparently failed to find all of them.   —*12/31/78*

"The Rabbit Place"

The National Park Service may use fire to return the Cherokees Tsistuyi, the Rabbit Place, to something more nearly resembling its former grassy loveliness.

What was the Rabbit Place for the Cherokees later became Gregory Bald for white men whose livestock fattened on its lush wild grass. For thousands who came later, it has been outstanding as the place where wild azaleas bloom in great variety and beauty.

According to James Mooney's *Myths of the Cherokee*, the rabbits had their townhouse on the grassy bald on the crest of the Great Smokies, high above Cades Cove. There lived their chief, the Great Rabbit, large as a deer, swift as the wind.

I doubt that adult Cherokees really believed this. More than likely it was a story told to the children. But then maybe some did believe it. For the Indians, as well as for some twentieth century white folks, there was a rather wide area where myth and reality merged.

For many years there has been disagreement over the origin of Gregory Bald and the other grassy balds of the southern mountains. Some people have insisted they were cleared by white settlers for livestock. Others believe the balds were there before the first white settler ever crossed the mountains.

The fact that Gregory had its place in Cherokee mythology lends weight to the latter belief.

I've read all sorts of theories about how the balds came to be. One fellow, whose name escapes me at the moment, wrote a rather convincing theory that goes all the way back to the Ice Ages. He said extreme cold killed the hardwoods at the high altitudes where the balds occur, and then hot periods killed the spruce and firs. And, he said, they never came back for lack of seed sources for the particular strains that would thrive there.

Recent history has done much to mess up that theory. For since the National Park Service banned grazing in the park nearly forty years ago, both hardwoods and softwoods have started invading the balds.

Great Smoky Mountains Conservation Association has been trying for years to get the Park Service to preserve some of the balds. But it is general Park Service policy to let nature have her way out in the boondocks.

For months, the Park Service agonized over how to preserve the balds as parts of the wilderness. This would require some natural means, of course. And, you may remember, it gave rise to speculation in this space about a year ago that elk might be reintroduced, in the hope that they would graze the balds and preserve them just as domestic livestock formerly did.

The agonizing seems to be over now. The Park Service has told the conservation association it expects to preserve Gregory and Andrews Balds as managed historic areas within the wilderness; not as parts of the wilderness.

In discussing this at the recent annual meeting of the conservation association, Park Supt. Vincent Ellis said fire is one possible tool to use to keep the forest out of the balds.

The Cherokees sometimes burned the forest to make for more

bountiful blueberry crops. And it's quite likely they knew a thing or two about game management, Mr. Ellis thinks. They likely knew that clearings in the forest provided good places for deer and elk to graze.

And, Mr. Ellis thinks, the Cherokees may have used fire at the Rabbit Place and other balds in the mountains. Then white settlers likely enlarged some of the balds they found in the mountains after they drove out the Indians.

One particularly fine thing about the balds is that nobody knows for sure how they came to be. And I hope nobody ever learns. The mystery probably is lots more fascinating than the truth would be.

—6/24/74

10

Pioneer Industry: The Water Mills

Back when this region was very young in terms of white folks occupancy, the very earliest industries probably were grist mills, though some might think blacksmith shops.

Settlers chopped down trees, or maybe merely girdled them, in rich meadows and planted corn. They gathered the corn and had to have some place to grind it. So as soon as every community had as many as five or six families, somebody built a mill.

Community grist mills lingered well into the twentieth century, but most of them were out of business by mid-century. I know of none still operating purely for the neighborhood farm folk. Of course, some serve mostly as tourist attractions.   —*3/6/75*

Well, I Was Wrong

"You go to showin' a man a team of mules and they'll act up every time," Charlie Coada said, as the belt jumped off the wheel for the third time in ten minutes.

This is the belt that transfers the power from the turbine shaft to the millstone in Charlie's gristmill, on Hesse Creek, in Blount County.

He said the cold, dry weather had made the belt loose. He sprinkled water here and there along the belt, and the mill was soon grinding Sam Gentry's ninety-five-pound turn of Hickory King corn.

I had stopped at the mill, hoping I would find Charlie grinding. For when I'd stopped there back in the summer, he had no customers. I stopped the first time after Clifford Leisure, Gatlinburg, told me about Charlie's mill. The reason was that I'd written earlier that I knew of no gristmill now operating "purely for the neighborhood farm folk."

Well, I was wrong. For Charlie's mill is nothing more or less than a mill that grinds corn for farmers who grow the corn themselves. Unlike all the other gristmills I know of in this region, Charlie's mill caters to tourists in no way. He couldn't if he wanted to, for when more than three cars park at the mill, there's a traffic jam.

The mill is less than a mile off State Highway 73, between Walland and Townsend. Going south from Maryville, turn right onto West Miller Cove Road. (It's the first road south of the Foothills Parkway.) Go about two-tenths of a mile to the stone church building on the left, turn left down the narrow gravel road. Keep going till you see the attractive two-story farm house on the right and the twin-gabled little weather-boarded building on the left. The one on the left is the mill.

When I stopped, Charlie had just finished grinding a turn for Giles Myers. We chatted a minute and I said I was disappointed that I'd arrived too late. But just as I was leaving, Giles said somebody else was coming with a turn.

It was Mr. Gentry. He and Mr. Myers carried the turn, in a clean meal sack, into the mill. Charlie weighed it. Then he grunted a little as he hefted it up to the hopper and poured the corn out of the sack. The broad, flat grains filled the hopper almost to overflowing.

Then came the trouble with the belt. But after it was behaving properly, Charlie conferred briefly with Sam Gentry.

"You want yours sorta fine, don't you?" he asked.

Mr. Gentry nodded agreement. Charlie turned a big iron ring an inch or two, thus lowering the upper millstone a bit closer to the lower one, to make for finer meal. Then both men caught a bit of the warm meal that was pouring down into the mealbox and rubbed it between their fingers. It was fine enough.

Then Charlie went up to the hopper and motioned me to join him. He took his "toll board" down from the wall beside the hopper and checked it to see how much toll he would take from Mr. Gentry's corn. The board, maybe eighteen inches long and eight or nine inches wide, is covered with numbers, showing how much toll to take. It starts with a sixteen-pound turn (from which two pounds of toll is taken) and goes up to 115 pounds (from which fifteen pounds is taken).

Then Charlie used his "toll dish" to dip his toll (about twelve pounds, as I recall) from the corn in the hopper. He poured it into a barrel already nearly full of Hickory King corn. He had two other containers of toll corn. One contained what Charlie called "old-timey white corn," and the other contained shoe-peg corn—very small pointed grains that look a little like shoe pegs.

Charlie, a retired Aluminum Co. of America employe, is sixty-eight years old. He and his wife, Eula, bought the house, mill and land in 1955. Their first intention was not to live there, at least not immediately. But Eula said it was so peaceful and quiet, and so much cooler than Alcoa in summer, that they moved there only weeks after they bought the place.

The mill still goes by the name of the Martin Mill, because John Martin built the house and either rebuilt or remodeled the mill many years ago. Eula said John Martin went by the name of "Snaky John Martin," to distinguish him from other John Martins in the area. She also said she once read in a history book that the first mill at this spot was built in 1796.

Charlie and Eula use the waters of Hesse Creek for many purposes. Charlie can use the same power that turns the millstone to run a cornsheller and an emery wheel. And he uses it to operate a water pump that irrigates his lawn and garden.

I suppose most of Charlie's customers are from Blount County. But some people bring corn from as far away as Newport, Madisonville, Englewood. Even North Carolina and Georgia.   —*12/7/75*

Family Mills

That small creek that hurries down the northwestern hollow of Mt. Le Conte and jumps over Rainbow Falls and goes rock-hopping on into Gatlinburg now is called Le Conte Creek. But it used to be called Mill Creek. And with good reason.

It might also have been called Ogle Creek. Or Oakley Creek. Or, to prevent any hard feelings in either family, Ogle-Oakley Creek. All with good reason.

On the last three and one-half miles of Le Conte (Mill) Creek, before it joins West Prong of Little Pigeon River, were fourteen grist mills. Make it thirteen, for the fourteenth one actually was on a small tributary called Oakley Branch, and, as you can see on the map, it belonged to Rev. Noah Ogle.

This map originally was made by Mrs. Lucinda Ogle and Bill Dyer redid it from her pen-and-ink sketch. Lucinda is the daughter of the late Wiley Oakley and Mrs. Rebecca Ann Ogle Oakley. Wiley was the "Roamin' Man of the Mountains," a happy, mountain-loving man given to telling wonderful tall tales. Well, Lucinda is a true daughter of her father. Or, to put it another way, she takes after her pa. She tells a good story.

A piece I wrote a few days ago about old grist mills set her to remembering the mills on Mill Creek and the people who owned them.

"All these folks are my kinfolks; so I am not afraid of them," she said. (Besides, most of them are gone now.)

"Every man who had a little land that bordered the creek owned a grist mill at one time. I just bet they didn't trust their kinfolk . . . to take the proper toll dish full out of their turn of corn. Could be they needed every grain of their own corn," Mrs. Ogle said.

Then she got down to what may be the truth of the matter: "My guess is that it was prestige. They wanted to be considered by one another . . . as prosperous folks. Like, nowadays someone owns a Cadillac automobile. The mill was their Cadillac."

She says she bets "no one else can find that many mills in so short a distance. Because this creek had so many small waterfalls and the contour of the land fell so fast, it lent itself so easy to putting in a millrace. Also, not all the millhouses stayed in operation long, for sometimes a spring freshet would wash them away."

When Lucinda drew that map, her memory told her that fourteen of the families in Mill Creek Valley owned mills and three did not. But she has since remembered a few other non-millers, and she thinks the total is about six.

One of the interesting non-millers was Indian Bill. She says Indian Bill was the only Cherokee she knows about who lived on the north side of the Great Smokies during this period. She does not remember him, for he must have died before she was born. But her mother remembers him.

Mt. LeConte

Balsam Top

Bullhead Mt.

Mill (LeConte)

RICHARD OGLE
SANDFORD OGLE and Others

JOHN (Bullhead) WHALEY

BIRDWELL HUSKEY

JUNGLE BROOK HOUSE & MILL (Mill Still Stands)

REV SAM OAKLEY

UNCLE HARVEY OAKLEY

OLD AUNT FRANKY OGLE

REV. NOAH OGLE

Oakley Branch

GRANDPA HENRY OAKLEY

UNCLE GEORGE OGLE

NICK HUSKEY & Others

ISIAH TRENTHAM

OLD JIM OGLE

■ = FAMILIES WITH MILLS —LIVED ON CREEK
□ = FAMILIES WITHOUT MILLS

GATLINBURG

Artwork by Bill Dyer

If Indian Bill had owned a mill, he'd have been just another miller on Mill Creek. (But he might have been the only miller who wasn't an Oakley or an Ogle or who wasn't married to an Ogle or an Oakley.) He served a different purpose. He was the man who knew which herbs to gather to keep people from getting sick. Or to make them well if they got sick.

Indian Bill's house isn't on the map. He was one of those Lucinda thought of after she'd made the map and sent it to me. He lived in the last house up the creek, beyond what is now Cherokee Orchard.

The Junglebrook Mill, built by Lucinda's grandfather Noah (Bud) Ogle, still stands, preserved by the National Park Service, along with the Junglebrook House. You see no millwheel with this mill. That's because it's a tub (for turbine) mill. The turbine is under the building, powered by water coming down the wooden sluice at right.

A small building near the mill was the Ogle Honeymoon House. As Noah Ogle's sons got married, each moved into this house with his bride. They lived in it until the next son married. Lucinda thinks each of her Ogle uncles—Leonard, Isaac, Matt and Wilson—lived in the house a year or two with their brides.

(Randolph Shields told me a long time ago about a house which served the same purpose in the family of one of his Cades Cove ancestors. But instead of being called a "honeymoon house," it was called the "weaner cabin," where the groom and his bride were "weaned" from their families.)

Doing all that remembering about grist mills made Lucinda remember something else—a "little man who was a real artist in his way. Aaron Reagan, who lived on Roaring Fork Creek . . . would go from mill owner to mill owner, during the winter months, sharpening the millrocks. I would sit hunkered down so fascinated watching him chip and peck on the beautiful design, which pattern made the corn turn to meal that worked its way between the two round flat rocks toward the spout that poured the meal into the big box.

"Sometimes I would almost be frozen when Aaron Reagan would look at me and say in the kindest voice, 'Little one, run and warm. I will be a long time finishing . . . '

"In the fall, this same little man, Aaron Reagan, would come with his mule and sled, loaded with his big molasses pan, scoops, etc., to make on shares the molasses for different mountain folks. Of course, they had already built the furnace of mud and rocks to fit the pan."   —3/30/75

How Did the Tub Mill Get Its Name?

Dr. R.S. Hines, a Cleveland, Tennessee, dentist, thinks the tub mill, that small, slow watermill with which some East Tennesseans used to grind their grain, did not get its name the way I said it did.

"In your article of March 30, you referred to a tub mill as a turbine mill and that the 'tub mill' derived from 'turbine,'" he said.

"I'm quoting from an old friend of mine (now deceased), Frank Oliver, Smoky Mountains ranger. I asked him why it was called a tub mill and he told me that it was because it could grind a 'tub' of corn a day."

Dr. Hines, I'm not positive where I came by my belief that "tub mill" is a corruption of "turbine mill." But I suspect that you and I got our different impressions from people in the same organization—the National Park Service (NPS). I believe mine came from something I've read about one or the other of the two tub mills in the Great Smokies—the little Junglebrook mill near Gatlinburg and the much larger Mingus Mill, in North Carolina.

So I talked with Ed Trout, the NPS historian for the Great Smokies, and asked could he shed any light on the matter. His belief jibes with mine, but proving it turned out to be a bit difficult.

He found a reference to tub mills in Eric Sloane's *Diary of an Early American Boy.* In it is an illustration of a tub mill turbine turning within a tub-like covering. Sloane says nothing about how such a mill came to be called a tub mill. But the fact that the turbine in his illustration is housed in a covering that looks something like a tub raises even another possibility.

Ed also looked in another book, *Flour For Man's Bread,* by John Storck and Walter Teague, and found material on tub mills dating all the way back to the fifteenth century. But the authors managed not to say why the thing is called a tub mill.

Now, another NPS man, Glenn Cardwell, heard it still another way: It's a tub mill because the little hopper holds only a tubful of corn.

Dr. Hines, I think we're going to have to ask for help on this one. Does anyone know positively, and can he prove, how the tub mill got its name?   —*4/13/75*

Now the time has come to try to settle, maybe once and for all, the business of how the tub mill got its name.

I think I've heard that James White, Knoxville's first settler, had a tub mill somewhere on First Creek. Maybe the Bicentennial buffs should recreate it. But I suppose that would be pretty difficult to do, since the road-builders a few years ago buried James White's section of First Creek.

Because its wheel usually was pretty well hidden under the mill-house, the tub mill wasn't as colorful as those with the big overshot (or undershot) water wheels.

A few weeks ago, I indicated that "tub" was a corruption of "turbine" and that this is why it's called a tub mill. Not so, responded Dr. R.S. Hines, a Cleveland dentist. He said he'd been told it was a tub mill because it could grind only a tubful of corn in a day.

But we now hear from another Cleveland gentleman, Ned Carter, who says:

"As an authority on this subject, I am here to straighten you out. Dr. Hines may be able to cure distemper but he sure is not an authority on mills. A 'TUB' mill is nothing in the world but a 'TURBINE MILL.' The 'TUB' is just how some fellows say 'TURB' which is only a shortening of the word TURBINE.

"When you get these problems, just sit down and use a little common sense."

Roy Bell, Morristown, put this note in the mail: "The book *Foxfire 2* . . . answers your questions regarding the tub mill. Pictures and drawings indicate why the name is 'tub.' "

Mr. Bell, I read the *Foxfire 2* chapter on the tub mill and found that editor Eliot Wigginton, like several other authors and editors, passed up a good opportunity to say directly and unequivocally why that mill is called what it's called.

True, the drawings do "indicate" the reason for the name. But they indicate two different reasons to me. He calls the wheel a "tub wheel" and the thing does look remotely like a tub. But the wooden covering for the top (or "runner rock") looks even more like a tub.

Also, here's a letter from Lucinda Ogle, Gatlinburg, who inadvertently started this fuss by giving me the picture of the Junglebrook tub mill published here a few Sundays ago. She says:

"No one has mentioned the big wooden band that goes around the two round stones to keep the meal from flying out. This is two mill rocks in a wooden tub—why the name tub mill, is what I was always told."

Next came John E. Kirkland, for years a hydraulic turbine specialist with TVA. And he was carrying a reprint of a 1954 article by Edward Uehling, published in the Allis-Chalmers Electrical Review. I think Mr. Uehling wrote what we've been looking for:

"Another form of wheel extensively used for grist mill applications was known as the tub mill. . . With a vertical instead of a horizontal shaft, the wheel ran in a circular wood enclosure, or tub without a bottom. In one sense it was merely a kind of vertical flutter wheel. The water was let on at an angle through a crude spout, and the tub, a continuous apron, confined the water to the wheel on its downward course."

What we've wound up with here is a whole bundle of reasons for calling a tub mill a tub mill. All of them sound reasonable. I'm inclined to think Mr. Uehling may have given us the original reason. But who can be positive?   —*4/20/75*

00000

The last time I wrote about tub mills, I resolved to lock up the subject and throw away the key. For I thought it was unlikely that anybody would add much of value to what others had already said here. But I was wrong.

Dr. Gregory Jeane, an assistant professor of geography at Auburn University, probably can qualify as an expert on the history of mills. He's been doing research on them for five years. So let's see what he has to say.

"The tub mill is generally accepted by mill scholars as being a modification of the Old World 'Greek' or 'Norse' mill. The exact origin of the prototype is yet to be resolved, but is believed to have originated in the (highlands) of the eastern Mediterranean as early as the second century B.C. From there it diffused westward throughout the Mediterranean and the rest of Europe. Eastward it may have diffused into China. Records indicate it was well known in ancient times there.

"The horizontal mill is the simplest form of mill machinery run by water. It apparently diffused rapidly along various frontiers because of its easy construction, and because it served a very basic need. Exactly when the horizontal mill became a part of various European cultures is simply educated guessing. It was certainly well established throughout Western Europe by Medieval times. When Europeans began migrating to North America, they had available a vast amount of milling expertise to carry with them.

"In America, the horizontal mill became synonymous with the frontier. It was frequently the first mill type constructed, often followed at a later date by some other, more sophisticated type of mill. The Americans, however, did something no European miller did, and that was to enclose the horizontal wheel in a wooden casing or 'tub.' I contend that this is the more probable origin of the name. It did increase the efficiency to a degree, although there is no indication that knowledge of the turbine came from it. The similarity was recognized later, after turbines had been introduced into America, but not at initial occupance. Interestingly enough, the French 'discovered' the modern turbine in the early part of the nineteenth century, basing early experience upon use of the horizontal mill. The theory, however, goes back at least as far as Leonardo de Vinci, possibly earlier. The first turbine recognized as such is attributed to Benoit Fourneyron."

After his five years of mill research, Dr. Jeane says he's convinced that "much mill information in America that is passed on to the public is highly suspect as to validity." He says there often is little concern about the correctness of it, so long as it sounds good.

With the nation's bicentennial rapidly approaching, "American pioneer industries, of which milling was certainly one of the most important, are receiving little or no recognition," Dr. Jeane says. "When they do, the material has been so romanticized that it no longer represents reality, rather some clouded version of it . . . Travels abroad have frequently confirmed that other nationalities have a more detailed, and accurate, knowledge about America than the average American citizen. As a teacher, it makes me wonder where we have gone wrong." *—5/19/75*

11

Welcome to the Park

Great Smoky Mountains National Park is putting so much realism into the pioneer farm exhibit at Oconaluftee, N.C., that some people don't believe it.

They can believe the chickens and geese and Tony the horse and Zeb and Zeek the oxen. They can believe Sandy and Bullet the farm dogs. They should be able to believe the sorghum molasses-making which will start this coming weekend.

But some of them have trouble believing that's real food Arvel and Jane Greene are eating there in the kitchen of the old log house.

"Is that plastic food?" somebody asked the other day.

Well, it's not plastic. Not by a long, long, long shot. Alberta and I had dinner with Mr. and Mrs. Greene, along with a couple of other guests, Mrs. Shirley McHan [Boykin] and Dick Zani, a few days ago. Dick is the park's interpretative specialist at 'Luftee.' Shirley is the manager of Great Smoky Mountains Natural History Association. The association and the National Park Service share the responsibility of the exhibit.

We arrived about 10 a.m. and started walking about the farm-building area. We entered through a picket gate held closed by the weight of an Oconaluftee rock on a wire attached to the gate.

We encountered a white Leghorn rooster, which Dick said is sort of a loner. He has little to do with the Rhode Island Reds, the Bantams, the Cornish, and several chickens of mixed ancestry that scratch around the garden and barnlot. We even found one trying to make a nest—or maybe just wallow a bit—in the charcoal and ashes in the fire pit of the forge in the blacksmith shop.

The barn probably is not a typical Western North Carolina or East Tennessee pioneer barn. But it's the barn the Enloe family built on this farm—but not on the specific ground where it now stands—many years ago. It has a large open shed on each side, and it was used as a drovers' barn. It was a stopping place for livestock which had summered on mountain grass and was being driven south to markets all the way to Charleston. The old Indian Gap Road, the only road which crossed the middle of the Great Smokies for many years, passed within a few yards of the barn.

We met Arvel, coming across from the hog lot to the barn, toting a sharpened stake he was going to use to repair the hog-lot fence.

Arvel is sixty-two years old, and you could search this country from end to end and from top to bottom and find no more authentic mountain farmer than Arvel Greene.

He can make you a hammer handle, or fashion you a chair with a split-oak bottom. He can make you a horseshoe in the blacksmith shop. Or rive shingles from red oak, and then nail them exactly the right way to the top of a house or barn to keep out the rain.

Arvel looked up at the three-year-old shingled roof of the barn and said some of the shingles were nailed on improperly before he arrived and got things straightened out. What was wrong was that the nail heads were exposed.

He explained that the nails are supposed to be always covered by the overlapping shingles. This barn roof is of shingles twenty-four inches long, with about seven inches of each shingle exposed. The roof is three shingles thick, and 18,000 shingles were required for the job.

Arvel wears bib overalls. He carries his watch in the bib pocket where it's supposed to be, and the watch is tied to a short leather string. This is not for show, any more than the leather thong around Arvel's broad-brimmed, sweat-stained hat is for show. They are almost as much a part of him as the wrinkles in his red-brown neck and his courteous manner and mountain accent.

"If a body could ever get time to do it, he could cut a yellow poplar and hollow it out and make an honest-to-goodness authentic trough for the springhouse," Arvel said.

The trough there now embarrasses Arvel a little. Anybody who knows wood would know this one is made of some Western wood. Sawed wood, at that.

And if he had time to do it, Arvel also could make a cider press that really would be more in keeping with pioneer times than the one now in the springhouse.

Earlier, I had asked Dick whether he'd considered a hog-killing as a demonstration when colder weather comes late this fall.

He said it had been discussed, but Paul McCrary, head of the interpretative program in the park, had turned it down on grounds it would be too bloody for the tastes of most park visitors.

I suppose Paul is right. For Arvel and Dick said some visitors are disturbed because the pigpen and the barnlot are a bit soiled at times, and some also are disturbed because the windows of the old log house where Jane and Arvel "live" aren't screened. This definitely is not a pioneer era.

The house originally was built on Indian Creek, north of Bryson City, seventy or eighty years ago by Old Man John Davis, according to Arvel. He and Jane "live" in it from 10 a.m. to about 6 p.m. Tuesday through Saturday. Jane cooks their noon meal on hot coals in the fireplace. (Actually, their regular home is a much older log house. Arvel said they were told it was 150 years old when they bought it thirty years ago.)

Jane rang the bell for us to come to dinner, which is what nearly all farm people used to call the noon meal. We sat on benches at an unpainted wooden table loaded with fried chicken, Clay peas, turnip greens, boiled potatoes, a mold of home-churned butter, a platter of sliced tomatoes, cucumbers, celery and peppers, along with a jar of beautiful currant jelly and another of honey.

And I must not forget the bread. Jane had baked gritted bread, plus biscuits. And two gritters were hanging on the wall.

Red peppers, beans (white half-runners and Kentucky Wonders) were hanging beside the fireplace. Several gourd containers hang on the wall, and Arvel used one of these to fill a wooden bowl with water to wash his hands.

We drank cider that was made on the farm only a few days ago. The pommy pile from the cider-making was still fragrant in the garden.

Tourists continually passed. Some looked in and said nothing. Others commented. Some obviously didn't believe what they were seeing. Not all of it, anyway. They doubted the food had been cooked in the fireplace.

Jane has a pretty face—dark complexion, dark hair, fine regular features. From the neck down she disappears into a long, loose dress of the type that pretty well concealed the figures of pioneer women.

There were two desserts—stacked cake and egg custard pie. These were not baked in the fireplace. After all, there is a limit to what can be cooked in a two-hour period on a rather small fireplace. One of Jane's friends had baked the cake and Jane had baked the pie at her regular home. But she said both could be baked in her Dutch oven in the fireplace.

At "dinner" with the Greenes I ate about three times as much as I usually eat at lunch.

Arvel dug into the ashes and found some hot coals, put on more wood, and soon there was a blaze to heat the dish-washing water in a kettle suspended from the fireplace crane.

Arvel works throughout the year at the farm. Jane's season there will end the last Saturday in October.

They've talked with lots of visitors the past summer. And lots of people have gone back to New York, Detroit, Akron, Knoxville, and Los Angeles with clearer comprehensions of what life was like on a mountain farm a hundred and more years ago.   —*9/23/73*

00000

Class, today we shall discuss sorghum molasses and the fact that we might all starve if we had to live under eighteenth century cooking conditions and twentieth century laws.

Stanley G. Canter, chief of interpretation for Great Smoky Mountains National Park, has asked me to tell you the sad news that molasses won't be sold at the park this year. Probably never again.

And Jane Greene can no longer give park visitors bite samples of the old-timey food she cooks in iron pots and ovens over the fire in the fireplace at Oconaluftee, in North Carolina.

Stan Canter says the problem is the strict laws of today on food preparation.

Great Smoky Mountains Natural History Association for many years has sponsored molasses-making demonstrations every autumn in Cades Cove and at Oconaluftee. And visitors could buy molasses.

"As you probably know, about 95 percent of what we sold was not made in the park," Stan Canter said. "It was purchased from a supplier in Georgia. Although it was cooked in open vats as we do, it was a more mechanized, commercial operation. We tried to inform visitors who bought molasses that it was not a product of the demonstrations at Cades Cove and Oconaluftee. However, most of them actually thought that it was . . .

"It is also becoming almost impossible to give an authentic demonstration and still meet public health standards for the production of . . . food . . . to be sold to the public," Stan said.

One problem with the molasses cut, stripped and cooked the way East Tennesseans and North Carolinians did it fifty to one hundred years ago was that a few insects got cooked in the process.

Stan said he's been told that aphids collect in a little groove in the cane. Old-time 'lasses-makers usually don't bother to brush every last aphid—and maybe not even the first aphid—out of that groove. Maybe the aphids added vitamins or protein to the finished product.

But food laws limit the percentage of insect material in food products. Stan said he heard that old-time molasses made in a demonstration at another national park was tested and shown to have 300 percent more insect matter than the law allowed.

So no more molasses sales in the park. But the demonstration will continue. And the law does not yet forbid your getting a noseful of the wonderful aroma of boiling molasses.

Technically, Jane Greene never was supposed to permit visitors to sample her open-fireplace cooking. But there was a time when nobody fussed at her if she forgot the rule and gave some hungry visitor a mouth-watering bit of hoecake cooked on the hoe. Or on a hot place on the hearth brushed clean of ashes.

But no more. The rule reigns. After all, some highly sanitized visitor might die of a speck of ash in a hoecake.

For this same reason, Bill Hooks' wild-food buffet was stopped a year or two ago. Bill used to cook up batches of ramps, sassafras tea, poke sallet and goodness knows what else. He would explain to visitors how mountain folk used to thrive on that stuff. Then he'd permit the visitors to sample it.

No more, no more!

But Bill does continue to do another of his food demonstrations.

This is his mountain Christmas dinner of Christmases past. He cooks it. He talks about it. People look and listen. But they no longer partake of it.   —*8/19/79*

Worth of Wilderness

Hazel Creek, Forney Creek, and the Middle Prong of Little River, three of my favorite streams in Great Smoky Mountains National Park, have "the lowest natural levels of mercury in the U.S."

That's one of the goodies I found in a 311-page volume entitled "Environmental assessment alternatives for the draft general management plan (for) Great Smoky Mountains National Park."

That statement is made in connection with impacts to be expected from construction of the controversial transmountain highway which was proposed several years ago to run from the vicinity of Bryson City, N.C., to near Townsend, Tennessee.

Authors of the assessment went on to say that water quality of the three streams would be "adversely affected by contaminated run-off from the proposed road," and the streams would "no longer be useful for baseline studies, which in turn will affect the value of the park as an International Biosphere Reserve."

This thing intrigued me because I'd never heard of the low mercury level in the streams, and because it is just one of literally thousands of examples of the worth of the wilderness of the Great Smokies.

The assessment contains other such matters of interest, and several alternative plans for different types of park use.

My own general idea is that it should be managed in a manner to preserve for visitors down through the centuries as much as possible of the freshness of the wilderness. To make it possible for a visitor two hundred years from now to see much the same thing that one saw two hundred years ago.

Other little factual nuggets I found and like include:

1. Three wildlife species on the U.S. endangered species list which live in the park are the red-cockaded woodpecker, the Indiana bat and the cougar.

(Park officials don't know whether the cougar [mountain lion,

panther] in the park is the Eastern cougar or the Florida panther.)
[Park authorities are now doubtful that either exists in the park.]

2. In the park are 333 streams big enough to support fish life and these have 735 fishable miles.

3. Precipitation in the park averages about sixty-four inches (or 890 billion gallons) per year. About 500 billion gallons of this is discharged as runoff and leaves the park by way of all those creeks and rivers. The rest of it evaporates, is transpired by plants, or seeps into the earth through permeable rocks.

4. Forests of the Great Smokies have been described as the "most complex and diverse in North America." Roughly 160,000 to 200,000 acres of the park are in virgin forest.

5. Another park resident fairly rare is the northern pine snake, which is on Tennessee's "threatened" list. This fellow is in the extreme western end of the park, in the general vicinity of Happy Valley.

6. Two Great Smokies bird residents which are on North Carolina's "threatened" list are the brown creeper and the golden-crowned kinglet.   *—1/17/77*

Mountain Miles Keep Him Lean

I didn't think I'd like to try keeping up with Dwight McCarter on a mountain trail if he took a notion to move in a hurry.

He's thirty-four years old, five feet and nine inches tall. And at 132 pounds, he's as lean as a hungry rabbit.

Dwight is a back-country technician in Great Smoky Mountains National Park. He walks all the trails on the Tennessee side of the park. He walked "pretty close to" 3200 miles last year. He's walked about 2600 so far this year. That means he averages walking eight to ten miles a day.

He usually walks only five days a week. That is, he walks for a living only five days a week. He may do a little walking here and there on his days off, usually Wednesday and Thursday. Some weeks he walks fifty miles, other weeks eighty miles or more.

If he had to walk forty miles in a day, it wouldn't bother him. But he might not carry as much on his back as he does on his shorter jaunts.

One tool he usually carries is a "pulaski," sort of a cross of a mattock and an axe. He cleans out trail water bars with the mattock part of it and chops out fallen trees with the axe. He sometimes carries a one-man crosscut saw.

On Fridays, his load is about forty pounds. For he usually carries camping gear for spending Friday night in the backcountry. On other days, he usually has only a twenty-pound load.

One recent typical day, Dwight and Ranger Bob Whiteman walked up the Hannah Mountain Trail from Sams Gap to Sheeppen Gap. At Sheeppen, they measured the bare ground at backcountry campsite Number 13. This involves carrying measuring equipment. The idea is to compare this year's measurements with last year's, to learn how much of an impact campers are having on the site.

Dwight also always carries a litter bag. A big one. Actually, a large plastic bag inside a tow sack. He picked up quite a bit of litter at the campsite and finished filling the sack at Moores Spring, off Gregory Bald. Then they walked down the Gregory Ridge Trail, stopping at the new backcountry campsite Number 12, near Forge Creek, to measure it.

You'd think a fellow doing all that walking in the mountains would see lots of snakes. He does see some, but not as many as you might think. He estimates he comes across twenty-five to thirty rattlers and copperheads a year.

He's been roaming about in those mountains long enough that he knows to be careful along creeks in July and August. Copperheads and sometimes rattlers hang out along the creeks in the hottest weather. A copperhead struck at him on Little River, above Elkmont, not long ago. Missed him by about a foot, he said.

He likes to meet people on the trail, talk, and answer their questions. The question tired hikers ask most is, "How far is it to . . . ?"

Most people Dwight meets on the trails are wholesome, OK folks. But once in a while he comes upon somebody who thought a few drinks of liquor would be helpful. He met one "boisterous, disoriented" fellow on the Alum Cave Bluff Trail not so long ago.

Also, not so long ago, when he was hiking off trail, he came upon two men he suspected were poachers. But he was not sure. He saw no guns. But he thinks they live not far from the park. And they were off the trail. That often adds up to poaching, but not always. Since they carried no rifles or shotguns that he could see, he legally could do nothing but speak to the two and go on his way.   —*9/16/79*

How Should the Smokies Be Used?

The view was not the same.

This was the first thing I noticed when I looked out the window of one of my favorite Gatlinburg motels three weeks ago.

This was where Alberta and I "camped" between the two legs of my transmountain hike described in the columns of June 14 and June 18. This motel is one of those on the west side of the river, high on the hillside.

It's high enough that, in times past, one looked out the window and saw the mountains, without seeing much of the town. The first time we stayed there, several years ago, our window served as sort of a frame for Mt. Le Conte.

Not now.

The first thing I saw was that tall structure which I believe is called the Space Needle.

A little later, while I was showering off the day's dried sweat, Alberta arranged a chair in such a way that I could sit in it and look out the window and miss the Space Needle.

But the view was still cluttered. Nearby was a segment of that aerial tramway that walks on concrete stilts over a large piece of the town. And, farther away to the southeast, another obstruction was rising— possibly that eighteen-story "motel" someone is building.

Clearly, Gatlinburg has changed a lot since the days when men and women with mountain accents started renting rooms and selling country ham and fried chicken to visitors who came to see the mountains.

I wanted to get up and eat an early breakfast in order to start walking again before 8 o'clock. Alberta asked that we be called at 6:30.

The clerk, a woman with a distinct British accent, responded with incredulity: "Six-thirty! In the morning?"

However, I'm not complaining about the British accent. It's not as out of place as those porpoises at Pigeon Forge.

And I may be one of a minority disturbed about the high-rise structures that clutter one's view of the mountains from Gatlinburg. Maybe only a minority of us still look upon Gatlinburg as an adjunct to the Great Smokies, mostly as a place to sleep and find an excellent meal while visiting the mountains.

For many, the roles of the town and the mountains have become reversed. Gatlinburg itself is the primary reason for their visits. The Great Smokies are secondary. Many come to Gatlinburg and never go up into the mountains.

No doubt, there are some who'd rather look at the Space Needle than Mt. Le Conte.

If somebody could move Gatlinburg, Space Needle and all, to flatlands 500 miles away, it would continue to draw visitors. I suppose it could go it alone.

Yet, it most likely couldn't go it as well. You can't ignore the fact that part of Gatlinburg's extraordinary success stems from its setting—a village in a valley at the foot of lofty mountains. Those who clutter the customers' view of the mountains may be doing Gatlinburg no favor.

—7/1/73

ooooo

Marion Randolph, Oak Ridge, is such an amiable gentleman that I'm going to lend him some space here, even though he's going to use it to say some things with which I don't agree. His subject is what to do about various problems of the Great Smokies.

"Could it be . . . that we have several factions involved in the Smokies problem and perhaps even . . . some right in each?" he asks.

"In that case, finding the right answer is going to be somewhat complicated. Let's pursue this approach just a bit farther. What if we could have hotels in the park, horse trails for horsepersons, foot trails for hikers, wilderness for the 'wilder,' trailer camps for those who trailer, nature trails for cars and those who have a need, swimming pools in a mountain valley, chapels by a rocky stream, guided tours for those who need guiding, summer training camps for youngsters, a

Bavarian village nestled high in the peaks, beautiful sunrises and sunsets, fresh mountain showers to bring out the wildflowers, uncontaminated air and clean mountain streams, rhododendron and azalea blooms to decorate the hills, a blanket of snow in winter to cover the sleeping hills till spring, silence yet noise, people yet privacy, dwellings yet wilderness, horses and people?

"Back to some suggestions now . . . being considered. The negative approach of charging, restricting, removing shelters and lodges, etc., seems so contradictory to what the prime purpose of what a national park is all about—for the enjoyment of the people . . . we should be proud of the numbers of people (who) are experiencing our mountains life . . . . We need to meet the needs of each and also provide for the growth that is certain to come. Wouldn't it be reasonable to strive for improvement of a system that is already Number One for national park visitation . . .? So, if we quickly get away from the negative treatment of this problem and exercise our efforts toward more positive solutions, maybe we can work something out."

(I haven't agreed with some of what Marion has said up to now, for I don't think the park can be all things to all people in unlimited numbers. We're going to skip next to one of his ideas that I do buy, completely.)

"Fortunately for all, the beauty of the Appalachian Mountains is not confined to the seventy-mile strip through the heart of the Smokies. The Smokies do comprise 505,000 very beautiful acres, but have you ever looked at a map showing the Cherokee National Forest, divided into two parts, north and south of the Smokies, bordering the Tennessee line from Virginia to Georgia, with 604,000 acres? And on the other side of the state line, North Carolina has Pisgah and Nantahala National Forests with 927,000 acres. So we do have a great potential for development of some kind. The Smokies represent only twenty-five per cent of this complex."

Yes, Marion, and there are lots of good acres in neighboring pieces of Virginia and Georgia, too.

The thing Marion is getting at here, I think, is that we should somehow tell people—both those here and those from far away—that there are good mountains outside the Great Smokies for fishing, hiking, riding horses and bicycles.

And, Marion, I think they're better than the Smokies for Bavarian villages and wild hog hunting.   —2/28/77

12

A Surviving People

This piece is about snakes, Cades Cove pioneers, Dr. Randolph Shields, grass, and over-population. I am going to mix it up so that you have to take the bad with the good or not take it at all.

Randolph, a native of Cades Cove in what is now Great Smoky Mountains National Park, is chairman of the Department of Biology at Maryville College. As an MC student some four decades ago, he walked thirty miles round trip on weekends between the college and his home in the Cove. At fifty-nine, he says he still could make the same walk, though he'd need a few shorter hikes for conditioning. He helped Kermit Caughron herd the last cattle on Gregory Bald in 1934 before the National Park Service declared the balds off limits to domestic livestock.

His great-great grandfather, Robert Shields, was one of the early settlers in the Cove in about 1822. His great-grandfather, Frederick (Fed) Shields, built the only three-story log house in the Cove to house himself, his wife, and sixteen children, thirteen of whom grew to "ripe old age."

Randolph thinks two is the maximum number of children any family should have now, and he'd feel more cheerful about the fate of humanity if the child producers simply would cease for a year or two.

But he does not hold it against Great-Grandfather Shields that he begot so many children. Times were different. Fed liked to hunt. He'd take his gun off the wall, call his dogs and be gone for days at a time. A man such as he needed stalwart sons to leave at home to work. A man who expected to get ahead in those days needed lots of sons to clear wilderness and grow crops in root-plagued new ground.

The world has changed considerably in the generations between Fed and Randolph. If there were any wilderness left to conquer, one son at the controls of one of today's mechanical monsters could knock down as much in a day as the whole Fed Shields brood could clear in a week. This country had maybe twenty-five or thirty million people when Fed was producing. It has six or seven times as many now. But not an acre more of land.

After Randolph got a diploma from Maryville College, he worked as an aquatic biologist for TVA, fisheries biologist for Tennessee, served in the Navy during World War II, went with the Tennessee Stream Pollution Control Board as an aquatic biologist, headed the North Carolina trout program, taught at Emory and Henry and Roanoke Colleges, got his doctorate at UT, then went back to Maryville College and the job he still holds.

During some summers, he served as a ranger-naturalist in the Great Smokies. One of the tasks he always enjoyed was guiding wilderness hikes up Mill Creek, the stream that rises high on Russell Field and tumbles down through the mountain forest into the Cove, then goes past the place where Randolph was born, and on to turn the wheel of the old Cable Mill, before it joins Forge Creek and then Abrams Creek.

Randolph is an expert on both the human and natural histories of the Cove and the mountains that rim it. On those hikes, he told wonderful stories about his ancestors and their neighbors.

Sort of a secular snake handler, Randolph occasionally encountered and picked up copperheads and timber rattlers as he guided tourists on the Mill Creek hike. Casually holding the reptiles, he told his awed audience of the snakes' role in the ecology of the region.

He remembers one copperhead, a snake which had freshly shed its old skin and was "beautiful" in its shiny new one. He stepped on the snake's head and grasped it just behind the head. But his foot was in the way of his hand, causing him to grasp the snake a fraction of an inch too far from the head.

As he held the snake and talked, the reptile managed to turn its head and bite Randolph on the thumb. Randolph is proud. And tough. He never batted an eye, cussed, or interrupted his talk. Only one man in the audience noticed the snake bite Randolph, and this fellow said nothing about it till later.

Randolph finished his talk on copperheads, then pitched aside the specimen and continued to lead the hike. The fang wounds bled freely, aided by some surreptitious sucking on Randolph's part. Though he got out most of the venom that way, he had a "dizzy spell" on the hike and some swelling for a day or two. But without further treatment, the thumb got all right.

He regards rattlesnake venom as a more serious poison than that from a copperhead. The former causes tissue to slough. Slashing the bitten area with knife or razor blade, once a recommended first aid treatment, spreads the venom and causes more tissue to slough, Randolph says.

Modern snakebite treatment is catching up with—and probably surpassing—a remedy some Smoky Mountains dwellers used long ago. Randolph said a fellow bitten on the leg or foot by a rattler would begin the treatment by killing the snake that bit him.

Then he'd carve out a slice of the snake's flesh and carry it with him to the nearest cold mountain stream. He'd stick the bitten foot or ankle into the cold water and keep it there for two or three hours. Then he'd get up, slap the slice of snake flesh over the wound and go about his business.

There was no magic about the snake flesh, but it probably served as well as anything for a dressing, Randolph says. What helped was the cold water. It slowed the circulation of the venom, gave the body time to adjust to it. Modern treatment is a spray can of a chemical freezing agent. But Randolph says this is dangerous if not properly used. The freeze can do as much damage as the venom.

Randolph doesn't kill the snakes he meets in the mountains. There, he says, he's the trespasser, not they.

Besides, Randolph doesn't think snakes rank very high on the scale of threats to human society. Nor does the atomic bomb. "I firmly believe man will control this machine of destruction (the bomb) because its use obviously will wipe out centers of cultural control," he says. "I have far greater concern for the more subtle elements of destruction that are prevalent and sure . . . The population increase and all this entails is *the* destroyer of our species."

Randolph voices this concern in a speech he sometimes makes when somebody invites him. The title is " All Flesh Is Grass" (from the sixth verse of the fortieth chapter of Isaiah).

With a lately grown beard that starts out brown at the temples and tips out curly white at the chin, Randolph may look a little like an Old Testament prophet as he deals out his harsh message. He might have happier audiences if he told some of his fine stories of snakes and bears and friends and kin of Cades Cove. But he figures this is not the proper speech for an ecologist and population biologist in 1972.

Holding up a symbolic blade of grass, Randolph tells his listeners: "Here is the only thing that stands between you and oblivion. Here is the intermediary between you and the ultimate source of energy that keeps you alive—the sun."

He laments the world's annual loss of a million acres of green things and the air pollution which threatens that which remains, the only source of free oxygen and the source, directly or indirectly, of nearly all food.

Don't talk to Randolph about our food surpluses. "The idea of a food surplus is fast becoming a fantasy," he says. " . . . If all the surplus food products were distributed equally among the hungry there would be only enough to give each person less than the equivalent of one cup of rice."

He laments the lack of discussion of population and environmental problems during the past presidential campaign. However, he does see one small reason to cheer: A "nucleus" of concerned people is growing.

He is doing all he can to speed its growth. He is one of the Blount County leaders who established the Maryville College Environmental Education Center at Tremont, in the Great Smokies. Fifth and sixth graders have come there from schools all over East Tennessee, plus a few from North Carolina.

At Maryville College, Randolph pushed successfully for a regulation which permits no one who intends to teach to get a degree without a course in environmental biology.

"That was a good step forward," he smiles, adding that elementary teachers are "the most important people in society today."

—11/26/72

John Walker Travels

Back in the days when the Walker Sisters of Little Greenbrier Cove were young women, people in the Great Smoky Mountains didn't travel a great deal. John N. Walker, the sisters' father, normally didn't venture far from home.

So it was pretty unusual when he once decided to visit one of his nine brothers, Thomas F. Walker, way over in the Jefferson City area. Tom was the youngest of the ten brothers and John was the oldest. There were five girls in the family.

Mel Walker, one of Tom's sons, phoned me a few weeks ago, not long after I wrote some pieces here about the Walker sisters. Mel was a group manager for the phone company and lived in Loudon County until he retired and moved to West Palm Beach, Florida, in 1958.

Tom Walker married Nannie Line, whose father, Alfred Line, operated the old Line Springs Hotel, and they moved all their possessions in an ox wagon to Jefferson County in 1880, Mel says.

Tom occasionally went back to the Great Smokies to see his folks, but they rarely visited him. He kept asking John to visit him and John finally agreed.

In 1907, John wrote Tom he was coming to see him and asked Tom to come to the depot and meet him. So Tom hitched a horse to his one-horse buggy and drove down to meet his oldest brother.

John didn't have much luggage. But he had a homemade wooden box. It was about eighteen inches long, twelve inches wide and ten to twelve inches deep. The top was a pane of window glass.

"In that box were two of the biggest rattlesnakes I ever saw," says Mel Walker, who was about fifteen years old at the time.

Rattlesnakes didn't live in the Jefferson City area, and John apparently thought Tom was lonesome for a pair of excellent snakes from the mountains of his childhood.

John had gone to the trouble of hunting and catching the rattlers. He built the box for their trip. Then he walked down from Little Greenbrier to Little River and caught the Little River Lumber Company train to Maryville.

The box of snakes drew a good deal of comment on the train and at the depot in Maryville, where John transferred to a Southern Railway train which took him to Jefferson City by way of Knoxville.

After all John's trouble, Tom didn't appreciate the snakes.

"My father said we didn't have any rattlesnakes at Jefferson City and we didn't want any," Mel remembers.

This must have cooled the brothers' reunion. If it didn't, Tom certainly cooled it a few mornings later.

Mel said he heard two shotgun blasts early in the morning three or four days after John arrived. Tom had killed both snakes. "It made Uncle John mad," Mel remembers.

John stayed a few days longer. Then he said, "Tom, if you'll take me back to the depot, I'll be leaving. If I was to die, there's no land around here fit to bury me in."   —9/5/71

Last Resident of the Park

Some of you remember Lem Ownby, the old mountain man who lives alone in a house on Jakes Creek in Great Smoky Mountains National Park. Well, here is a story of two U.S. Supreme Court justices and some other citizens in the legal business who went to visit Lem. It comes from Knoxville lawyer Foster D. Arnett:

About four years ago, the U.S. Sixth Circuit Court of Appeals was having its annual conference in Gatlinburg. Justices Potter Stewart and Harry Blackmun were honored guests. On an afternoon when no conference activities were scheduled, Foster invited the two justices, Mrs. Stewart, and Knoxville lawyer and Mrs. McAfee Lee to relax at the Arnett cottage in Elkmont.

All accepted. They enjoyed it.

After his guests had rested, Foster told them a little about Lem Ownby and asked whether they'd like to go up Jakes Creek to meet the old mountain man.

They thought that was a great idea.

They went to the seventy-five-year-old mountain home where Lem lives alone. Foster knocked. The following is not a word-for-word record of what was said, but it comes pretty close:

"Who is it?"

"Uncle Lem, this is Foster. I have some guests with me who would like to meet you."

"Who are they?"

Foster, visualizing Lem seated in his chair beside the stove, gave him the names of everyone in his party, along with the titles of the two members of the highest court in the land.

"I don't want to see those people," Lem said.

Naturally, Foster was embarrassed. He told Lem what fine people he'd brought to see him and how much they wanted to meet him.

Lem was unchanged. He said he didn't want to see them.

Foster was about the only one who was unhappy. The two justices were bent over laughing at the situation. They enjoyed Lem's stubborn independence. And they left without seeing him.   —*6/30/80*

00000

Bent and blind and ninety-one years old, Lem Ownby lives alone beside the singing waters of Jakes Creek. He's the last of his kind in Great Smoky Mountains National Park.

The buzz of bees blends with the creek music. An empty beehive and a bee smoker lie on Lem's front porch, under the crosscut saw hanging on the porch wall. Though he is blind, Lem still works with his bees.

"I still put in the supers," he said, "though I can't see the hives."

Lem hasn't always been blind, but his vision was never better than about half of normal. However, it was considerably better the first time I saw him than it is now.

That time, a dozen or more years ago, I had hiked from the Sinks, intending to meet Alberta in Elkmont, near the Jakes Creek trailhead. To my surprise, the trail led me to the edge of a clearing. There stood a house, barn, fruit trees, lots of beehives. And I found Lem and a pair of dogs there.

He had far more hives then. He says he had 145 hives when his vision was relatively good and he was stronger. He says he's getting "tottery" now and has only twenty hives.

I hadn't known that Lem existed until I hiked into his clearing that day. Yet, he was in the same class with the widely known Walker spinster sisters who lived in Little Greenbrier Cove.

Lem and his wife, the Walker sisters, some families in Cades Cove and a few other families scattered about the park chose to accept a little less money for their land when it was bought for the park, in exchange for the right to live out their lives on the land that had been theirs.

By the 1960's, many of this group had died. Some had changed their minds and moved outside the park. The last Walker sister, Louisa, died in 1964 at eighty-two. This left only Lem and his wife, Mimmie. Mimmie died thirteen years ago. This left only Lem.

Kermit Caughron and Hugh Myers live in Cades Cove under a different arrangement, as do the summer people in the Elkmont colony. Park officials also permit Roy Ownby, great-nephew of Lem, and Roy's wife, Jean, to live in a mobile home a few yards from Lem's house. They're available to help Lem in an emergency.

But Lem has had few emergencies. In this age when humans orbit the planet and walk on the moon, Lem has traveled in a smaller orbit. He was born Feb. 24, 1889, in a house that stood near where the Wonderland Club Hotel now stands. When he was two, his father, Tom Ownby, moved the family less than two miles to the place on Jakes Creek. They lived in a log house. Some 75 years ago, the log house was replaced, in nearly the same spot, by the one in which Lem now chews his Bloodhound tobacco and lives out his years.

He has plowed oxen, mules, horses on the forty-four acre farm on Jakes Creek. But he has never owned or driven an automobile. He worked for Little River Lumber Company when it was harvesting the big trees of the virgin forest of the mountains around him. But he has never held a job outside the Great Smokies.

Lem has crossed only one state line, the one at the top of the mountain dividing Tennessee from North Carolina, going as far as Tow String Creek, still in the Great Smokies, "to buy a dog from a feller."

He has never been farther from the Great Smokies than Knoxville. His wife was hospitalized there. He spent five weeks and one day in St. Mary's Medical Center when he had pneumonia ten years ago. He didn't like it, couldn't stand the water. Somebody finally had to bring him water from the mountain spring that's piped constantly to his back porch.

The spring is one hundred yards from his house, up in the edge of the woods. The path to it is winding. But Lem can go to it night or day, in snow or sunshine. Being blind is "unhandy," he says. But he manages.

He cooks his breakfast and supper, and sometimes his dinner (midday meal). But Jean Ownby often cooks the midday meal and leaves it for him to heat.

He washes his clothes and bed linens. He washes his dishes. He cleans the house. He feeds the chickens. He planted pumpkins this spring. He set out tomato plants and drove stakes into the ground beside them.

He has a shotgun in the house, and if the need arose he could shoot it. Last time he shot it was about two years ago. He heard a bear up in the Golden Delicious apple tree in the front yard. The bear was chomping apples. Lem yelled at him. The bear kept on chomping. Then Lem got the shotgun and fired away. He couldn't see the bear, but he heard it leaving. However, the bear came back a night or two later and harvested all the grapes from the vines that grow on the garden fence.

An electric fence circles the cluster of beehives and keeps out the bears.

Why has Lem lived so long?

He says he's not sure why, "but I lay it to honey. I never took a dose of doctor medicine till I was fifty-five years old." He said he has eaten honey "might nigh every day" for more than fifty years.

He called attention to the fact that his ninety-one year old face is unwrinkled. Maybe honey is to be credited with that, too.

Lem knows honey, knows bees. Blind though he is, he's not the least afraid to walk among the bees constantly buzzing around the hives. In his opinion, the best honey is made from linn nectar, and the linn (basswood or linden) trees will be blooming soon. He remembers chestnut honey, and he said oldtime beekeepers always claimed the bees "got a heep iller, would sting you quicker," when they were working on chestnut bloom.

Two Chinese chestnut trees are beginning to bloom in Lem's yard. He has a low opinion of Chinese chestnuts, compared with the sweet American chestnuts that used to grow in the Great Smokies. He holds a similar bad opinion of the rainbow trout that swim in Jakes Creek, where he used to catch "speckles" (brook trout).

Lem's life winds down in unhurried grace. Year by year, his activities diminish. His realm is within a progressively tightening circle. The wilderness advances upon his clearing, now only about an acre.

Young poplars grow where Lem's cattle used to graze on grass. He has left not one cow or horse. Nor has he a dog to bark at bear or timber rattler.

But he has a few chickens. An old black hen trailed by a brood of two-week-old chicks squawked loudly as I walked past, and a big red rooster also registered disapproval.

More and more, Lem sits and listens to the tick of the clock he's listened to for seventy-five years. He cannot see them but he knows his parents are together in a photograph on the fireboard. A framed photograph on the wall is of his maternal grandfather, Dave Watson. Lem said Dave Watson was one of seven brothers who came home together from the Civil War and found their mother praying for them "in the chimney corner."

With the pride of mountain men of an earlier era, Lem says he's never been on relief. He said he's eligible for food stamps, and some have tried to persuade him to use them. He has refused.

Will he live to be one hundred?

He doubts it. He doesn't seem much concerned about when he departs. He says he's "got the rocks bought" for his grave. He's going to a "better place."

But don't bet that he'll like the water when he gets there.

—*6/15/80*